CHAUCER
1340–1400

*The Life and Times
of the First English Poet*

RICHARD WEST

CARROLL & GRAF PUBLISHERS
New York

Carroll & Graf Publishers
An imprint of Avalon Publishing Group, Inc.
161 William Street
New York
NY 10038-2607
www.carrollandgraf.com

First published in the UK by Constable,
an imprint of Constable & Robinson Ltd 2000

First Carroll & Graf edition 2000

First Carroll & Graf trade paperback 2002

ISBN 0–7867–0925–1

Printed and bound in the EU

Contents

List of Illustrations

Chronology

1340   Geoffrey Chaucer, son of a vintner, born in London, between 1339 and 1346, although most scholars agree on an earlier date, about 1340.

1348–9   The Black Death, which has ravaged continental Europe, arrives in England during the summer of 1348, killing a third of the population until it subsides in 1350. For some of this period, Geoffrey's father John Chaucer was living in Southampton as a butler or purchaser of wine for King Edward III. By 1350, the Chaucers were back in their London home at Thames Street, near the river.

1350s   Thanks to John Chaucer's employment with King Edward III, he obtains for Geoffrey the position of page in the retinue of the Countess of Ulster, wife of the Duke of Clarence, a younger son of Edward III. The household records show that Geoffrey accompanied the countess on visits to Windsor, Oxford, Liverpool and Yorkshire.

1359   Chaucer takes up arms as a *valettus*, a page or squire, in Edward III's invasion of France. He joins in the siege of Reims. The defenders include two French poets, Guillaume de Machaut and Eustache Deschamps, whose work Chaucer came to admire.

1360   Chaucer is captured by the French at Rettel, west of Reims and ransomed by Edward III.

1365/6   Chaucer marries Philippa, eldest daughter of Paon de Roet, from Hainault in the Netherlands, an official in the household of Edward III's queen, Philippa of Hainault. Philippa Chaucer's sister Katherine de Roet was to become the mistress and then the wife of Edward's second son John of Gaunt, Duke of Lancaster, the virtual ruler of England during the early years of the reign of Richard III.

1367   At about this time, Chaucer appears to have entered the service of John of Gaunt as well as that of King Edward III.
Birth of Geoffrey Chaucer's first child, Thomas.

1368	John of Gaunt's first wife Blanche dies in a recurrence of the plague. Chaucer commemorates her in one of his most beautiful early poems, *The Book of the Duchess*. He goes on to write part of *The Romaunt of the Rose*, a verse translation of *Le Roman de la Rose*, and *Boece*, a prose translation of the *Consolation of Philosophy* by Boethius. These are followed by *The Parlement of Fowles* and *The House of Fame*.
1360s	Chaucer employed on military and diplomatic missions to France, Flanders and Spain.
1371	John of Gaunt marries Constanza, daughter of King Pedro 'the Cruel' of Castile.
1372	Philippa Chaucer is granted an annuity by John of Gaunt for services in the household of the new Duchess Constance.
1372–3	Chaucer joins trade and diplomatic mission to Genoa with a side trip to Florence where he gets to know the works of Dante, Petrarch and Boccaccio.
1376–7	To Lombardy on diplomatic mission to Bernardo Visconti of Milan and the English mercenary captain Sir John Hawkwood.
1378	A schism in the Church results in rival popes at Rome and Avignon.
1380	Cecilia Champaign drops her charge of rape against Chaucer.
1381	Peasants' Revolt in Essex, East Anglia, Kent and London.
1382	Archbishop of Canterbury condemns the teachings of the Oxford theologian John Wyclif and his followers the Lollards.
1385	Chaucer appointed justice of the peace in Kent.
1386	Member of Parliament for Kent for one session. Gives up lease on Aldgate house and moves to Greenwich in Kent. Probable start of writing of *Canterbury Tales*.
1395	Chaucer receives fine gown of scarlet from John of Gaunt's son the Earl of Derby, the future Henry IV.
1397	Richard II returns from military campaign in Ireland to crush his domestic enemies 'the Appellants'. Gaunt's brother, the Duke of Gloucester, murdered at Calais, probably on the orders of Richard II.
1399: Sept.	Deposition of Richard II by Henry IV.
1400: Feb.	Body of murdered Richard II returned from Pontefract to London. 'The Complaint of Chaucer to his Purse', addressed to Henry IV.
June	Chaucer's pension renewed.
25 Oct.	Chaucer dies. He is buried in Westminster Abbey.

Acknowledgements

The author and publisher wish to thank the following for permission to use copyright material:

A. P. Watt Ltd. on behalf of The Royal Literary Fund for excerpts from G. K. Chesterton, *Chaucer* (1932).

Benson, Larry D., ed. (1987) *The Riverside Chaucer*, 3rd edn. Houghton Mifflin.

Curtis Brown Group Ltd., London, on behalf of the estate of the author for excerpts from Neville Coghill, trans. *Chaucer: Troilus and Criseyde*, Penguin Classics. Copyright © 1971 the Estate of Neville Coghill.

Peters Fraser and Dunlop Group Ltd. on behalf of the estate of the author for excerpts from David Wright, trans., *Chaucer: The Canterbury Tales*. Copyright © 1985 David Wright.

Laurence Pollinger Ltd. on behalf of the author for excerpts from Charles H. Sisson, trans. *The Inferno, Purgatorio,* and *Paradiso* from *Dante: The Divine Comedy*, Oxford University Press (1981).

Penguin Books Ltd. for excerpts from Froissart, *Chronicles*, translated by Geoffrey Brereton, Penguin Classics (1968). Copyright © Geoffrey Brereton 1968; and Giovanni Boccaccio, *The Decameron*, trans. by G. H. McWilliam, Penguin Classics (1972), revised edition (1995). Copyright © G. H. Mcwilliam, 1972, 1995.

Every effort has been made to trace the copyright holders but if there have been any inadvertently overlooked the publishers will be pleased to make the necessary arrangement at the first opportunity.

North
Sea

DENMARK

IRELAND

ENGLAND

• London

• Hamburg

Calais

Cologne

Erfurt

GERMANY

HOLY

Cherbourg

• Coucy

Paris

ROMAN

Nuremburg

BOHEMIA

Brest

BRITTANY

• Rennes

Strasbourg

VOSGES

EMPIRE

Augsburg

BAVARIA

Munich

Vienna

Atlantic
Ocean

FRANCE

Orléans

Basle

Zurich

Constance

JURA

Berne

La Rochelle

Poitiers

Limoges

Lyon

Geneva

ALPS

Clermont

SAVOY

Turin

Milan

Venice

Bordeaux

AQUITAINE
(GUIENNE)

Avignon
(PAPACY)

PROVENCE
(to Naples)

PIEDMONT

Genoa

LOMBARDY

Florence

Adriatic

Toulouse

Marseille

TUSCANY

PAPAL
STATES

NAVARRE

PYRENEES

Narbonne

Najera

CASTILE

ARAGON

CORSICA

Rome

Madrid

Barcelona

• Toledo

SARDINIA

BALEARICS

• Seville

• Granada

Cadiz

Gibraltar

AFRICA

Tunis

Mahdia

CHAUCER'S
EUROPE

N

W   E

S

0   300   600 miles

A Note on the Text

IN WRITING THIS BOOK on Chaucer and the fourteenth century, I have not presumed to trespass into the field of university Chaucer studies, medieval literature or linguistics, which are the jealously guarded preserve of professionals. Although I became very interested in the effect on Chaucer of European literature, especially the thirteenth-century French poem *Le Roman de la Rose*, and the three great Italians, Dante, Petrarch and Boccaccio, I have approached these writers as an enthusiastic amateur and have used translations available to the general reader, notably C. H. Sisson's *Divine Comedy*.

Like anyone writing of Chaucer for the general public, rather than for school and university students, I have had to face the problem that much of his language is hard to understand without a note and glossary. Even in the seventeenth century, publishers put out versions of *Troilus and Criseyde* in Latin or in modern English 'for the satisfaction of those who either cannot or will not take ye paines to understand the excellent Author's farr more exquisite and significant expressions, though now grown obsolete and out of use'.

On the other hand, there must be many readers who have studied Chaucer at school or university and can easily get the hang of it again. They may even resent having explained to them quite common archaisms such as 'sooth' for 'truth', 'wight' for 'person', and 'hir' for 'her' or 'their'.

Obviously I would hope that anyone who is interested enough in Chaucer to have begun this book would want to go back to the original to get the full flavour of the poetry but, for the sake of ease and enjoyment, I have fallen back on using revised or modernized versions. This is the more excusable because in the case of Chaucer – as distinct from Shakespeare, the King James Bible or the Book of

Common Prayer – there are very few passages or even lines that have entered the language.

One of the few long passages from Chaucer in the *Oxford Dictionary of Quotations* comes from the Palinode at the end of *Troilus and Criseyde* and is easily understandable to the modern reader. However for most quotations from *Troilus* I have used the brilliant modernisation by Neville Coghill which capture Chaucer's humour and narrative verse, while sticking close to the literal meaning.

For most of Chaucer's poems, except for *Troilus and Criseyde* and the *Canterbury Tales*, I have used the text of the great Victorian scholar Walter W. Skeat, in the 1920 edition handed down to me by my mother who was a devotee of Chaucer and added some interesting pencilled annotations. In many cases I have altered the text or added explanations in brackets to make it easier to enjoy and understand. This practice evidently goes back to the days of Chaucer complained of the scribes who 'misurryte and mismetre' his poetry.

Even while Skeat was editing the definitive text, other Chaucer scholars were trying to produce a version that presented less difficulty to the general reader. One of the most successful of these attempts was the *Canterbury Tales* in the 1908 Everyman edition, revised by Arthur Burrell, who preserves much of the sound and flavour of the original, while modernizing phrases and words which have lost or altered their meaning. Thus, for example, in the *Knight's Tale* 'The shepne brenning with the blake smoke' becomes 'The stables burning with the black smoke'. While I have generally followed Burrell's version, I have on occasions altered a line for greater clarity and on occasion restored a pleasing word or line from the Skeat text.

In his refreshingly old-fashioned Introduction, Arthur Burrell explains why he has not tried to modernize the bawdy poems in the *Canterbury Tales*. 'To begin with, certain tales, seven out of the twenty-four, have been left untouched. They are so broad, so plain-spoken, that no amount of editing or alteration will make them suitable for the twentieth century.' Burrell then goes on to say that with the remaining seventeen tales he has modernized just enough to leave the 'quaintness'. Perhaps unconsciously, Burrell has touched on the heart of the problem, since 'queynt' in Chaucer can mean either 'ingenious, clever and strange' or what the Victorian glossaries called 'the female pudenda'. In short, it is our modern c-word, which still has the power to offend and shock, so it is often avoided even in vulgar circles by some kind of euphemism such as the rhyming slang 'berk' (from Berkeley Hunt) or the jocular 'See you next Tuesday'.

Having always favoured restraint, if not censorship, in the printed word, I thought at first of leaving the bawdy *Tales* in medieval obscurity. Then I slowly began to realize that in Chaucer's case the q-word was sometimes necessary. This is especially true of the *Miller's Tale* which describes the naughty wife of the carpenter. I therefore turned to the brilliant verse translation of the *Canterbury Tales* by the late David Wright (Oxford University Press) whom I had known in Soho and at Appleby-in-Westmorland.

By a cunning use of half-rhymes and assonance, David managed to capture the music and rhythm of Chaucer's poetry while getting across his satire and jokes. His word picture of Alison in the *Miller's Tale* seems to me almost as beautiful as the original. David's sensitivity to Chaucer's poetry may have had something to do with his love and understanding of the great South African author Herman Bosman, who wrote in English a cycle of comic stories about his fellow Afrikaners. Bosman himself was a devotee of the *Canterbury Tales* and shared Chaucer's skill at letting his stories bring out the character of the narrators.

Introduction

DURING THE 1970S, WHEN Alexander Chancellor was editor of the *Spectator*, he indulged my passion for travelling round England writing of places in terms of their history, especially the Middle Ages. In 1980 my friend the publisher Jeremy Lewis, then working for Chatto & Windus, suggested I write a book along the same lines, which appeared the next year as *English Journey*. In the early summer of 1981 I persuaded Alexander Chancellor to let me write a series of articles on the sixth centenary of the Peasants' Revolt, which raged along the route of Chaucer's pilgrims between Southwark and Canterbury. Soon afterwards the *Spectator* published my first attempt to draw a comparison between Chaucer's Wife of Bath and the modern feminist movement, especially with regard to Chaucer's alleged rape of Cecilia Champaign.

The idea of writing a book on Chaucer took shape in 1996 when I had just completed *The Life and Strange Surprising Adventures of Daniel Defoe*, another literary man who had lived at a critical time in English history. I thought of tackling William Cobbett, who like Defoe was not quite sure if this country belonged to Europe or to the English-speaking world, but decided instead to go right back to Chaucer, who was in at the birth of England as a separate nation and could be regarded as the first true Englishman. It also occurred to me that the sixth centenary of Chaucer's death fell when the book might be ready for publication. I immediately started a course of reading all Chaucer's work and anything I could find on the history of the fourteenth century. Since we were selling our London home, I persuaded my wife to buy a small house in Deal on the Kent coast near Canterbury.

However, it was not until Christmas 1997 that my literary agent Christopher Sinclair-Stevenson rang me in Dublin to say that Constable had made an offer for the Chaucer book. I am hugely grateful to Blen Glazebrook, the chairman of Constable, for backing the idea and giving encouragement in the years that followed. During this time Constable merged with another small and independent publishing house, Robinson, whose editorial management, notably Nick Robinson and Jan Chamier, have shown great sympathy and patience in getting the book through its final stages.

During the years I have spent on this book I have relied very heavily on those of my family and friends who have given me encouragement and borne with my ramblings about the Black Death, Boccaccio and the iniquity of friars. At times I must have seemed like a Mr Dick in *David Copperfield*, who also scribbled away on the Kent coast, vainly trying to keep King Charles's head out of his never finished memorial.

I must thank most of all my dear wife Mary, who has been an unfailing support, psychological, moral, medical, editorial and not least financial, to the detriment of her own work on books and journals. I am also most grateful to my sons Patrick and Edward for transferring onto computers my handwritten versions of medieval English and French and Italian. Their work was completed by two skilled typists in Deal, Rachel Sleavalle and Angela Sanderson.

It has been an encouragement over the past few years to discover how many old friends and acquaintances turned out to share my enthusiasm for Chaucer, confirming me in my hunch that he is second only to Shakespeare among the favourite poets in the English language. This was brought home to me on the evening I began this work when I happened to be dining with the great Irish historian Conor Cruise O'Brien and his wife Maire, a distinguished poet in the Irish language. It turned out that Maire had done a postgraduate course in Chaucer, while Conor was able to give me a commentary on Richard II's Irish policy in the last decade of the fourteenth century.

Among the many friends who gave me advice or encouragement I should like in particular to mention Clive Allison, Nick McConnell and Joe and Julie Steeples in Deal, Tom Margerison and Majorie Wallace who came with Mary and me to Reims where Chaucer served as a soldier, and Clive and Cordelia Unger-Hamilton who entertained us at Ely.

Finally, I must thank the two freelance editors who saw the book through its production, first James Young, who gave it a scholarly vetting, then David Blomfield, who knocked it into a briefer and more coherent form.

Needless to say, the book's errors and deficiencies are my own.

1

Canterbury Pilgrims

On 28 DECEMBER 1999, a pilgrimage of Christians was making its way to pay respects to the memory of Archbishop Thomas Becket at Canterbury. Although these pilgrims had begun their walk from 'every shire of England' and from every part of the British Isles, they converged on the route from Southwark to Canterbury that Chaucer's pilgrims had followed in 1386. Geoffrey Chaucer died on 25 October 1400. Thus Kent and its famous cathedral took the lead in celebrating not only the end of the second millennium but the sixth centenary of the county's favourite poet.

Chaucer's age was the first when people began to think in these hundred-year terms, but there was still no agreement on how they should be numbered, so that what in England has come to be known as the fourteenth century was called by the Italians the 'three hundred' (*trecento*), a constant cause of bewilderment to students of the Renaissance. Moreover the keepers of calendars in those days reckoned the start of the new year not in mid-winter but in early spring, not in January but in March, and so Chaucer's pilgrims set out for Canterbury 'When that Aprille with his showres swoot/The drought of Marche hath perced to the root . . .'.

The pilgrims who walked through Kent in those dying days of December 1999 were passing the scenes of the great events of Chaucer's lifetime. As a soldier and diplomat on missions to France, Spain, Italy and the Netherlands, Chaucer frequently took the Canterbury road to the Channel ports, such as Sandwich, Deal and Dover. As an official of customs and excise, he supervised the export of goods from London and Kent, especially the sale of wool and cloth through the staple, or monopoly, at Calais, which had been won from France in 1349. Later, as superintendent of public works,

Chaucer combined with the architect Thomas Yevele to rebuild the nave of Canterbury Cathedral, as they had done in Westminster Abbey. Through his connections at Canterbury, Chaucer acquired the lucrative post of ward to the son of a wealthy landowner at nearby Betteshanger.

Although no vestige remains at Southwark of the Tabard Inn where Chaucer's pilgrims assembled, the nearby Church of St Mary's is now Southwark Cathedral, newly refurbished and given access once more to the Thames. Here one can see the tomb of Chaucer's fellow poet and friend John Gower, who lived here during the Peasants' Revolt of 1381, when a mob released the prisoners from the Marshalsea, looted St Mary's Church, and murdered the Flemings who ran Southwark's brothels.

Anti-immigrant feeling still runs high in south-east London and the Medway towns. It was here that some white thugs murdered a young black man, Stephen Lawrence, while further east at Gravesend a Kosovar refugee died in a gangland knifing just before the new millennium.

Most of the pilgrims in December 1999 must have spared a thought or at least a glance for the much-trumpeted Dome at Greenwich with its 'Faith Zone' for multi-religion, multi-ethnic Britain. Chaucer was living at Greenwich for the last few years of his life but did not speak well of the town in his writing. The Host in the *Canterbury Tales* calls Greenwich contemptuously 'an Inne of Shrews', or nest of thieves – perhaps a reference to the occasion when Chaucer was held up or mugged there, twice in the same day.

And so, at the close of the millennium, two columns of pilgrims came together at Rochester on the Medway to start the final leg of their walk to Canterbury. It was here in the *Canterbury Tales* that the Host, Harry Baily, called on the Monk to contribute a tale after those told by the Knight, the Miller, the Reeve and the Man of Law.

> 'My lord Sir Monk,' quoth he, 'be merry of cheer,
> For you shall tell a tale trewely.
> Lo, Rochester here standeth faste by.'

Chaucer's bantering tone is all the more odd since at this time, when the pilgrims were passing through Rochester, all this part of the Kent coast was living in fear of a French invasion. From the start of the

Hundred Years' War, which lasted through Chaucer's lifetime and into the fifteenth century, the French had repeatedly raided and sacked the Cinque Port towns such as Hastings, Sandwich and Rye, usually in revenge for English atrocities. During the 1380s, when England was losing the war, Richard II called out the Watch, or militia, along the Thames Estuary and the Channel coast, while Parliament warned that France meant 'to destroy the English language and occupy English territory, which God forbid, unless a remedy of force is found'. The churches of Kent were forbidden to ring more than one peal of bells except in the case of a French invasion.

Then in 1386, the year in which Chaucer set his *Canterbury Tales*, King Charles VI of France decided to carry the war from the coast to the heart of Kent. A high Mass was celebrated at Notre Dame Cathedral in Paris to bless the proposed invasion. The largest fleet of the war so far was assembled at Sluys, the port of Bruges, equipped with huts to serve as a base camp on English soil. The French hoped to exploit the political troubles of Richard II, especially the absence abroad of his uncle and best commander John of Gaunt, who had left for Spain to pursue his claims to the throne of Castile. As the Earl of Salisbury warned King Richard in Parliament: 'Your majesty must not be surprised if our adversary the King of France prepares to invade us; for since the death of our most potent and famous prince Edward [Richard's grandfather, Edward III, or perhaps Richard's father, the Black Prince] this kingdom has incurred several risks of becoming destroyed by its own subjects.'

On the advice of Parliament, which included Geoffrey Chaucer as a member for Kent, King Richard sent archers to reinforce some of the coastal towns which the French might attack. According to Sir John Froissart, the leading chronicler of the Hundred Years' War, the English were ready to let the French put ashore in Kent for a few days, then starve them to death. To this end they proposed to destroy the bridge over the Medway at Rochester. This alone would have stopped the pilgrims getting from Southwark to Canterbury in 1386.

Moreover, St Thomas's shrine at Canterbury was at risk, since both sides in the Hundred Years' War regarded holy relics as the richest form of booty. The governor of Dover Castle, Sir Simon Burley, who feared that the French would soon land on the coast near Deal, took it upon himself to warn the abbot of Christ Church Canterbury to hand over St Thomas's relics for safe keeping. According to Froissart, who was a friend of Burley, the abbot gave him short shrift: 'How, Sir, can you wish to despoil the church of its jewel? If you are afraid you can shut yourself up in your castle at Dover: however, the French are not bold enough to advance so far!'

The abbot was right, for Charles VI abandoned his plans to invade Kent, as did Louis XIV, Bonaparte, Kaiser Wilhelm and Adolf Hitler.

Yet where they failed, other invaders had succeeded long before, making Kent the political and cultural heart of England.

Julius Caesar and his army put ashore in 55 BC on the beach that runs north from the cliffs at Dover only miles from the old Kentish settlement on the Stour that would become the city of Canterbury. When Caesar went on to conquer the people of south-east Britain, he claimed to have found that of all the Britons, 'by far the most civilized are those who inhabit Cantium, which is an entirely maritime region, nor do they differ from the Gallic custom.' Admittedly Caesar's first-hand knowledge of Britain was confined to Cantium, or Kent, but his observations were nevertheless correct. Although south-east England had broken away from the Continent in a geological shift about six thousand years earlier, both sides of the Channel were inhabited by the same Celtic people, known to the Romans as Belgae, who spoke the same language and shared the same attributes of civilization, such as horse-drawn chariots, sailing ships and a silver or copper currency.

Julius Caesar's failure to come back to Britain after the campaign season of 54 BC did not mean that Cantium lost touch with the empire. The British leader Cassivelaunus continued to pay tribute not to Rome itself but to the flourishing Roman colony of Gaul, which was run by Latinized Belgae, similar to their cousins, the Cantii. There was also a flourishing trade across the Straits of Dover, with Britain exporting corn, cattle, gold, silver, iron, hides, slaves and hunting-dogs, and importing luxury goods such as wine, oil, bronze furniture, pottery, silver and glass-ware.

The Romans returned in AD 43 to occupy and rule Britain for the next four hundred years. They brought with them the apple trees that would help to make Kent the orchard as well as the garden of England. They also began the extraction and smelting of iron ore between

Tunbridge Wells and the Channel. The Kentish settlement on the Stour developed into the fortress town of Durovernum, complete with the Roman amenities of an amphitheatre, public baths and a grid of streets between the gateways. Much of Durovernum was brought to light by workers clearing the rubble after the Luftwaffe raid on Canterbury of 1 June 1942, and can now be seen in the Roman museum near the cathedral.

Roman officials and the British collaborators built farms and elegant villas throughout those parts of Kent that now form the outer suburbs of London. It was here in Kent that the Romans built their most famous road, the Watling Street joining London and Westminster to the Channel Ports. In Chaucer's time this still formed most of the route of the Canterbury pilgrims.

Although Latin did not take over popular speech in Britain as in Italy, Spain, France or even distant Romania, it lived on in the law, the Church and above all in education, as we shall see from Chaucer's knowledge of Ovid and Virgil. He often makes fun of the struggle the English had in coping with French and Latin as well as their own developing language. Two of the most villainous pilgrims use dog Latin to cheat and baffle the ignorant. The Pardoner tries to squeeze more money out of his congregation by preaching upon the text that avarice is the root of all evil ('*Radix malorum est cupiditas*'), while the Summoner frightens his victims with Latin tags before hauling them up in court on sexual offences:

> And when that he well drunken had the wyn,
> Then would he speke no word but Latyn.
> A few terms had he, two or three,
> That he had learned out of some decree . . .
> But who-so would him try on other things,
> He had then spent all his philosophie.
> 'Ay, *questio quid juris*' wolde he crye,
> He was a gentil felow and a kynde;
> A better summoner shulde men nowher fynde.
> He wolde suffer for a quart of wyn
> A good felaw to have his concubine
> A twelve month, and excuse him utterly.
> And fooles coude he deceive privily.

Chaucer would have loved the nineteenth-century Irish story about the judge in a case of cattle theft who asked the defending counsel: 'Is your client aware of the saying "*Questio quid juris?*"' (or some such tag) and received the answer: 'My lord, on the Connemara mountain top, where my client dwells, they talk of little else.'

The funniest use of Latin in Chaucer is made by the barnyard cock Chaunticleer in the *Nun's Priest's Tale*. He has been quarrelling with his favourite hen about dreams, predestination and other abstruse matters, but now wants to make it up with her and enjoy her sexual favours:

> 'Now let us speke of mirthe, and stay al this;
> Madame Pertilot, so have I blis;
> Of one thing God hath me sent large grace;
> For when I see the beautee of your face,
> Ye be so scarlet red about your eyen,
> It makith al my drede for to dyen,
> For, al so sure as "*In principio*
> *Mulier est hominis confusio*".
> (Madame, the sentence of this Latyn is,
> Womman is mannes joye and mannes blis.)
> For when I feel a-night your softe syde,
> Al be it that I may not on you ryde,
> For that your perche is made so narrow, allas!'

Here is a joke within a joke, within a joke, for the Latin words really mean: 'In the beginning, woman is man's confusion, or downfall.' But does his wife Pertelot spot the deception? Does Chaunticleer himself know what the Latin words really mean? Chaucerian scholars have never agreed on this, as G. K. Chesterton pointed out: 'I suspect that he [Chaucer] has made a good many jokes that his critics cannot see; and one or two which the commentators have sat down grimly and resolutely to prove not to be jokes at all!'

It was during the Roman occupation of Britain that Christianity spread from Palestine westward across the Mediterranean until it established itself in the cities of Rome and Constantinople. This was the age of the Acts of the Apostles, the early fathers and eremites, the saints and martyrs who suffered under Nero and Diocletian.

Christian missionaries also preached the faith throughout the British Isles, apparently winning most converts in northern England and Wales. It was a Roman general stationed at York who later won power as the Emperor Constantine, ended the persecution of Christians and himself took up the Cross and joined the Church after the Battle of the Milvian Bridge in 312. Only two years later, bishops from York, London and Colchester attended a Church council at Arles in Provence.

Some modern scholars believe that when the pagan cults were outlawed, British Christians joined in looting the now illegal temples, rather as Protestants took advantage of Henry VIII's dissolution of the monasteries. The British also joined in the theological squabbles that splintered early Christendom. The monk Pelagius (c.360–420), the founder of the Pelagian heresy, was a Welshman said to have lived at Bangor-is-y-Coed, on the River Dee.

It was from this period, when the Rome of the Caesars was turning into the Rome of the Popes, that the Second Nun takes her tale of the martyrdom of St Cecilia. The saint emerges as one of those tough pious women so admired in the fourteenth century, who brings on her death by insulting the Roman chief of police. The Second Nun introduces her tale of the early Church with a very medieval hymn to the Virgin Mary, translated almost verbatim from Dante's *Paradiso* Canto 33: '*Vergine madre, figlia del tuo figlio*'. Dante's hymn is supposedly sung by St Bernard of Clairvaux, the twelfth-century mystic, theologian and founder of the Knights Templar Crusading Order of monks.

> Thou mayde and mother, daughter of thy son
> Thou well of mercy, sinful soules cure
> Whom that high God in bounty chose alone
> Humblest and best of every creature.

Cecilia is pushed into marriage with a man she does not know but succeeds in staying a virgin on her wedding night. She persuades her husband to leave their bridal chamber and meet the leader of the Christians, Pope Urban, in the Catacombs. For this she is taken before the imperial chief of police, Almachius, who orders her to sacrifice to Jupiter and, when she refuses, starts an interrogation:

'What maner woman art thou then?' quoth he.
'I am a gentil-woman born' quoth she.
'I axe thee' quoth he, 'though thee it greve,
Of thy religioun and of thy byleve.'
'Ye have bygone your question foolishly,'
Quoth she, 'that wolden two answers conclude
In one demande; ye axen ignorantly.'

Cecilia is condemned to be boiled to death in a bath but escapes triumphant:

The longe night and eek a day also,
For all the fire, and eek the bathes heat,
She sat all cold, and felt of it no woe;
It made her not one drope for to sweat,
But in that bath her deth she moste get.

Chaucer's favourite Latin author and philosophical mentor, Anicius Manlius Boethius (c.475–524), or Boece in English, lived in Rome during the age sometimes called 'The Barbarian Disruption' between Pope Urban of the *Second Nun's Tale* and Pope Gregory the Great, 'the apostle of the English', who sent Augustine to Canterbury in 596. Between the start of the third and the end of the sixth century, southern Europe came under attack from wave after wave of hordes from eastern Europe and Asia, including the Huns, Teutons, Goths, Avars, Slavs and Vandals. The city of Rome was twice conquered and looted, first by the Visigoths in 410 and then in 476 by the Ostrogoths under their King Theodoric.

Ever since Gibbon, most historians have roughly concurred with the view of Henry Osborn Taylor: 'The Goths were the best of the Barbarians and Theodoric was the greatest of the Goths. Under Theodoric the relations between Goths and "Romans" were friendly. It was from the Code of Theodosius and other Roman sources that he drew the substance of his legislation. His aim was to harness the relations of the two peoples and assimilate the ways of the Goths to those of their more civilized neighbours.'

Boethius was born about AD 475 and went into public service under Theodoric, at one time becoming Consul. He was also a poet, scholar and follower of the late Roman Stoic philosophers, whose teaching of fortitude – stoicism – has entered the English language. Boethius devoted his spare time to translating Greek authors such as Plato and Aristotle, and compiling texts of ancient knowledge on mathematics, music and geography.

As a champion of 'Roman' liberties under a foreign occupation, Boethius fell out with his Visigothic masters, was thrown into jail and tortured to death at Pavia in about 524. While in prison, Boethius wrote the book for which he is still famous, the *Consolation of Philosophy*, a series of meditations in prose and verse. Like Dante before him, Chaucer adapted passages of the *Consolation* in his poetry, but also translated the whole of it into English prose. 'It must be supposed that Chaucer would apply more than common attention to the author of such celebrity,' wrote Samuel Johnson, who prided himself on his Latin, 'but in fact he has attempted nothing higher than a version strictly literal, and has degraded the poetical part of prose, that the constraint of versification might not obstruct his zeal for fidelity.'

Johnson forgot or did not know that Chaucer had adapted much of Boethius in the *Canterbury Tales*, *Troilus and Criseyde* and some of the shorter poems. The fact that Chaucer wanted to give a translation in simple English prose (much homelier and less Latinate than Johnson's polysyllables) suggests that he also sympathized with the efforts of Wyclif to make the Bible available to a broader public.

The *Consolation of Philosophy*, as its name suggests, was written by Boethius to counteract the fear and loneliness of prison. To develop his argument and provide himself with companionship, he wrote in the form of a three-way conversation between himself and two female spirits, representing Fate and Philosophy – the first of them cold, if not malign, but the second kind and encouraging. However, Philosophy scolds Boethius when he forgets his lesson:

'But say me this, remember thou what is the end of things, and whither the intention of all things tendeth?'

'I have heard it told, sometime,' quoth I, 'but dreryness hath dulled my memory.'

'Certes,' quod she, 'thou knowest whennes that alle things bien comen and procede?'

'I woot well,' quod I, and answered that God is bygnnynge of al.

'And how may this be,' quod she, 'that syn thou knowest the bygnnynge of things, that we knowest not wher is the ende of things?'

On such occasions we feel that Philosophy's schoolmarmish catechism must have been worse than secret police interrogation.

Like failed politicians of every age, Boethius is keen to settle scores with his rivals and enemies:

'How often have I resisted and withstonden thilke man hight Conigaste that made always assaults against the proper fortunes of poor feeble folk . . . How often eke have I cast out him, Trygiwille, Provost of the King's house, both of the wrongs that he had begun to do and eke fully performed.'

Boethius even records the quarrel with Theodoric which no doubt led to his arrest: 'When that Theodoric, the kyng of Goths, in a dere yeer, had his garneeris [granaries] full of corn, and commanded that no man shulde byen no corn til his corn was soold, and that at a grievous dere prys, Boethius withstood that ordenaunce and overcome it, knowing all this the King himself!'

The *Consolation* is a ragbag collection of philosophical moralizing, nostalgia for family life, nature notes and snippets of classical myth and history, such as the poem on Nero, to which Chaucer supplies a gloss in brackets.

We han wel known how many grete heroes and destructions were i-doon by the Emperor Nero. He leet brennen the cite of Rome, and made sleen the senatours; and he cruel whilom sloughe his mother, and he was maked moist with the blood of his modir (that is to seyn, he leet sleen and slitte the body of his modir to seen where he was conceyved); and he looked on every halve [side] upon her cold deede body, he no teer wette his face but he was so hardhearted that he might been domesman or judge of hir deade beaute.

Chaucer recalls this gruesome passage in the *Nun's Priest's Tale* when the abduction of Chaunticleer by the fox causes consternation to his loved ones:

O Woful hennes, right so cried ye,
As when that Nero brente the citee
Of Rome, cride the senatoures wyves,
For that there housebondes losten alle there lyves,
Withouten gilt this Nero hath them slayn.

Boethius was the origin of most of the verses in which Chaucer appears to give an opinion on morals, politics, or the events of his day. This goes especially for *The Former Age*, a lament for primitive innocence, which has often been cited for Chaucer's attitude to the Hundred Years' War, the feudal system, the rise of capitalism, monarchy and the Peasants' Revolt, yet it is little more than a paraphrase of Metrum 5 in Book II of the *Consolation of Philosophy*, written almost a thousand years earlier.

Here is the start of the prose translation:

> Blissful was the first age of men. They heelden hem apayed [satisfied] with the metes that the trewe feeldes broughten forth. They ne destroy-eden ne desseyvede hemself with outrage [excess]. They were wont lyghtly to slaken hir hunger at even with acornes of ookes . . . They slepen holsome slepes upon the gras, and dronken of the rennynge watres and layen under the shadowes of the heye pyn-trees.

And here is the first stanza of *The Former Age*:

> A blissful life, a paisible [peaceful] and a sweete,
> Ledden the peoples in the former age;
> They helde hem payed of fruites that they ete,
> Which that the feldes yave hem by usage;
> They were not for-pampred [over-pampered] with outrage.
> Unknown was the quern [hard mill] and eek the melle;
> They eten mast, hawes, and swych pounage [pig-food],
> And dronken water of the colde welle.

Boethius condemns the man that first 'dalf' or delved up the 'gobettes or the weightes of gold covered under earth and the precious stones that wouldest han be hydde', especially since their acquisition has put many men in danger.

The Former Age also attacks the mining industry:

> But cursed was the tyme, I dare wel saye,
> That men first dide hir swety bysiness
> To grobbe up metal lurkinge in derknesse,
> And in the riveres fyrst gemmes soghte.
> Allas, than sprang up all the cursedness
> Of covetyse, that fyrst our sorwe broghte!

In the mid-afternoon of 29 December 1999, I joined with hundreds of others at Canterbury Cathedral to pay respects to the memory of Archbishop Thomas Becket who was murdered there at the same time and day of the year in 1170. This annual ceremony and the one on 8 July, to mark the 'translation' of Becket's remains after his canonization, have been at the heart of the Becket cult which flourished during the Middle Ages and still continues into a new millennium. Becket's shrine and reputation for working cures were also the reasons why, in about 1386, Chaucer's pilgrims gathered at Southwark

> . . . from every shire's end
> Of Engelond, to Canterbury they wende,
> The holy blisful martir for to seeke,
> That them hath holpen when that they were weeke.

As is now customary on 29 December and on the Saint's Day, 8 July, there were two separate services in the cathedral, one for the Church of England and one for the Roman Catholics, who also claim Becket as their own. Indeed, at the 'Martyrdom', the spot where Becket was murdered, there is a plaque to commemorate the occasion on 20 May 1982 when Pope John Paul II and Archbishop Robert Runcie knelt side by side in prayer.

The murder of Becket in 1170 has come to be seen by medieval historians as a catalyst for the great events of Chaucer's lifetime, especially the breach with France, and the start of a separate English Church.

Becket became a hero to the nationalist historians of the nineteenth century, English, French and Irish. For Lord Macaulay, who celebrated the triumph of Protestant, constitutional power, Thomas Becket was a hero of the common English people, 'an enemy of their enemy', the Norman barons. To the French nationalist and republican Jules Michelet, he was a victim of the breakaway Anglo-Norman Henry and the detested Eleanor who had given all western France to her new husband. Michelet also saw Becket as the victim of Norman racial pride: 'His origins were against him. He was, it is said, the son of a Saracen (i.e., Muslim) woman who had followed a Saxon back from the Holy Land. His mother seemed to bar him from the Church, his father from the state!' In fact Becket was a pure-blooded Norman Christian on both sides, his father hailing from Caen and his mother from Rouen.

At the time his murder revived old stories and prophecies of a curse hanging over the heads of Henry, Queen Eleanor and their children. The stories went back to Eleanor's reprobate grandfather William IV of Aquitaine, who had kept a private brothel disguised as a nunnery. An angry hermit had prophesied that William and his descendants through the male and female lines would never know any happiness in their children. When Eleanor was an old woman, Bishop Hugh of Lincoln (St Hugh) used to repeat this story, saying he had heard it from Henry II, who must have heard it from Eleanor.

Eleanor of Aquitaine (1122–1204) was in fact more important than Becket as an influence on Chaucer's age. She was the richest woman in Europe as well as a famous beauty who left King Louis VII of France to marry Henry II of England, taking with her as a dowry all the lands from the Loire to the Pyrenees. She was seen by the French as a traitress who condemned her country to centuries of war until redeemed by Joan of Arc.

By Henry II Eleanor bore and raised two disastrous English kings, Richard the Lionheart and John, whose unstable bloodline continued throughout the fourteenth century with the homosexual Edward II and the still more neurotic Richard II, before the Plantagenet dynasty came to an end in 1485 with the death of Richard III at Bosworth. Eleanor's fantastic career, which included crusading in Palestine with her first husband and several years' imprisonment by her second, has made her the villainess of Shakespeare's *King John*, as well as the subject of two fine biographies eight centuries later.*

Although Henry II was an intelligent, learned man who spoke Latin better than his archbishop Thomas Becket, it was Eleanor who made the English court the centre of a poetic revival. She had grown up in her native Aquitaine listening to the *chansons de geste*, or songs of valiant deeds, celebrating the knights such as Roland and Oliver who had fought back the first Islamic invasion. Since the *chansons*, like modern war and action films, had little appeal for female audiences, a vogue grew up in Eleanor's time for 'Arthurian' poems telling of knights in love as well as in combat. Although the Arthurian poems flourished in France, they were generally set in a misty Celtic land that could be Brittany, Cornwall, Wales or Ireland.

---

* Desmond Seward's *Eleanor of Aquitaine, The Mother Queen* (1978) is especially good on the Second Crusade and Eleanor's relationship with the Church. Alison Weir's *Eleanor of Aquitaine, By the wrath of God, Queen of England* offers feminine understanding without feminist propaganda.

One of the first Arthurian poets was Marie de France, later Abbess of Shaftesbury in Dorset, whose 'Breton' romances delighted Henry II and Eleanor. The royal couple commanded their court 'reader' Wace to make a French translation of Geoffrey of Monmouth's Latin *History of the British Kings*, a collection of Welsh legends which gave Shakespeare the plots of *King Lear* and *Cymbeline*. These twelfth-century Arthurian poets invented the story of the Round Table as well as the pious tale that Joseph of Arimathea came to Glastonbury in Somerset, along with the Holy Grail, the Ark of the Covenant and other sacred relics.

Queen Eleanor became the patron of the French poet Chrétien de Troyes, one of whose early works was based on her own adventures in Palestine on the Second Crusade. She encouraged Chrétien to write a series of poems about the Arthurian knights, including the story of Percival and the Holy Grail, Tristan's love for Yseult, and Lancelot's for Guinevere.

Chaucer in the *Nun's Priest's Tale* shows that he acknowledged the power of Arthurian romance over women:

> Now every wise man let him harken me,
> This story is as true I undertake
> As is the book of Lancelot of the lake
> That women hold in full great reverence.

Yet perhaps because he regarded them as women's books, Chaucer himself borrowed little from Arthurian stories, except to make fun of them, as in the *Wife of Bath's Tale*. However, he studied and came under the spell of the twelfth-century *Roman de Troie* (Romance of Troy) by Benoit de Maure, who also was a protégé of Eleanor of Aquitaine and indeed dedicated this epic to 'the rich lady of the rich King, whose kindness knows no bounds'. Benoit's flattery is more subtle when for the first time he shows Helen of Troy as an admirable as well as a beautiful woman although, like Eleanor, she started a war by leaving her husband for another man.

Eleanor gathered around her poets and troubadours of the southern French dialects known collectively as Languedoc or Provençal, a language of vernacular poetry which preceded and deeply influenced Dante's Italian as well as Chaucer's English. Even those of us who barely discern the nuances of modern French can nevertheless under-

stand why an expert like Helen Waddell called twelfth-century Provençal a 'language softer than sleep', whose poetry 'demands no other
intellectual background than of a morning, the far-off singing of birds,
a hawthorn tree in blossom and a crusade for the holy sepulchre. It is
the Middle Ages in the medium of a dream.'

The same dreamy images recur in the thirteenth-century *Roman de
la Rose* which Chaucer translated, and in many of Chaucer's own
fourteenth-century poems such as *The Book of the Duchess, The
Parliament of Fowls, The Legend of Good Women* and even the
General Prologue to the *Canterbury Tales*, if we substitute a pilgrimage for a crusade to the holy sepulchre.

Eleanor judged the poetry contests or 'courts of love' in which
troubadours vied in singing devotion to their ladies, first as aspirants,
then as suppliants and suitors, and finally as accepted lovers who got
their reward of a hand to kiss, but nothing more, since the rules
demanded chastity, or at any rate secrecy. The spectacle of a young
man wasting away for love was agreeable to middle-aged ladies then
as now, not least to Eleanor. As the young Queen of France she had
thrilled to the amorous compliments of the Gascon poet Marcabru.
Thirty years later, as Queen of England, she could still succumb to the
flattery of a German student who strummed his harp and sang:

> Were the world all mine
> From the sea to the Rhine,
> I'd give it all
> If so be the Queen of the English
> Were in my arms.

Eleanor's favourite troubadour and reputed lover was Bertrand de
Born, a swaggering bully-boy from the Dordogne who lived by
extortion and plunder. It was certainly with Eleanor's encouragement
that Bertrand became a boon companion of Henry 'the young King',
her eldest son, and prompted him to revolt against his father in 1173.

Henry II crushed the revolt and incarcerated Eleanor for most of the
next twenty years, but he was broken by the ingratitude of the son he
dearly loved. Dante, in one of the lowest circles of the *Inferno*,
encounters a bloody torso holding a severed head and swinging it
like a lantern, which says to him:

> Know that I am Bertrand de Born.
> I am he who gave the young King evil advice
> I made father and son rebel against each other.

Although Eleanor spent sixteen years confined in castles because of her part in the young Henry's rebellion, she had already poisoned the minds of her three remaining sons, Geoffrey, Richard and John. It was Geoffrey who said that, in the Plantagenet family, sons always hated their fathers, and he too went to an early, embittered death. But it was Richard, the brave and handsome Coeur de Lion or Lionheart, on whom Eleanor worked her most baneful corruption by love. Their relationship has been the subject of a play and film, *The Lion in Winter*, and could serve as a Freudian psychological case-history on how a selfish woman can turn her son into a homosexual.

Eleanor fostered such a vicious hatred between father and son that when Henry II lay on his death bed, he whispered in Richard's ear: 'God grant that I don't die before I take revenge on you.' Monster though Eleanor had become, it is hard not to admire the spirit which drove her, in her sixties, to ride to Madrid to find a suitable wife for her son, then lead the young woman across the Pyrenees and the Alps to Sicily, where Richard declined to marry her until he had finished with his boyfriend. She stood by Richard when he led a crusade to the Holy Land, as disastrous in its way as the one she had taken part in forty years earlier. She stood by Richard when he was captured and held to ransom in Austria, abusing the Pope for his inactivity in a letter signed 'Eleanor, by the wrath of God, Queen of England'.

When Richard was freed from his dungeon, Eleanor went up the Rhine to meet him and take him back to Sandwich, from where they went over to Canterbury to pray at the shrine of St Thomas. She was one of those present in Nottingham at the scene so often portrayed in Hollywood films of Robin Hood, when Richard revealed himself as king to the jubilant English people.

There is reason to believe that Chaucer did not go along with the medieval cult of Richard I which held him up as a model of chivalry and a Christian crusader against Islam. A well-known example of the cult was Geoffrey de Vinsauf's *Poetria nova*, a pompous Latin treatise on rhetoric which the author illustrated with flamboyant examples of his own. One of these is a lament for Richard the Lionheart.

In the *Nun's Priest's Tale*, when Chaunticleer the barnyard cock is carried away by a fox on a Friday in spite of his warning dream, Chaucer pokes fun at Geoffrey de Vinson's elegy:

> O Gaufred, deere maister soverayn,
> That when the worthy King Richard was slayn
> With shot, complainedst his death so sore,
> Why ne hadde I nought thy cunning and thy lore . . . ?

These lines can be taken to mean that Chaucer laughed at Richard the Lionheart and the cult of chivalry. This interpretation conforms to the twentieth-century view that Richard and his fellow crusaders went to the Holy Land for plunder or to indulge their blood-lust, rather than from religious conviction. The question will be discussed in the chapter on Chaucer's Knight.

Just as modern historians tend to debunk King Richard I, so some have tried to revive the reputation of John, his younger brother. It has been said that he helped to rebuild the navy, introduced copper coins, and granted incorporation to Liverpool. Medieval historians saw him more accurately as a cruel greedy brat who said he would gladly sell London if he could find a buyer, and who managed to pick and lose quarrels with the Church, the King of the French and the barons of England, before they obliged him to endorse Magna Carta, the Great Charter of English rights, including habeas corpus.

Shakespeare in *King John* calls Eleanor of Aquitaine a 'monstrous injurer of heaven and earth' and a 'cankered grandam' with a 'sin-conceiving womb'. The playwright was echoing the dying words of St Hugh of Lincoln in 1200:

> The descendants of King Henry must bear the curse pronounced in Scripture, 'The multiplied brood of the wicked shall not thrive,' and again 'The children of adulterers shall be rooted out.' The present King of France will avenge the memory of his virtuous father, King Louis, upon the faithless wife who left him to unite with his enemy. And as the ox eats down the grass to the roots, so shall Philip of France entirely destroy this race.

As St Hugh of Lincoln predicted, Philip threw John out of Normandy and would have defeated him in England as well, had John not died from eating 'a surfeit of lampreys', as the chroniclers record.

King John's loss of Normandy has come to be seen by historians as the catalyst which created the two separate nations of England and France, each with its own frontiers, language, culture, system of government and patriotism. Yet although England and France were growing apart in the thirteenth century, they remained loosely attached by the French lingua franca, by family ties and above all by adherence to the Roman Catholic Church. Both countries experienced the transformation of the Church caused by its new-found militancy against the Orthodox faith of the East, against Jews, and against the heretical sects which now can be seen as the forerunners of Protestantism. This new and often intolerant militancy was bound up with the decline of monasteries and the rise of the mendicant friars in the thirteenth century. This is a major theme of the French poem *Le Roman de la Rose* which Chaucer helped to translate into English and which also inspires the satire in the *Canterbury Tales*.

Like so many major events in English history, the débâcle of King John revolved around Canterbury and another strong archbishop, Stephen Langton, who was one of the witnesses to Magna Carta. After John's death in 1216, Archbishop Langton attempted to reconcile the warring factions in England by setting up shrines to two of his martyred predecessors: St Elphege, killed by the Danes, and St Thomas, killed by the Normans.

Even during the reign of King John, the offerings of the pilgrims were enough to pay for a shrine to Becket within the new Gothic Choir and Trinity Chapel, near the east end of the cathedral. When it was thought that the saint had a worthy resting place, the relics were brought up from the crypt in a translation ceremony conducted by Archbishop Langton and watched by the boy Henry III on 7 July 1320. During that first year alone, the visitors to the Becket shrine gave £1,142 in money, gold, silver and jewels, while the monks replaced the design of their ancient seal with one showing a representation of Thomas's murder. This was the start of a souvenir trade which also embraced St Thomas badges and phials or ampullae of holy water, said to contain drops of his blood.

Chaucer never mentions Becket's relics but makes clear his opinion of some of the relics peddled by the Pardoner:

> For in his bag he hadde a pilow there
> Which that he saide was oure Lady's veil:

He seide he hadde a gobet of the seyl
That seynt Peter hadde, when that he wente
Upon the see, til Jesus Crist him hente.
He had a cros of brasse ful of stones
And in a glas he hadde pigges bones.
But with these reliques, whenne that he found
A pore persoun dwellyng upon ground,
Upon a day he gat him more moneye
Than that the parsoun gat in monthes tweye.

Edward I, the 'Hammer of the Scots' and the strongest King of England before his grandson Edward III, was a frequent worshipper at the shrine of Thomas Becket after he offered a successful prayer for the healing of his favourite falcon, and it was Edward I's son Edward II who instituted the custom of anointing kings with 'Becket's Oil' at their coronation. This did not avert disaster from his own ignominious reign which is now chiefly remembered for the loss of the Battle of Bannockburn to the Scots, and his flagrant homosexual affairs. Indeed, Edward II's horrible murder at Berkeley Castle, by having a red-hot poker pushed up his rectum, was interpreted by some contemporaries as revenge for the sins of Henry II and Eleanor of Aquitaine.

After a time of civil anarchy, Edward III was crowned at Westminster Abbey on 1 February 1327. He was fifteen years old. Chaucer's contemporary and fellow poet Sir John Froissart begins his *Chronicles*** with his compliment to King Edward III, his own and Chaucer's patron: 'It is commonly believed among the English – and this has often been borne out since the time of good King Arthur – that in between two brave and warlike Kings, there has always reigned one less gifted in mind and body. This was illustrated by the parentage of King Edward III. His grandfather Edward I was a brave, wise and resourceful ruler, enterprising and very successful in war. But when he died he was succeeded by the son of his first marriage [i.e., Edward II] who was quite unlike him in wisdom and courage, and governed the country harshly on the advice of others.' (Here Froissart means Edward II's homosexual favourites such as Piers Gaveston and Sir Hugh Despenser, whose execution at Hereford he describes in revolting detail.)

---

* Penguin Classics, 1968, selected, translated and edited by Geoffrey Brereton.

In the next two chapters I examine the state of England from 1327 up to the year 1340, the approximate date of the birth of Chaucer. In the first chapter, I shall try to explain how Edward repaired the damage done to the realm by his father, and then won the confidence of the barons, the Church and Parliament, including a now assertive House of Commons. Next I examine Edward's early military exploits, as chronicled by Sir John Froissart, who remains the best historian of England in the fourteenth century. The second chapter explains how Edward III helped to make England a great commercial power by advancing the merchant class to which Chaucer belonged.

2

Edward III Goes to War

BY THE TIME OF his father's murder, the fifteen-year-old King Edward III had moved with his court and his counsellors up to York, to repel a Scottish invasion. King Robert the Bruce of Scotland was now afflicted with leprosy but saw in the troubles of England a chance to repeat his triumph at Bannockburn and thus guarantee his dynasty and his nation's independence. Soon after Easter 1327, the English army in the north watched the smoke of burning villages rising over the moors and knew that the Scots had once again entered their country.

Chaucer's *Man of Law's Tale*, relating how Constance is shipwrecked on the Northumberland coast, conveys the terror with which the medieval English regarded the Scottish border. From Froissart's *Chronicles* of 1327, we understand why the knights of the fourteenth century dreaded having to serve in this theatre of war:

> Young King Edward and his army rode all that day over those hills and desolate heaths, finding no towns and following no road, with only the sun to guide them over those trackless wastes. By the late afternoon they had reached the Tyne. Exhausted by the day's journey, they forded it with much difficulty, because of the great stones that lay in it. When they reached the other side, each chose a piece of ground along the bank on which to spend the night, but before they had all found a pitch the sun was setting . . . Towards noon the next day some peasants told them they were about forty-two miles from Newcastle and about thirty-three from Carlisle. There were no nearer towns in which they could get provisions . . . In this way they had gone three days and nights without food, wine, fodder, candles and everything else . . . Some were so famished that they snatched the food from their comrades' hands, which gave rise to serious brawls among the men. As an added misery,

it never stopped raining the whole week . . . At nightfall the Scots in the mountain-slope opposite always lit great fires and raised such a din by blowing on their horns and whooping in chorus that it sounded to the English as though all the devils in hell had been let loose.

When the young King Edward failed to defeat or even to find the Scottish army at Easter 1327, he returned to Durham in despair. To make matters worse, his mother, Queen Isabella, under the influence of her lover Roger Mortimer, was insisting that he make peace with Robert the Bruce. One hundred Scottish knights were called to a Parliament at York in February 1328 for the express purpose of ratifying Scottish independence. The resulting treaty recognized Robert as king of a sovereign nation; it restored the frontier established by Alexander III, and it cancelled all obligations implying subjection to England. So Scotland obtained the separate status it was to lose again by the Act of Union of 1707 but seems largely to have recovered at the end of the twentieth century.

Although English chroniclers condemned what they called a *turpis pax* or cowardly peace, it did not satisfy Scottish pride or aspirations. A few years later Scotland renewed its 'Auld Alliance' with France, just as centuries later Irish nationalists would look for help to Spain, France and Germany. King Edward and many Englishmen blamed this *turpis pax* on Isabella the Queen Mother, and still more on Mortimer, who was proving as greedy as Edward II's favourites. Edward III joined in a plot to enter Nottingham Castle at night to seize Mortimer and Isabella. She is said to have begged her son to 'have pity on gentle Mortimer', but he received no better treatment than he had handed out to Edward II. After a trial by his peers in London, Mortimer was hanged, drawn and quartered. Once Mortimer was out of the way, King Edward III showed his natural magnanimity of spirit. The Queen Mother, Isabella, was allowed to retire in comfort at Castle Rising in Norfolk, where she was visited each year by her son, and eventually joined the Franciscan order of St Clare. Edward III was equally generous to the friends and adherents of Isabella, and even of Mortimer.

When in 1330 Edward III began his half century of independent rule, it seemed to the monkish chroniclers of the time like Israel's delivery from the house of bondage. The king was in his nineteenth year – strong, brave and married to the attractive Princess Philippa of

Hainault, in the Netherlands, who had already borne him the first of many children, Edward, the future Black Prince. It is true that from an early age Edward III was prone to embark on affairs with married women, but this was acceptable in an age which took its sexual morality from poems about King Arthur's court. After his failure in Scotland King Edward was keen to win his spurs by a crusade to the Holy Land, perhaps at the side of his cousin, King Philip VI of France. When this plan fell through, the two kings slowly came to accept the idea of fighting against each other, like Palamon and Arcite in Chaucer's *Knight's Tale*.

The quarrel between the Capets and the Plantagenets went back to 1154 when Eleanor of Aquitaine divorced Louis VII and married Henry II of England. Almost two centuries later, Henry's descendant Edward III still owed feudal allegiance to the French king who was suzerain of Eleanor's lands in Aquitaine. These included the port of Bordeaux and the vineyards of Gascony, which now, in the fourteenth century, brought Edward more revenue than did England itself. Since Edward III was chronically short of money and by nature extravagant, he liked the idea of obtaining sovereignty over Gascony, just as Philip wanted its revenue as well as its feudal ownership. Both kings were aware of this in 1329 when Edward was summoned to Amiens to render homage, as his Plantagenet ancestors had all had to do. Philip was not pleased when Edward, his vassal, turned up in a robe of crimson velvet worked with leopards in gold, and wearing a crown, sword and spurs. He demanded the proper liege homage, bare-headed and with ungirt sword, but Edward refused.

In spite of such posturing, neither Philip nor Edward was yet ready to meet the cost of all-out war, though both were recruiting allies – the French at Edinburgh, the English in Flanders. Both competed for the allegiance of the barons of Gascony and the other provinces of Aquitaine. At first they moved cautiously, as with the pawns in chess, but when Philip announced the confiscation of Gascony, Edward replied by laying a formal claim to the French throne, by right of succession through the female line.*

Edward had the advantage over Philip by his control of most of the Netherlands. His marriage to Philippa gave him Hainault, with which

---

* Like all such dynastic disputes, it holds little interest for the modern reader. However, legal experts still consider Edward's case tenable in law, if not in common sense.

came the provinces of Holland and Zeeland. Since England supplied the wool to the weaving towns of Ghent, Bruges and Ypres, Edward was virtually master of Flanders and knew how to play on the Flemish hostility to the French, which persists to this day. Knights from Hainault joined Edward's campaign against the Scots in 1327, and one of their number gave the account of its hardships to Froissart, who was himself a Hainaulter.

The cost of hiring Hainault soldiers and subsidizing the burghers of Bruges, Ghent and Ypres put a further strain on Edward's finances and made him dependent on Parliament, which met forty-eight times during his reign. So it was during Chaucer's lifetime that England developed the unwritten principles of government by consent, and no taxation without representation, the principles that eventually caused the American Revolution. This meant that kings governed with the consent of the temporal and spiritual lords, the knights of the shires and the burgesses of the towns, of which seventy-five were represented during the reign of Edward III and eighty-three in the reign of Richard II. The temporal peers included most surviving descendants of William the Conqueror's barons, to which Edward added a number of wealthy newcomers as well as the royal dukes from among his own sons, notably Chaucer's patron John of Gaunt, 'time-honoured Lancaster' as he is known to us from Shakespeare. It was during the fourteenth century that senior prelates first normally sat in the House of Lords, including the primates of York and Canterbury, the bishops of London, Durham and Winchester, and the abbots or priors of some of the wealthy monasteries. These men had the power to grant or refuse the payment of tithes to the Crown.

Since much of Edward's revenue came from taxes on wool and manufactures, he paid special attention to the knights of the shires and burgesses of the towns, who were 'elected' by the sheriffs – more in the sense of 'picked' or 'chosen' rather than gaining most votes in a ballot.

It was accepted in Chaucer's time that men of property in a shire, whether knights or not, were fit to represent it in Parliament. King Edward preferred to have 'Knights girt with the sword and having the honour of Knighthood', especially those who had proved themselves in war, but he could not always persuade them to take a seat. Nor was the king always successful in excluding lawyers from Parliament on the grounds that they used it in the interest of their private clients. The parliamentary knights of the fourteenth century ranged from the younger sons of earls to prosperous yeomen, some of whose ancestors had been serfs. Probably most had served their county as sheriffs, coroners, justices of the peace or tax collectors. They brought to Parliament a wide range of administrative experience and knowledge of local conditions. Gradually they began to merge with the burgesses of the towns into a common interest group in the House of Commons.

The *General Prologue* to the *Canterbury Tales* points out the difference between a knight with 'the honour of knighthood' and a 'knight of the shire' who is chosen to sit in the House of Commons. The first, who heads the pilgrims and tells the first tale, was

> . . . a worthy man
> That from the time that he first began
> To riden out, he loved chivalrye
> Trouth and honour, fredom and courtesie
> Full worthy was he in his Lordes warre,
> And thereto had he ridden, no man so far,
> As well in Christendom as in heathenesse . . .

The knights of the shire are represented by the sybaritic Franklin, or landowner, whose honour derives from wealth and the open house he keeps in the country:

> His bread, his ale was always best of all;
> His store of wine was known in special.
> Withoute bakemeats never was his house,
> Of flesh and fish, and that so plenteous
> It snowed in his house of meat and drink,
> And alle dainties that men coulde think.
> After the sundry seasons of the year,
> He changed them at meat and at souper.
> Full many a fat partridge had he in mew,
> And many a bream and many a luce in stew . . .
> His table dormant in his halle alway
> Stood redy covered all the longe day.
> At sessions there was he lord and sire.
> Full ofte tyme he was Knight of the shire . . .
> A sheriff and a counter [auditor] had he been,
> Was nowhere such a worthy Frankeleyn.

In spite of his wealth and office, Chaucer's Franklin was aware of not being a gentleman, like the Knight, for when the Knight's son, the Squire, has finished his tale, the Franklin says ruefully that his own son is addicted to gambling and low company:

> I have a son, and by the Trinity
> I rather would than twenty pound worth land,
> Though it right now were fallen in my hand,
> He were a man of such discretion
> As that ye be; fie on possession,
> Unless a man be virtuous withal
> I have my son rebuked, and yet shall,
> For he to virtue listeth not to entende,
> But for to play at dice, and to dispende,
> And lose all that he hath, is his usage;
> And he had rather talken with a page
> Than to commune with any gentil wight
> When he might lernen gentillesse aright.

Chaucer himself had something of both the 'parfit gentil Knight' and of the Franklin. He had served in the war in France and his son was enrolled as a squire, but he lacked the honour of knighthood. However, like the Franklin he was a knight of the shire and sat for Kent in the House of Commons. He was amply qualified by his work as a justice of the peace and his civil service duties with the customs, roads and forestry departments. Moreover he did not carry the stigma of being a lawyer, and clearly rather despised the Sergeant of Law who dealt in property and liked to bamboozle his clients with jargon and mumbo-jumbo:

> All was fee simple to him in effect,
> His word of law might never be suspect.
> Nowhere so busy a man in any case,
> And yet he seemed busier than he was.

Edward III understood from the start the need to keep the good will of all three estates of Parliament: the lords temporal and spiritual and the House of Commons. He made sure that the members claimed and were given their travelling and attendance fees, and made a point of thanking all those who made the arduous journey north when Parliament met at York. Thanks to this broad support, Edward won his first political confrontation with his own appointed Chancellor and Archbishop of Canterbury, John Stratford, who at one time threatened to become another Thomas Becket.

The trouble began in 1339 when Edward's Florentine bankers ran out of funds and he tried to raise cash by increased taxes and tithes from the Church. First in his role as Chancellor, then as archbishop, Stratford rebuked the king for his costly military plans. In November 1340 Edward arrested some of his privy councillors and threatened Stratford who beat a retreat to Canterbury. The king sent out tax commissioners to step up the rate of collection. He wrote to the Pope at Avignon, accusing Stratford of plotting against him and even planning his murder. He sent an official to Canterbury with a request to Stratford to come to London, prepared to go abroad as a hostage for debts due to the merchants of Louvain, one of the Netherlands towns which England was subsidizing.

Stratford played for time, so it was not till 29 December, the anniversary of Becket's murder and now his saint's day, that he proclaimed his political views. Speaking in English from the cathedral pulpit, Stratford declared that the loss of Henry II's overseas lands was a punishment for the killing of Becket, and he even made a connection between the English defeat at Bannockburn and the monarchy's treatment of the Church. The archbishop then pronounced sentence of excommunication, the royal family excepted, on anyone who violated Magna Carta, the peace of the land, or the liberties of the Church. The bishops were ordered to have this sentence read out in all the parish churches in England.

Archbishop Stratford's sermon at Canterbury on St Thomas's Day, 1340, the probable year of Chaucer's birth, was meant as a warning to Edward III not to make the same mistakes as his ancestor Henry II and could be seen as a prophecy of the folly and pride of Henry VIII, two centuries later, when Becket's remains were exhumed and scattered. But Edward III was to prove a loyal son of the Church of Rome and Canterbury, and a frequent suppliant at St Thomas's shrine.

In return Archbishop Stratford became a loyal supporter of Edward's government and of his war against France. He advocated in Parliament the tithes and taxes which Edward required to raise his armies and to subsidize his allies in the Netherlands. He backed Edward's claim to the throne of France and blessed his invasion of Normandy as part of a 'just war', as defined by Thomas Aquinas, the greatest theologian of the Middle Ages. Only a few years after his critical sermon at Canterbury, Archbishop Stratford preached another at St Paul's in London supporting Edward's war. In particular he endorsed as genuine the document which the English claimed to have found at the sack of Caen, announcing a plan by the Valois kings to reconquer Britain and make French compulsory as its national language.

This was not, as many supposed at the time and for centuries afterwards, an early example of 'black propaganda', comparable with the 'captured documents' so often found in modern wars. According to Keith Fowler, who has edited and introduced a recent collection of essays on the Hundred Years' War, the original *ordonnance* not only survived but can still be seen at the Archives Nationales in Paris.*

The popularity of Edward's war among the bishops, as well as among the temporal peers, the House of Commons and the English people at large, increased with his early success against the French and their Scottish allies. In the words of a recent historian of the reign: 'The victories of Crécy, Neville's Cross and Poitiers persuaded the higher clergy that the King was fighting a just war.'† Both as a strategist and a field commander Edward was claiming a place as one of the great war leaders in English history, the first in a line stretching through Marlborough, Wellington and Winston Churchill.

Although Edward used to be best remembered for introducing the rites and mottoes of chivalry such as the Garter, *Ich Dien* and *Honi soit qui mal y pense*, he can also be seen as a pioneer of modern, total war, a precursor of Ludendorff, Hitler and North Vietnam's Vo Nguyen Giap. Just as Napoleon argued that an army marches on its stomach, Edward saw the importance of logistics and supplies. Early on in the war against France, he banned the export of horses to the Continent in case they should fall into enemy hands. To keep his soldiers supplied with fish on Fridays, he equipped his invading forces with portable leather boats to go out on rivers and lakes.

---

* *The Hundred Years War*, London, 1971, p. 7, note 24.

† W. M. Ormrod, *The Reign of Edward III: Crown and Political Society 1327–1377*, 1990, p. 20.

Edward III may have celebrated chivalry, but his innovations hastened the end of the age of the knight on horseback. The use of longbow archers and dismounted men-at-arms, which he had learnt in fighting the Scots on the border, was just as revolutionary in its time as were the tank and machine-gun in the First World War. He was the first military leader to understand the potential of the cannon. It was used at first in sieges to break down walls more effectively than a battering-ram or stone-firing ballista.

If cannons were used at Crécy, however, they probably played little part except to frighten the horses; nor was naval gunfire used in the English triumph at Sluys, though it played a part in a subsequent battle off La Rochelle. Still, Chaucer was so excited by this innovation that he brought it into a poem (from the *Legend of Good Women*) about the Battle of Actium, where Antony and Cleopatra encountered the fleet of Octavian. Here the 'grete gonne' adds to the more conventional means of attacking ships with claw-like grappling hooks and shears to cut the rigging, as well as anti-personnel devices like scattering peas on the enemy decks to make them slippery, or throwing lime in enemy eyes:

Up goeth the trompe, and for to shout and shoot
And peyne hem to sette on with the sonne.
With grisly sound out goeth the grete gonne
And hotly they hurtelen all at once,
And from the top down came the great stones.
In goeth the grapnel so full of crooks;
Among the ropes renne the shearing hooks.
In with the pole-ax presseth he and he;
Behind the mast beginneth he to flee,
And out again, and driveth him overbord;
He stingeth him upon his spear's ord [point];
He rent the sail with hooks like a scythe;
He bringeth the cup and biddek them be blithe;
He poureth peasen upon the haches slidere;
With pottes full of lime they go togidere;
And thus the longe day in fight they spende,
Till at the last, as everything hath ende,
Antony is schent [destroyed] and put him to the flyte,
And all his folk to-go that best go might.

Fleeth eke the queen, with all her purple sail
Because of the strokes that went as thick as hail,
No wonder was she might it not endure
And when that Antony saw that aventure,
'Alas' quoth he 'the day that I was born!
My honour in this day thus have I lorn!'

From contemporary chroniclers it would seem that Edward III had the same gift for inspiring his troops with discipline and morale that Shakespeare attributes to Henry V in a later stage of the Hundred Years' War. The discipline was apparent at Crécy when English archers faced the advance of thousands of Genoese crossbow-men in the pay of France. Froissart writes: 'The Genoese began to utter loud whoops to frighten the English but the English waited in silence and did not stir. The Genoese hulloa'd a second time and advanced a little further, but the English still made no move. Then they raised a third shout, very loud and clear, levelled their crossbows, and began to shoot. At this the English archers took one pace forward and poured out their arrows so thickly and evenly that they fell like snow. When they felt those arrows piercing their arms, their heads, their faces, the Genoese who had never met such archers before, were thrown into confusion. Many cut their bowstrings and some threw down their crossbows.' The same patience and discipline of the English bowmen destroyed the French cavalry at Poitiers.

Besides inspiring the common soldiers, Edward III had the rarer gift in a king or commander of holding on to the loyalty of his generals and counsellors, without arousing jealousy or contention. His principal commanders on the first campaign in France – Henry, Earl of Derby, the Earls of Warwick, Northampton and Suffolk, Sir Reginald Cobham and Sir Walter Manny – were with him still on his last. Although his beloved son Edward the Black Prince was to alienate the people of Aquitaine by his arrogance and cruelty, no chronicler ever questioned his courage or patriotism. In striking contrast to his ancestor, Henry II, Edward III enjoyed the love and loyalty of his children, including Chaucer's patron, John of Gaunt.

Moreover, from Froissart's account of the naval battle of Winchelsea, one of the great sea battles of his reign, it sounds as though Edward was fond of the rough male heartiness which today we associate with a stag night or rugby club dinner.

On that day, I was told by some who were with him, he was in a gayer mood than he had ever been seen before. He told his minstrels to strike up a dance tune which Sir John Chandos who was there beside him, had recently brought back from Germany. And out of sheer high spirits he made Sir John sing with his minstrels to his own vast amusement . . . While the King was enjoying this gaiety and his Knights were cheerful at seeing him so cheerful, the look-out shouted 'Ship ahoy. And it looks like a Spaniard.' The minstrels stopped playing and the man was asked if he saw more than one. In a moment he answered: 'There are so many, God help me, I can't count them' . . . The King therefore had wine served to himself and all his Knights. Then he and the others put on their battle-helmets . . .

Although the war developed into a contest of nation states, most of the fighting took place not in the heartlands of England and France but in peripheral regions such as the Scottish borders, Brittany, Flanders and Gascony, the last two being the principal sources of wealth, from cloth and wine respectively.

Before he set off on campaigns in France, Edward ensured the defence of his own island kingdom, especially the south-east coast and the Scottish border. Soon after the triumphs at Crécy and Calais he hurried up north to repel an invasion and win the Battle of Neville's Cross, near Durham. From the account of Froissart, it seems that Edward wanted to turn the English into a nation at arms: 'It was next proposed and decreed that no one in the realm of England, on pain of decapitation, should practise any game or sport other than that of shooting with bows and arrows, and that all craftsmen making bows and arrows should be exempted from all debts.

'It was also decreed that every knight, squire and fighting-man serving the King in his war should draw the King's pay but that each should maintain himself according to his standing for half a year out of his own funds, any prisoner or other war-gains which he might make remaining with him for his personal profit.

'It was also decreed that in the coastal areas and islands, such as Cornwall, Guernsey, Wight, Hampshire and Sheppey, no men-at-arms or defence personnel should be moved away regardless of any levy called by the King, but should guard their coasts and borders and should train their children in the use of arms and archery, in return for two pence each day drawn from the duties on the wool within their districts.'

Edward III's mobilization for total war in 1340 was comparable to Churchill's in 1940 except that on the earlier occasion England was the aggressor nation preparing to launch an invasion across the Channel. This partly explains why the Hundred Years' War is no longer glorified in modern school history books, its very name suggesting that it was futile as well as long drawn out. Moreover, with hindsight it is obvious how the early English triumphs at Crécy and Poitiers would end in the French reconquest of Aquitaine in 1453, the shameful burning to death of Joan of Arc, and the rebirth of French military pride. But Edward III at the start of the conflict could not be expected to look ahead to the fifteenth century, still less to the empires of Louis XIV and Napoleon Bonaparte.

Like even the wisest statesman, Edward III belonged to his age and worked for his own and his country's advantage, as he saw it. If he had stopped to list his war aims, these would have included maintaining sovereignty over Aquitaine and its vineyards; disrupting the Auld Alliance of Scotland and France; remaining an ally of Bruges, Ghent and Ypres; and after the capture of Calais in 1337 repopulating the town with English settlers.

We can never know if Edward III really believed in his claim to the throne of France or whether this was a bargaining ploy to maintain the loyalty of Aquitaine and Flanders. The monarchs of England did not relinquish their claim to the throne of France till the Peace of Amiens of 1802, when the most recent French king had perished by the guillotine. Certainly Edward did not intend to occupy the whole of what is now France, any more than the Valois kings hoped to repeat the achievement of William the Conqueror.

To understand how the Hundred Years' War was seen by Chaucer, we cannot do better than stay with Froissart. Indeed, some scholars believe that Chaucer's hymn to the marguerite or ox-eye daisy in the prologue to the *Legend of Good Women* derives from Froissart's *Ditte De La Jonece,* with their '*Joli mois de may*' and other overworked phrases of medieval poetry:

> Whan that the month of May
> Is comen, and that I hear the fowles singe,
> And that the flowers ginnen for to springe
> Farewell my book and my devocioun . . .
> As I said erst, whanne comen is the May

> That in my bed, there dawneth me no day
> That I nam [am not] up and walking in the mede . . .

If such lines of Chaucer were really derived from Froissart, it is easy to understand why Froissart himself is less regarded in France as a poet than as the author of the *Chronicles*.

But like many literary men of the age, Froissart earned his bread as a minstrel and clerk at the court of patrons, who included kings and queens, for whom he wrote verses to flatter and amuse. Froissart was born in about 1337 at the now-French town of Valenciennes, then the capital of the county of Hainault, whose territory in the Netherlands included modern Holland and Zeeland. The county's political and economic ties with England were strengthened when Edward married Philippa of Hainault. She in turn took Froissart into her service in London and Windsor, to compose 'fine ditties and writings on love', as he explains in the prologue to the *Chronicles*.

On his first visit to England, in 1361, Froissart crossed the Channel with Chaucer and an official party escorting the King of France and other prisoners held as hostages after the Battle of Poitiers. To gather material for the chronicle he had already begun to write, Froissart travelled to Edinburgh for a six-month stay which included a trip to the Highlands, then followed this up with a tour of the equally unexplored Welsh Marches.

During a truce in the war, Froissart journeyed through Brittany, then down the Rhône to Avignon and across to Bordeaux, where he was present 'sitting at table' when the future Richard II was born. During his travels throughout the Continent and then back to England again to witness the final years of Richard II, Froissart sought out and interviewed veteran knights, whose reminiscences compose this rich blend of war reporting, deeds of chivalry, sexual gossip and political commentary, including accounts of the Peasants' Revolt in England and the Jacquerie in France. Although, unlike Chaucer, he never saw action, Froissart served as a diplomat and adviser to some of his patrons, such as the King of Bohemia. During the 1360s he took holy orders and later acquired rich livings to supplement the money he earned by his pen.

As a Hainaulter, sympathetic to what we might well call Belgian or Dutch aspirations, Froissart aimed to be neutral between the warring English and French, enjoying the confidence of both high commands.

When he came to England in 1386, at the height of a French invasion scare, it did not seem to occur to anyone at Dover or Canterbury that he might be spying out the defences. The only trace of national animosity in the *Chronicles* comes after the Battle of Chevy Chase, when Froissart praises the way that the Scots and English treated each other's prisoners, comparing both nations favourably with the Germans: 'It would be better for a knight to be captured by infidels, out-and-out pagans or Saracens, than by the Germans.'

Froissart has been accused of flattering his employers, or their families, as when he writes of his patron's father, the blind King of Bohemia, at the Battle of Crécy. Generations of children have thrilled to the story of how the old man, determined to get in the action against the English, ordered his horse to be tied to those of his knights: 'They were found the next day lying around their leader with their horses still fastened together.'

Froissart managed to please two patrons at once when he told how, after the fall of Calais, Queen Philippa pleaded with Edward to spare the lives of its burghers, a scene now familiar from the sculpture outside the Houses of Parliament. Although Froissart portrays them both as wise and forgiving, he also suggests that Edward was still more swayed by the argument of Sir Walter Manny: 'My lord, you may well be mistaken, and setting a bad example for us. Suppose one day you sent us to defend one of your fortresses, we should go less cheerfully if you have these people put to death, for then they would do the same to us if they had the chance.'

Froissart is sometimes blamed for the glorification of fourteenth-century war in Victorian history books and novels. Certainly he was acclaimed by Sir Walter Scott: 'Whoever has taken up the *Chronicles* must have been dull indeed if he did not feel himself transported back to the days of Crécy and Poitiers.' Froissart is also clearly the principal source for Sir Arthur Conan Doyle's two swashbuckling novels about the Hundred Years' War, *Sir Nigel* and *The White Company*.

Doyle wrote these books when he was bored with Sherlock Holmes and Dr Watson, although, like the detective stories, much of their action is set in the comfortable surroundings of Surrey and Hampshire, where his typical readers lived or aspired to live. The inscription on the frontispiece to *Sir Nigel* suggests that Doyle wanted fourteenth-century chivalry to inspire his and Cecil Rhodes's dream of a world-wide empire, reuniting Britain with the United States: 'In the Hope of the future Reunion of the English-speaking Races, this little Chronicle of our common ancestry is inscribed. South Norwood. September 29, 1891.'

Doyle's Victorian readers were offered two separate fantasies of the fourteenth century. Some would identify with valiant Sir Nigel Loring, whose ancestors had arrived with William the Conqueror, and who now feared that England was 'a degenerate land which has fallen away from the old standards of Knightly courtesy'. Other readers, influenced by Victorian left-wing ideas of medieval Merrie England, could identify with Doyle's yeomen and sturdy peasants in the tavern where the landlady carried 'a broad platter upon which stood beakers and flagons charged to the brim with the brown ale or the ruby wine'.

Although the characters in these novels owe much to the Knight and Squire of the *Canterbury Tales*, Chaucer himself appears in a seedy role as one of those war correspondents so disliked by Victorian generals:

'It is well to have a learned clerk in every troop,' said Sir Nigel. 'By St Paul, there are men so caitiff that they think more of a scrivener's pen than of their lady's smile, and do their devoir in the hopes that they fill in a line in a chronicle or make a tag to a jongleur's romance. I remember well at the siege of Retters there was a little sleek, fat clerk of the name of Chaucer who was so apt at tondel, Sirrente or tonson, that no man dare give back a foot of the walls, lest he find it all set down in his rhymes and sung to every underling and varlet in the camp.'

Froissart did not disguise his view that the English invasion of Normandy in 1346, which led to the Battle of Crécy and the acquisition of Calais, was motivated throughout by desire for plunder. Edward III had prepared an expedition for the relief of Gascony but was turned back by a change of wind. It was Sir Godfrey Harcourt who counselled a change of plan. 'Normandy,' said Sir Godfrey, 'is one of the richest countries in the world. You will find large towns and fortresses completely undefended, in which your men will win wealth enough to make them rich for twenty years to come.'

The English found Barfleur undefended because its people surrendered in order to save their lives. The victors emptied the town of its gold, silver and jewellery. The 'very servants in the army turned up their noses at fur-lined gowns'. At Saint Lô, the English seized such quantities of cloth 'that they would have to let it go cheap if they had had anyone to sell it to'. Some inhabitants of Caen opened their strong-boxes and chests to the English, in return for their lives. King Edward himself sent back from Caen a batch of prisoners he had bought from Sir Thomas Howard in cash, including the Count of Guinea, the Constable of France.

Froissart concludes his account of this Normandy campaign: 'So the King sent back his fleet full of conquered spoils and of good prisoners, including more than sixty knights and three hundred wealthy citizens, with a host of loving greetings to his wife, my lady Philippa, the gracious Queen of England.'

When Edward landed at Sandwich on 14 October 1347, before going on to Canterbury to offer thanks at St Thomas's shrine, the whole country appeared to join in his triumph. In the words of Thomas Walsingham, the leading chronicler of the reign and by no means always approving of Edward: 'A new sun seems to have arisen over the people in the perfect peace, in the plenty of all things and in the glory of such victories. There was hardly a woman of any name who did not wear some ornament or have in her house fine linen or some goblet, part of the booty the King sent back from Caen or brought back from Calais.'

3

The Rise of the English Merchant

EDWARD'S VICTORIES AT THE start of the Hundred Years' War gave rise to the French national myth that England's pre-eminence is always due to commerce rather than courage. Once again it is the nineteenth-century Michelet, in one of his purple passages, who explains how the myth began at about the time of the birth of Chaucer:

A new crusade is beginning but of a quite new kind, not in search of the Holy Grail or the lance (which pierced the side of Christ on the cross), or the Empire of Trebizond. If we stop a ship on the sea we are likely to find not the second son of a noble Frenchman, going in search of a kingdom, but a Venetian or Genoese wanting to sell us sugar or cinnamon. This new religion of wealth has also its pilgrims, its monks and martyrs, ready to spend the best years of their lives in distant counting houses in Tyre or Novgorod. Lonely and celibate in their fortified barracks, they sleep fully armed beneath their desks, guarded by fierce hounds . . .

All this explains the events which are shortly to follow. The secret of the battles of Crécy and Poitiers is to be found in the merchant counting houses of London, Bordeaux and Bruges. Even before this charter, the foreigners poured into England. When one sees the boom in commerce which had begun in the thirteenth century, it is no surprise to find in the fourteenth an English merchant playing the host to five kings. Historians of the Middle Ages speak of English commerce just as one might today.

O England, the ships of Tharsis, famed in Scripture, could they compare with thine? Spices arrive from the four climatic zones of the world. Genoese and Venetians bring sapphires and emeralds washed down by the rivers of paradise. Asia for purple dyes, Africa for balm,

Spain for gold, Germany for silver, all are thy humble servants. Flanders, thy seamstress, has woven thy wool into precious cloth . . .

It is true, as Michelet goes on to say, that Edward III employed the profits of commerce to hire Welsh, Irish and even Genoese mercenaries in the war against France. The same French grievance against the English recurred in the seventeenth, eighteenth and even nineteenth centuries. The series of wars against Louis XIV were fought largely by foreign mercenaries. The army which William of Orange took to Ireland in 1689 to raise the siege of Derry and beat King James at the Battle of the Boyne was largely composed of German troops under General Schomberg. The Duke of Marlborough's army during the War of the Spanish Succession depended largely on mercenaries from the present Croatia, whose appetite for plunder and rape was satirized by writers such as Defoe and Jonathan Swift. The same resentment lingered on into the late nineteenth century as France lagged behind England in industry and colonial empire.

Michelet was right in saying that Edward III was fighting an economic war against France. Indeed, sometimes he took more risks to get money than to win a battle. To finance his early campaigns, Edward obtained loans from Italian bankers amounting to almost a million gold florins from the Bardi family, and two-thirds as much from the Peruzzi, on the security of what he hoped to obtain from the tax on wool. When Edward defaulted, the Peruzzi went bankrupt in 1343, the Bardi the following year, and their crash brought down a third firm, the Accaiuoli. Small wonder that the historian of Florence, Matteo Villani, raged at the behaviour of '*il piccolo re di Enghilterra*' (the little King of England) or that the Florentine author Boccaccio devoted a story of the *Decameron* to the danger of doing business in London. When Edward was desperate for a Flemish alliance, he made promises to the people of Ghent which they did not trust, so he had to leave his queen and children there as hostages.

Since the Hundred Years' War took place at about the same time as the rise of capitalism in Europe, the one is sometimes used to explain the other. Certainly the demands of the war effort may help to explain why England eventually led the rest of Europe in the development of commerce and industry. But England did not lead at the start of the fourteenth century. Italy was the axis of economic development, with the Tuscan and Lombard banks providing the capital, the ports of

Venice and Genoa serving the eastern and western Mediterranean, and Florence its centre of manufacture, the Manchester of the Middle Ages. The Rhine and the Rhône were the two great trade routes joining the Mediterranean to the north of Europe. Although Europe had not yet begun the seaborne exploration of Africa, Asia and the Americas, Marco Polo had visited China overland, or at any rate published a book about his travels (its authenticity remains a matter of scholarly debate).

From the early fourteenth century, Tuscan merchants recounted a story that later went round Europe and eventually entered English folklore. This was about a young merchant who arrived by ship at one of the Canary Islands and was entertained to dinner by the local king. He was astonished to notice beside each place a club for killing the rats which infested the island and even invaded the dining hall to steal the food. The smart young Italian returned the next day with the ship's cat which he gave to the islanders to rid them of the vermin. In return he was given a monopoly of trade with the island. The story was attributed in England to the fifteenth-century merchant and Lord Mayor of London, Richard Whittington. He and his cat have been immortalized by the children's story and pantomime.

Why England eventually led all Europe in the development of capitalism has been debated by historians ever since. In the days when religion rather than politics ruled men's minds, a connection was made between the commercial spirit and Protestantism, a thesis advanced by R. H. Tawney in *Religion and the Rise of Capitalism*. Certainly Calvin preached the virtue of making money, though without bringing prosperity to Geneva, where his Church held sway. Eventually Holland and Scotland were held up as models for the 'Protestant work ethic'. This still does not explain why commerce flourished in fourteenth-century England, when Protestantism was still just an idea in the quarrelsome mind of John Wyclif.

Michelet explains the economic rise of England in just two words: wool and meat.

> *La laine et la viande.* It is that which originally made England and the English race. Before becoming the chief producer of iron and textiles, England was a producer of meat. From time immemorial they were an animal-raising and pastoral nation, a race nourished on meat. From this comes their fresh complexion, their beauty, their strength. Their

greatest man, Shakespeare, began as a butcher. In their climate, hungry man has to work to live. Nature forces him to do it, but nevertheless does well by him. He makes Nature work herself. He subjugates her by fire and iron.

All England is breathless from struggle. Man is as if in a state of shock. Examine that red face, that wild expression. You could easily think him drunk. But his head and his hands are steady. He is drunk only with blood and struggle. He treats himself as he does his steam engine which he feeds and fills to excess, to win for it still more power and speed.

Michelet was not the first nor the last to remark on English carnivorousness. From Canterbury at the start of the seventh century, St Augustine wrote to Pope Gregory that the newly converted English loved their meat so much that they would not eat fish on Fridays. When Edward III wanted the Flemings to come to England, bringing their 'mystery' with them, he promised them fine clothes and beautiful women for their beds, adding: 'Here they should feed on fatt beef and mutton till nothing but their fullness could stint their stomachs.'*

Long before Michelet wrote his history of the Middle Ages, French cartoonists depicted the typical Englishman as 'Monsieur Rosbif', his face the colour of rare entrecôte. But meat in the Middle Ages was not an important item of export, nor therefore of revenue for the war. It was not wool and meat but wool and wine that financed Edward's war, and incidentally enriched the Chaucer family.

Chaucer's great-grandfather came from Ipswich in Suffolk, a port for shipping wool to Flanders, and bringing in wine from nearby Germany as well as distant Bordeaux. The wealth of Suffolk from wool in the late Middle Ages can still be seen in the huge and beautiful churches of towns like Bury St Edmunds, Lavenham and Southwold, though Ipswich itself was unlucky enough to prosper during the nineteenth century, when the townspeople replaced earlier buildings with what was then in fashion.

East Anglia in the Middle Ages was one of the great wool-producing regions along with the Cotswolds, the West Riding of Yorkshire, Devon and Lincolnshire. Thanks to its soil and climate, England has

---

* Thomas Fuller, quoted in May McKisack's *The Fourteenth Century*, p. 367, in the *Oxford History of England*.

always produced better wool than any country in Europe except for Spain, as Daniel Defoe remarked in the early eighteenth century: 'Bring foreign sheep hither with wool like dog's hair matted and coarse. I'll undertake how to make the wool fine, the staple large, and the fleece heavy, and that without mixing the breed. Carry English sheep into most countries, Spain excepted, though when they were here their wool was rich, large and fine; it shall degenerate, grow coarse, short and thin; no soil, no climate but this shall uphold them.'

Huge flocks of sheep grazed on the flat East Anglian hinterland of the port of Ipswich. The Earl of Lincoln had more than 13,000; the Fenland abbeys of Crowland and Peterborough between them had 16,300, the priory of St Swithin's 20,000. The monks of Christ Church, Canterbury, already rich from the gifts at St Thomas's shrine, made further profit from sheep in what was largely a corn-growing part of England. The prior in 1322 had 13,730 sheep; their manure was valued at £9 6s 8d, the milk of 6,000 ewes at £96; the lambs were worth £150 and their wool £50; while the main wool crop of fifty sacks brought an annual revenue of £300.

During the course of the fourteenth century the English developed a cloth-weaving industry almost as lucrative as the export of wool to Flanders and Tuscany. Although Michelet attributes this to the Flemish immigrants bringing their skills or 'mystery', economic historians put it down to improvements in fulling, the process of shrinking the cloth to thicken and felt it until the fibres are so interlaced that the woven pattern is indistinguishable. From the start of the reign of Edward III, water-powered fulling mills replaced the old method of trampling the cloth underfoot with soap or fuller's earth. These fulling mills were as revolutionary in their time as the new textile technology of the eighteenth century. They also created a manufacturing class in the west of England, exemplified by Chaucer's Wife of Bath: 'In cloth-makyng she had such judgement/She passed them of Ypris and of Ghent.'

Geoffrey Chaucer's paternal great-grandfather in Ipswich was known as Andrew de Dinnington but his son became Robert Malyn le Chaucer, and Robert's son simply John Chaucer. The apparent confusion is partly explained by the way that widows remarried (witness the Wife of Bath) and young men took their stepfather's surname. By the end of the thirteenth century, Robert Chaucer the grandfather and Mary his wife had moved to London, but John their son was abducted by one of his aunts who wanted to marry the boy to her own daughter in order to keep the family's Ipswich property. This abduction is sometimes quoted to explain the puzzling incident when Geoffrey the poet was charged with the 'rape' (*raptus* in legal Latin) of a young woman called Cecilia Champaign. The question of whether this was a kidnapping, a physical rape, or what we would now call 'date rape' will be discussed in a later chapter.

To tell the truth, we know very little of Chaucer's background, not even if he was Anglo-Saxon as the name Dinnington suggests, or Norman French as Chaucer (from *chaussier*, a shoemaker) indicates. The last of the poet's male descendants died in the Tower of London in 1539, and nobody else of that name lived on into modern times. Chesterton in the 1930s lamented that he had never met a namesake of the greatest Englishman of the Middle Ages. A look at the modern London telephone directory shows not one Chaucer among the dozens of Chaus and Chaudhuris who, today, form the elite of England's merchant class.

Chaucer's family at Ipswich were engaged not only in shipping wool to the Continent but in collecting duty for the royal exchequer. The poet himself was appointed by Edward III in 1374 as controller of customs (the tax on wool, sheepskins and leather) and of the 'subsidy', a heavier tax on the same items of merchandise. Since wool was England's largest export, these taxes financed Edward's war in the 1340s and 1350s and helped to pay for the smaller military expeditions in the 1370s and 1380s. Wool taxes also accounted for most of the cost of civilian government and of the upkeep of the royal court. During his tenure of office, Chaucer controlled receipts of an average £24,600 per year.

Wine rather than wool was the line of business which brought Chaucer's father from Ipswich to London, specifically to his warehouse and home in the Vintry Ward, on what is now Thames Street, a block away from the river. Just as wool was England's largest export, wine was its overwhelmingly largest import, most of it coming from Edward's province of Gascony in south-west France: of the 90,000 to 100,000 tuns of wine shipped annually from Bordeaux at the beginning of the fourteenth century, a quarter came to this country.

The price of wine was as low as £3 a tun wholesale and 3d a gallon retail, sold by the 350 tavern-keepers in London alone. The king was a principal gainer from this enormous trade. His chief butler bought 2,000 tuns a year for the royal household, as well as supervising the tax on every tun entering English ports. Geoffrey Chaucer's father John was at one time an assistant royal butler, at Southampton. Once John Chaucer accompanied Edward III on a trip to Cologne, the principal entrepôt for Rhenish wine, as well as a place of pilgrimage to the shrine of St Engelbert – who was, like Thomas Becket, a former archbishop who had been murdered by his political foes.

Before visiting Canterbury, Chaucer's Wife of Bath had visited 'In Galice at Seint-Jame and at Coloigne'. The connection of these two cities with their stunning cathedrals and martyred archbishops would be renewed in 1941 when the Royal Air Force flattened Cologne and in revenge the Luftwaffe wiped out most of Canterbury. It is a tribute to medieval architects that both cathedrals survived as monuments of a more civilized age.

The Gascon wine trade suffered early on in the Hundred Years' War when fighting ravaged the Dordogne Valley and the Entre-Deux-Mers vineyards, then once again in 1369 when the French army reached the gates of Bordeaux. Nevertheless the Bordeaux merchants remained loyal to the English kings who had given them their municipal liberties, and to the merchants of London, such as the Chaucer family.

Even when Gascony was at peace, the wine merchants suffered the depredation of pirates and of their own equally villainous sea captains, such as the Shipman in the *Canterbury Tales* (David Wright version):

> He'd tapped and lifted many a stoup of wine
> From Bordeaux, when the merchant wasn't looking,
> He hadn't time for scruples or fine feeling,
> For if he fought, and got the upper hand,
> He'd send his captives home by sea, not land.
> But as for seamanship, and calculation
> Of moon, tides, currents, all hazards at sea,
> For harbour-lore, and skill in navigation,
> From Hull to Carthage there was none to touch him.

Several biographers have suggested that Chaucer's early life in the Vintry Ward may have introduced him to foreign traders and even taught him the rudiments of Italian. One of the best writers on Chaucer, the Roman Catholic apologist G. K. Chesterton, has even suggested that Chaucer's background in the wine trade meant that he shared his (Chesterton's) fondness for alcohol and by implication a preference for the Mediterranean over the north European culture. Like his boon companion and fellow Catholic Hilaire Belloc, Chesterton liked to imagine himself as a medieval troubadour striding from tavern to tavern through France on the way to Rome or Compostela. Like many admirers of Chaucer, he tended to picture the poet in his own image:

> Now Chaucer did come of a line of men that did deal directly with wine barrels . . . For there was natural magic and the world's desire stored in positive pots, solid as those that poured for Christ the incredible wine. He came of people who had dealt with the stuff and substance of things, and in his case with a highly appropriate sort of thing . . . Forth from among those mighty vats of the vine, brought by the Shipman from the lands of Froissart and Petrarch, he came to walk the world; who went singing all his days as if wine were in his very veins, and hidden in his northern blood, the very secret of the sun.

Unlike Chesterton, who often wrote as though he had wine or something stronger in his veins, Chaucer was obviously an abstemious man. Two of the few surviving documents about him record that on 23 April 1374 King Edward III granted the poet a gallon of wine a day, or enough to satisfy even Chesterton, but that early on in the following reign Chaucer commuted this grant to an annual payment in cash.

Chaucer never created a lovable and amusing male drunkard like Falstaff or Mr Micawber. The boozers among the Canterbury pilgrims range from oafs such as the Cook and the Miller to the revolting Summoner whose body has been corrupted by over-indulgence. Here in the David Wright version:

> All covered with carbuncles; his eyes narrow;
> He was as hot and randy as a sparrow.
> He'd scabbed black eyebrows, and a scraggy beard,
> No wonder if the children were afraid!
> There was no mercury, white lead or sulphur,
> No borax, no ceruse, no cream of tartar,
> Nor any other salves that cleanse and burn,
> Could help with the white pustules on his skin,
> Or with the knobbed carbuncles on his cheeks.
> He'd a great love of garlic, onions, leeks,

Also for drinking strong wine, red as blood,
When he would roar and gabble as if mad.
And once he had got really drunk on wine,
Then he would speak no language but Latin.

Chaucer's virtuous women, such as Griselda in the *Clerk's Tale*, the daughter in the *Physician's Tale* and the Widow in the *Nun's Priest's Tale* are shown as abstainers while the Wife of Bath confesses that wine makes her randy, the word 'likerous' meaning both liquorous and lecherous:

And after wyn on Venus moste I thynke
For al so siker [sure] as cold engendreth hayl
A likerous mouth must have a likerous tayl

The hypocritical Pardoner will not begin his tale until he has wet his whistle at an inn:

'But first,' quoth he, 'here at this ale-stake
I will both drink and byten on a cake.'

Here some of the other pilgrims protest that they do not want to hear any drunken ribaldry but a moral tale. He agrees to this: 'But I must think/Upon some honest tale, while that I drink.'

After his 'draught of corny ale', the Pardoner begins his sermon on the theme that the love of money is the root of all evil, which also contains a warning about the danger of wine, especially from Fish Street, close by the Chaucer family warehouse (David Wright version):

Wine stirs up lechery and drunkenness,
Is full of quarrelling and wickedness.
You sot, how blotched and altered is your face,
How sour your breath, how beastly your embrace;
And through your drunken nose there seems to come
A noise like 'Samson, Samson, Samson, Samson' –
Though Samson never touched a drop of wine ! . . .
Keep clear of wine then, whether white or red,
Especially of the white wine of Lepe
They have on sale in Fish Street, or Eastcheap.

Because this Spanish wine, in some strange way,
Creeps into other wines that grow near by;
Such vapours rise from it, the man who thinks
He's in Eastcheap at home, after three drinks
Finds he's in Spain right in the town of Lepe . . .
And that's when he starts snorting, 'Samson! Samson!'

Some admirers of Chaucer have been embarrassed by his bourgeois, or what he called 'burgeys', origins. The Elizabethan Thomas Speight wrote in his introduction to Chaucer's *Works*, published in 1598, that although the poet's father was a vintner he probably descended from 'some ancient but decayed noble line'. In rather the same way, the Victorians could not believe that Shakespeare came from the trades-man class and therefore suggested that his plays were written by someone of noble origin. Unlike his contemporary Boccaccio, Chaucer himself does not appear to have felt any shame in his family which had given him a good career at court. The distinction between the nobility and 'trade' is less apparent in Chaucer's *Canterbury Tales* than in the novels of Jane Austen or Dickens.

The portraits of the Merchant and of the unnamed Guildsmen in the *General Prologue* of the *Canterbury Tales* give an impression of self-importance and even a hint of the greed, fraud and usury with which their class was charged. One fine modern critic, Jill Mann, has gently reproached Chaucer for not denouncing merchants, doctors and law-yers or writing about the damage done to their victims. But as she acknowledges, Chaucer wanted to make his readers laugh rather than feel indignant. Nevertheless, Chaucer's introductory sketches of the Merchant and the Guildsmen show us his attitude to the new English capitalism, and merit close study in the original text (Riverside edition):

A Marchant was ther with a forked berd,
In mottelee, and hye on horse he sat;
Upon his heed a Flaundryssh bever hat,
His bootes clasped faire and fetisly.
His resons he spak ful solempnely,
Sownynge alwey th'encrees of his wynnyng.

The Merchant is one of the best turned-out pilgrims with his beaver-skin hat and elaborately buckled shoes, and his high horse is superior in every way to those of the other pilgrims. In modern terms he is driving an expensive car. Since Chaucer is shown in an early illustration wearing a forked beard, this is probably one of his self-deprecatory jokes. The Merchant talks solemnly about the increase in his profits, probably because he is really losing money. The Merchant may be from Ipswich, for he wants the seaway kept safe from pirates between the Orwell River and Holland.

> He wolde the sea were kept for anything
> Betwixe Middleburgh and Orewelle.
> Wel could he in exchange sheeldes selle.
> This worthy man ful wel his wit bisette:
> Ther wiste no wight that he was in dette,
> So estatly was he of governaunce
> With his bargaynes and with his chevyssaunce.

In just seven lines, Chaucer exposes the hollow man beneath the exterior. The Merchant is first heard pompously complaining that the government should do something about the pirates, when it is really his currency deals that have landed him in trouble.

The exchange shields were tokens used in the fourteenth-century money market and were probably as obscure to most of Chaucer's readers as 'futures' and 'commodities' are to most of us today. Like many a modern City dealer, the Merchant did his best to prevent people knowing whether or not he was really in debt, so dignified (or 'estately') was his conduct of bargains and his 'chevyssaunce', a polite term for usury.

The Haberdasher, Weaver, Dyer and Tapestry-maker who appear in the *General Prologue* but not in the rest of the *Canterbury Tales* are evidently in the same clothing guild or fraternity, while the Carpenter is perhaps an honorary member. In the fourteenth century, as still in our modern age, these City gentlemen loved dressing up in their finery to sit in a guildhall on a dais:

> A Haberdasshere and a Carpenter
> A Webber, a Dyere, and a Tapycer
> Were with us eek, clothed in one lyveree
> Of a solempne and a greet fraternitee.
> Ful fresh and newe their geere y-trimmed was;

> Their knives were y-sette not with brass
> But al with silver, wroght ful clene and faire,
> Their girdles and their pouches every where.
> Wel seemed ech of hem a fair burgeys,
> To sitten in a gildehalle on the dais.

Every one of them had the knowledge, property and rent to be an alderman, or so their wives hoped, for these ladies loved to be called 'madame' and lead the procession at the feasts on the eve of a holy day, with their gowns carried royally in their train.

> Everich, for the wisdom that he can,
> Was shaply for to been an alderman.
> For catel had they enough and rente,
> And eek hir wyves wolde it wel assente;
> And elles certeyn were they to blame.
> It is ful fair to been ycleped 'madame'
> And goon to vigilies al bifore
> And have a mantil roialliche ybore.

If merchants' wives enjoy the pomp and privileges of a public occasion, they are not always happy in their private lives, so Chaucer suggests in the *Merchant's Tale* and the *Shipman's Tale*, which concerns a merchant from St Denis, near Paris.

The *Sea-Captain's Tale*, as David Wright prefers to call it, sounds at first like an expression of anger against the wealthy landlubbers whose merchandise he carries:

> There was a merchant living at St Denis
> – As he was rich, most people thought him wise –
> Who had a wife, a woman of great beauty,
> A sociable girl, and fond of parties,
> Which is a thing that causes more expense
> Than all the regard and the compliments
> Which men pay them at dinners and at dances
> Is worth. Such pretences and salutations
> Pass like a passing shadow on a wall;
> But hard on him who has to pay for all!

At this point it becomes apparent that the *Shipman's Tale* was originally meant to be told by a woman, perhaps the Wife of Bath, for it reflects her cynical view, or even that of the prostitute La Vieille in Jean de Meun's *Roman de la Rose*:

> The wretched husband always has to pay;
> It's for the sake of his own standing he
> Keeps us in dresses and in finery,
> In which array we revel merrily!
> And if it turns out that he can't endure,
> Or won't put up with such expenditure,
> But thinks it all a waste and a dead loss,
> Then someone else has got to pay for us,
> Or lend us cash – and there the danger is.

In the tale that follows, the Merchant's wife has run into debt and asks for a loan of a hundred crowns from her husband's cousin, a monk, who first borrows the money from the husband. The wife is more than ready to repay the monk with her sexual favours, but nevertheless persuades herself that her husband is also to blame for thinking too much of his forthcoming business journey to Bruges:

> Three days went by; and then the merchant rose,
> And soberly took stock of his affairs;
> So up into his counting-house he goes,
> To reckon up how matters stood that year,
> What his expenses and outgoings were,
> Whether he'd made a profit or a loss.
> He spread his books and money-bags across
> The counting-board in front of him, then shut
> And locked the door (his treasure-hoard was great),
> And, having made quite sure that for the mean time
> He wouldn't be disturbed at his accounting,
> Remained there until past nine in the morning.

While the Merchant sits up all night with his accounts, his wife and his cousin meet for a rendezvous:

The monk, who'd risen with the dawn also,
Was walking in the garden to and fro,
Having recited, most punctiliously,
His office.
   Quietly the good lady
Stole to the garden where he paced sedately,
Greeted him as she'd often done before.

A few days later, the monk has promised to lend the Merchant's wife a
hundred francs, and has taken a kiss and a squeeze in advance of what
was to follow, but the Merchant is still preparing his trip to Bruges:

And off she goes, as happy as a lark,
To tell the cooks that they must hurry up,
So that they all could dine without delay.
Then up to find her husband goes the lady
And knocks upon his office door so boldly.
'*Qui la?*' says he – 'It's me, for heaven's sake!
And tell me, sir, when do you mean to eat?
And how long are you going to be at
Your sums and ledgers and accounts and stuff!
The devil take part in all such reckonings!
As if God hadn't given you enough!
Come down, and leave your money-bags alone.
Aren't you ashamed to think that Brother John
Has been miserably fasting all day long?
Come, let us hear a mass, and then we'll dine.'

When the monk asks for a loan to buy some cattle – in fact to give to
the Merchant's wife – the reply is a subtle blend of generosity and
caution:

'Dear cousin,' the good man returned politely,
'Now surely that's a very small request!
My money's yours whenever you may want it,
Not just my money but my merchandise.
For heaven's sake don't stint! Take what you please!
But there's one thing about us, as you know:
With businessmen, their money is their plough.

We can get credit while we've a good name,
But when we're out of cash, why, that's no fun.
When it's convenient you can pay it back
I'm glad to do my best to help you out' . . .
And so, when morning came, the merchant rides
To Flanders, with his apprentice as guide,
And after a good journey, reaches Bruges.
There he goes busily about his business,
Buying and borrowing, but never dicing,
And never dancing, but in short behaving
Just like a businessman . . .

The Merchant returns from Bruges to his wife at St Denis, then goes on to Paris to pay back the twenty-thousand-franc surety on a loan:

The first man that this merchant went to see
For his own pleasure, was this Brother John;
All out of fondness and deep affection,
And not to seek or borrow any money,
But to see him, ask after his welfare,
And gossip over business and affairs,
As old friends do when they are met together . . .
There was one snag: he'd somehow got to raise
As best he might, a loan to meet his debt,
Before he could relax in peace and comfort.

Here, in the same spirit of false bonhomie, the monk not only declines to help but pretends he has paid back the previous loan to the Merchant's wife.

'I'm truly glad to see that you've come home
From Bruges safe and sound,' said Brother John.
'And, heaven be my witness, were I rich,
For twenty thousand crowns you would not lack.
It's after all only the other day
That you so kindly lent those hundred francs –
By God above, and by St James, I say
I'm hardly able to express my thanks!
But I've returned that money, none the less;

> I took it to your home to your good lady
> Your wife, and laid it on your counter; she'll
> Be sure to know of it, as I can tell,
> I gave her certain vouchers – Now farewell . . .'

The Merchant repays his debt to the Lombard bankers in Paris and goes back to St Denis:

> As merry as a grig, for well he knows
> That over and above his gross outlay
> He stood to make a thousand francs that trip.

Now only the wife has lost out financially from this double-dealing, but later in bed she soon persuades the Merchant to forget the hundred francs:

> 'And so forgive me, my own dearest husband,
> I'll cheer you up if only you'll turn round.'

The *Shipman's Tale* is a naughty but light-hearted joke. The Merchant is cuckolded but he is not much worthier than his wife or cousin. The reader tends to agree with the Host's jocular comment:

> 'How that monk made a monkey of the fellow,
> And, by St Augustine, his wife also!
> Never ever bring a monk into the house.'

4

The Black Death:
Chaucer and the Jews

WHEN CHAUCER WAS A little boy during the years 1348 to 1350, there descended on England, as on the rest of Europe, one of the worst natural disasters in the history of mankind: an epidemic of bubonic and pneumonic plague, which has come to be known as the Black Death.

To many chroniclers of the time, the plague appeared like the end of the world. In Florence, Giovanni Villani paused from writing his *Storia Fiorentina* to ask himself why this horror had struck his beloved city, concluding that it was God's chastisement for the sins of avarice and usury – Villani himself was a partner in the banking house of Peruzzi and had been accused of malpractice. A few days later he died while writing a sentence about the plague (. . . *e dure questa pistolenza* . . .). His brother Matteo, who took on the task of writing the history of Florence, compared the disease to the biblical flood in its purpose, and thought he might be recording 'the extinction of mankind'. In the Irish market town of Kilkenny, which still has a merchant's house from the Middle Ages, Brother John Clyn, the only monk left alive in a community of the dead, set parchment aside to continue his record 'if perchance any man survive and any of the race of Adam escape this pestilence and carry on the work which I had begun . . .'. Someone else added on the parchment the news that Brother John had died.

The Black Death, like many subsequent epidemics of plague and other deadly diseases down to the Hong Kong 'chicken flu' of 1997, is thought to have started in eastern Asia, afterwards making its way to the Black Sea along the 'spice route' travelled by Marco Polo and other merchants from the Mediterranean.

The Venetians and Genoese on the Black Sea coast were at first delighted to hear that a pestilence had appeared in the army of Tartars which threatened to overrun their trading posts. Delight turned to panic when the invaders besieging the Genoese town of Caffa (now Feodosia) started to catapult the corpses of plague victims over the walls – the first recorded instance of biological warfare. The defenders picked up the rotten bodies and dropped them into the sea, but later took ships home to the Mediterranean. Early in 1348 these galleys, with some of the rowers dead at their oars, began to arrive at Venice, Genoa and Marseilles, but it was from the Sicilian port of Messina that plague spread through Italy and then all over Europe.

When the plague struck Messina, the people of nearby Catania at first offered their hospitals to the sick but later excluded them. The division among its victims brought by the plague was shown when the Messinese appealed to their patriarch archbishop to let them have the relics of St Agatha at Catania. But the Catanians allowed them only some holy water dipped in St Agatha's remains. When this water was sprinkled about the Messina churches, 'a black dog, bearing a drawn sword in his paws, appeared among them, gnashing his teeth and rushing upon them, and breaking all the silver vessels and lamps and candlesticks on the altars'. This account by Michael Piazza (quoted in Philip Ziegler's so far unrivalled history of the disease, *The Black Death*) suggests that the Sicilians were confusing the new disease with the more familiar rabies. Philip Ziegler remarks: 'The Black Death is associated more closely with Florence than any other city, so much so that in contemporary and even more recent accounts, it is sometimes referred to as "the plague of Florence". Partly because it was one of the greatest cities of Europe, and certainly the first of them to feel the full force of the epidemic. Partly it is because the plague raged there with exceptional intensity – certainly more severely than in Rome, Paris or Milan, and at least as violently as in London or Vienna.'

For the purpose of this book, Florence is still more important as one of the cities where Chaucer afterwards went, and the home of the three writers he most admired – Dante, Petrarch and Boccaccio. Indeed, he probably read and had certainly heard of Boccaccio's account at the beginning of the *Decameron*, perhaps the most vivid account of any epidemic in history.

In Sicily, as on the Italian mainland, the coming of plague was linked with seismic and other natural disasters. Shortly before the disease arrived, a series of earthquakes had shaken Rome, Pisa,

Bologna, Padua and Venice. From July 1345, six months of almost continual rain had devastated crops and made sowing impossible, as well as killing off livestock and poultry. Near Orvieto, the bridges were washed away by flood and hundreds died in the landslides, which still so often afflict modern Italy. As inheritors of the Latin tradition, many Italians recognized in the Black Death the plague which Ovid said had been visited by Juno on the Greek island of Aegina: 'At first the sky, dark and heavy, pressed down upon the earth, shutting in beneath its clouds a sultry heat which sapped all energy. And all this time the south wind blew with hot and deadly blasts. It is common knowledge that even the lakes and springs became infected, thousands of serpents crawled over our neglected fields, and polluted the rivers with their poisons. The violence of the disease and the suddenness with which it struck were first realized when dogs and birds, sheep and oxen, and wild creatures began to die. The wretched farmers watched in dismay as their sturdy oxen collapsed at work and sank to the ground in the midst of ploughing.'

Descriptions of the Black Death seldom mention its effect on animals, though Arab chroniclers related that birds fell dead from the trees as they did in the Hong Kong 'chicken flu' of 1997. Odder still, no mention is made of the death of rats, which later scientists thought were carriers of the Black Death and were seen to fall in huge numbers during the nineteenth-century plague epidemics in China and India.

Italian doctors were among the first to blame the Black Death on foul or infected air. 'Bad air', or malaria, was the name Italians gave to paludism, which was then endemic in various parts of the country, especially Sardinia, Valdichiana in Tuscany, and the Tuscan Maremma, or coastal marshes.

The Black Death was then ascribed to 'the air so full of sickness' (*l'aer si pien di maligia*). Pneumonic plague, as opposed to the more contagious bubonic type, was spread by coughs and sneezes from infected lungs.

The appearance of this harrowing and dismal passage in what is a book of salacious and comic stories has puzzled generations of readers of the *Decameron*. Many have leafed through in search of one of the saucy bits, to recoil in horror from the description of bodies rotting in the street. It is as though D. H. Lawrence had begun *Lady Chatterley's Lover* with an eye-witness account of the Battle of the Somme. The reason for this is partly explained by G. H. McWilliam in the introduction to his translation of the *Decameron*, from which I quote in this chapter. The passage about the Black Death, he says 'acts as the sombre and frightening prelude which medieval rhetoricians regarded as the essential component of comedy, to which the *Decameron*, like Dante's great poem (*La Divina Commedia*) was intended to belong.' Both works, in fact, despite their obvious difference in form and subject matter, respect the definition of comedy formulated, for instance, by Uguccione da Pisa in his *Derivations*: '*a principio horribilis fetidus, in fine prosperus desiderabilis et gratus*' (foul and horrible at the beginning, in the end felicitous, desirable and pleasing). The plague also serves to explain why the young people who tell the stories have left Florence to gather at a villa up in the hills.

Boccaccio begins the *Decameron* with an apology for its 'awkward and ponderous' introduction about the havoc wrought by the recent plague, but assures his readers that they are not to be subjected to a torrent of tears and sobbing. On the contrary, he continues: 'You will be affected no differently by this grim beginning than walkers confronted by a steep and rugged hill, beyond which there lies a beautiful and delectable plain.' He then plunges into the story of the plague:

In the face of its onrush, all the wisdom and ingenuity of man were unavailing. Large quanties of refuse were cleared out of the city by officials specially appointed for the purpose, all sick persons were refused entry, and numerous instructions were issued for safeguarding the people's health, but all to no avail. Nor were the countless petitions humbly directed to God by the pious, whether by means of formal processions or in all other ways, any less ineffectual. For in the early spring of the year we have mentioned, the plague began, in a terrifying and extraordinary manner.

It did not take the form it had assumed in the East, where if anyone bled from the nose it was an obvious portent of certain death. On the contrary, its earliest symptoms, in men and women alike, was the appearance of certain swellings in the groin or armpit, some of which were egg-shaped, while others were roughly the size of the common apple. Sometimes the swellings were large, sometimes not so large, and they were referred to by the populace as *gavoccioli*. From the two areas already mentioned, this deadly *gavocciolo* would begin to spread, and within a short time it would appear at random all over the body. Later on, the symptoms of the disease changed and many people began to find dark blotches and bruises on their arms, thighs and other parts of the body, sometimes large and few in number, at other times tiny and closely spaced. These, to anyone unfortunate enough to contract them, were just as infallible a sign that he would die as the *gavocciolo* had been earlier, and as indeed it still was.

Perhaps the nature of the illness was such that it allowed no remedy: or perhaps those people who were treating the illness (whose numbers had increased enormously because the ranks of the qualified were invaded by people, both men and women, who had never received any training in medicine), being ignorant of its causes, were not prescribing the appropriate cure. At all events, few of those who caught it ever recovered . . .

But what made this pestilence even more severe was that whenever those suffering from it arrived with people who were still unaffected, it would rush upon these with the speed of a fire racing though dry or oily substances that happened to come within its reach. Nor was this the full extent of its evil, for not only did it infect healthy persons who conversed or had any dealings with the sick, making them ill or visiting an equally horrible death upon them, but it also seemed to transfer the sickness to anyone touching the clothes or other objects which had been handled or used by its victims.

As an example of this contagious power, Boccaccio relates an unforgettably frightening incident which he claims to have witnessed himself (although there is no definite proof that he came to Florence during the plague there, from Ravenna where he was living for much of 1348):

Whenever an animal other than a human being touched anything belonging to a person who had been stricken or exterminated by the disease, it not only caught the sickness, but died from it almost at once . . . One day, for instance, the rags of a pauper who had died from the disease were thrown into the street, where they attracted the attention of two pigs. In their wonted fashion, the pigs first of all gave the rags a thorough mauling with their snouts, after which they took them between their teeth, and shook them against their cheeks. And within a short time they began to writhe as though they had been poisoned, then they both dropped dead to the ground, spread-eagled upon the rags that had brought about their undoing.

This is one of several passages where Boccaccio may have been playing down the horrors of the Black Death in Florence, for it is just as possible that the pigs were feeding upon the corpses rather than sniffing at their clothes. Chaucer remarks on the man-eating habit of pigs in the passage in the *Knight's Tale* on the horrors of anarchy and civil war:

> The tiraunt, with the prey by force y-refte;
> The town destroyed, there was no thing lefte.
> Ther burnt the shippes daunsing up and down;
> Ther died the hunter by the wilde lion.
> The sowe eating the child right in the cradel;
> The cook y-skalded, for all his long ladel.

Boccaccio nevertheless gives a harrowing picture of life in the stricken city. Whereas some people locked themselves in their houses, followed a moderate diet in food and drink, refused all contact and entertained themselves as best they could:

> Others took the opposite view, and maintained that a way of warding off this appalling evil was to drink heavily, enjoy life to the full, go round singing and merry-making, gratify all one's cravings, whenever the opportunity offered, and shrug the whole thing off as one enormous joke. Moreover they practised what they preached to the best of their ability, for they would visit one tavern after another, drinking all day and night to immoderate excess; or alternatively (and this was their most frequent custom) they would do their drinking in various private houses, but only in the ones where the conversation was restricted to subjects that were pleasant or entertaining . . . Hence most houses had become common property and any passing stranger could make himself at home as naturally as though they were the rightful owner.

Most people steered a middle course between debauch and isolation. 'Instead of incarcerating themselves, here people moved about freely, holding in their hands a posy of flowers, or fragrant herbs, or one of a wide range of spices, which they applied at frequent intervals to their nostrils, thinking it an excellent idea to fortify the brain with smells of that particular sort; for the stench of dead bodies, sickness and medicines seemed to pollute the whole of the atmosphere.'

Boccaccio remarked with sadness upon the breakdown of ties of friendship and family: 'It was not merely a question of one citizen avoiding another, and of people almost invariably neglecting their neighbours and rarely or never visiting their relatives, addressing them only from a distance; this scourge had implanted so great a terror in the hearts of men and women that brothers abandoned brothers, uncles their nephews, sisters their brothers, and in many cases wives deserted their husbands. But even worse, and almost incredible, was the fact that fathers and mothers refused to nurse and assist their own children, as though they did not belong to them.'

Boccaccio believed that the plague caused a decline in female modesty:

> As a result of this wholesale desertion of the sick by neighbours, relatives and friends, and in view of the scarcity of servants, there grew up a practice almost never previously heard of, whereby when a woman fell ill, no matter how gracious or beautiful or gently bred she might be, she raised no objection to being attended by a male servant, whether he was young or not. Nor did she have any scruple about showing him every part of her body as freely as she would have displayed it to a woman, provided that the nature of her intimacy required her to do so; and this explains why those women who recovered were possibly less chaste in the period that followed.

Boccaccio estimates that more than 100,000 people died within the walls of Florence in spite of its opulence and its medical science. 'Ah, how great a number of splendid palaces, fine houses, and noble dwellings, once filled with retainers . . . were bereft of all who lived there, down to the tiniest child. How many gallant gentlemen, fair ladies, and sprightly youths who would have been judged hale and hearty by Galen, Hippocrates and Aesculapius, having breakfasted in the morning with their kinsfolk, supped that same evening with their ancestors in the next world!' Boccaccio's sardonic reference to the leading medical experts of the classical age was to be echoed by Chaucer in the *Canterbury Tales* and the *Book of the Duchess*, an elegy for a victim of the plague.

In Italy, as throughout western Europe, the Black Death created a labour shortage, wage increases and social unrest. In 1383 Matteo Villani complained of the greediness of the labouring classes: 'Serving girls and unskilled women with no experience in service, and stable boys want at least twelve florins a year, and the most arrogant among them eighteen or twenty-four per year. Nurses and minor artisans want three times the usual pay, and labourers on the land all want oxen and seed before they accept a lease, and they demand to till only the best land.'

The shortage of labour led to labour disputes in the Tuscan cloth industry and the militant protest of I Ciompi, 'the clogs'. It also brought a revived demand for domestic slaves, not only from the traditional suppliers in Spain and North Africa, but from the Balkans, Constantinople, Cyprus, Crete and, above all, the Black Sea ports, from which the plague had originally come. The slaves were taken to Venice and Genoa or to the international markets on the Balearic islands of Majorca and Ibiza. By the end of the fourteenth century, according to Iris Origo in The Merchant of Prato, 'there was hardly a well-to-do household in Tuscany without at least one slave; brides brought them as part of their dowry, doctors accepted them from their patients in lieu of fees – and it was not unusual to find them even in the service of a priest.'

From the correspondence of merchants quoted in Iris Origo's book, it appears that the slaves often tried to escape to their homes in North Africa or the Balkans: 'We hear from Ibiza that Ser Antonio Delio has arrived there with many moorish captives in their ships, and twelve of them ran away with his rowing boat . . . but because of the weather, the said moors came here [Majorca] and for the present have been imprisoned, which has been a great piece of good fortune.' A letter from Barcelona to Avignon appeals for help in catching two runaway slaves: 'One of them is named Dmitri, a big man and very handsome. His flesh is good, fresh and rosy. The other lacks a tooth in front and has rather greenish skin. I pray you, Senor, have them caught, let them be fettered and send them back by boat to me.'

Although at the time of the Black Death the papacy was at Avignon, and the Pope, Clement VI, was a Frenchman, he nevertheless offered a plenary indulgence to anyone making a pilgrimage to Rome in 1350. The Florentine Matteo Villani was astonished by the number that headed for Rome, not just from Italy but from north of the Alps: 'The multitude of Christians who went to Rome was impossible to count,' he wrote, and the numbers he gives were probably bumped up in medieval fashion. 'By the estimate of those living in the city on

Christmas Day and in Lent until Easter, the pilgrims to Rome were from one million to 1,200,000. And then from Ascension to Pentecost, more than 800,000. In summer, the heat and the demand for harvest workers reduced the number to 200,000, but never before had there been such a pilgrimage.' Many of those who did join in the pilgrimage took the plague as a warning to repent their sins and commit themselves to prayer. Among these were the poet Petrarch who lost his beloved Laura as well as many among his friends and family. 'There was a crowd of us and now we are almost alone,' he wrote. 'We should make friends, but how can we when it looks to me as if the end of the world is at hand?' Even Boccaccio, who had described the plague in *Decameron* with irony and detachment, grew increasingly sombre and serious. In a letter to a friend in 1373, he lamented having written his masterpiece: 'I am certainly not pleased that you have allowed the illustrious women in your house to read my trifles; indeed I beg you to give me your word that you will not permit it. You know how much of them is less than decent and opposed to modesty, how much stimulation to wanton lust.'*

Some of the Genoese galleys which had brought the plague from the Black Sea to Italy went on to Marseilles and along the coast of Provence, from where the plague spread quickly north. One of the first French cities to suffer its onslaught was Avignon, where Clement VI took measures to ease the suffering of the afflicted. He hastened the granting of absolution to the sick and at first encouraged penitential marches until they led to excesses in which people of both sexes went barefoot 'some in sackcloth, some covered with ashes, wailing as they walked, tearing their hair and lashing themselves with scourges, to the point where blood was drawn'. This was the first appearance of the flagellants who infested Germany over the next two years, their piety often turning to anticlericalism and violence against the Jews. Pope Clement therefore banned the processions, probably to the benefit of public health, since large assemblies spread the pneumonic plague as they did the 'Spanish flu' of 1918.

Clement VI, as a patron of science, also encouraged the Avignon doctors to dissect the plague victims 'in order that the origins of the disease might be known'. These autopsies failed – not surprisingly,

---

* Quoted in Meiss, *Painting in Florence and Siena after the Black Death*, 1951.

since the secrets of the bubonic plague are still not clear to modern scientists using the most sophisticated instruments.

Pope Clement's physician, Guy de Chauliac, ordered that two fires be lit in the papal apartment, and that his holiness should sit between them even in the heat of summer. According to Daniel Defoe in his *Journal of the Plague Year*, the London doctors in 1665 also recommended a coal fire in summer to ward off infection.

The hatred of friars by the rest of the clergy, which Jean de Meun expressed in *Le Roman de la Rose*, did not abate in the face of common danger. The English canon regular, Knighton, wrote in his *Cronicon*, a lively record of events in the middle and late fourteenth century: 'Of the Carmelite friars at Avignon, sixty-six died before the citizens knew the cause of the calamity; they thought that these friars had killed each other. Of the English Austin friars at Avignon, not one remained. Nor did men care. At Marseilles, of one hundred and fifty Franciscans, not one survived to tell the tale, and a good job too!'

Until late in the twentieth century, the people of Nuits St Georges, in Burgundy, remembered the lines: '*En mil trois cent quarante et huit/ A Nuits de cent resterent huit.*' And at Beaune: '*En mil trois cent quarante-neuf/ De cent ne demeraient que neuf.*'*

The jingle was used by Chaucer's contemporary Guillaume de Machaut in one of his poems about the Black Death in France:

> For many have certainly heard,
> Heard it commonly said,
> How in one thousand three hundred and forty-nine
> Out of one hundred there remained but nine.
> Thus it happened that for lack of people
> Many a splendid farm we left untilled.
> No one ploughed the fields
> Bound the cereals and took in the grapes.
> Some gave triple salary
> But none for one denier was twenty enough
> Since so many were dead.†

---

* Quoted in Joan Evans's *Art in Mediaeval France*, 1948.
† Quoted by David Herlihy in *The Black Death and the Transformation of the West*, 1998.

In France, as in all western Europe, the labour shortage led to high wages, social unrest and the loosening of feudal ties. However, as Robert S. Gottfried has pointed out:

> In eastern Europe, plague led to serfdom. On the flat plains of Poland, Prussia and Hungary, grain-growing could be profitable only by using cheap unfree labourers, and many eastern lords used force to keep the peasants in place. Without kings to appeal to for aid, or towns to flee to as an alternative, eastern European peasants lacked the resources and mobility of their counterparts in the west. For them depopulation was a disaster; it led to the serfdom and misery of peasants which persisted in some places until the nineteenth century.

The plague penetrated even the pine forests and icy wastes of Scandinavia. It was the Swedish language that gave us the term Black Death or '*swarta döden*', and a Swedish director, Ingmar Bergman, who gave us the only film on the subject, *The Seventh Seal*, with Max von Sydow as a knight confronted by Death, the 'sallow rider' of the Apocalypse.

The history of the Black Death is perhaps most upsetting to modern readers because of its fourteenth-century intimations of twentieth-century hatred against the Jews. However, these pogroms must be examined not so much for their modern parallels as to help us answer the question of whether Chaucer too was an anti-Semite.

The accusation that Jews were causing or spreading the plague was first heard in the south of France in the early spring of 1348, shortly followed in May by massacres at Narbonne and Carcassonne. The anti-Semitic fury then moved east to Savoy, Switzerland and the Rhine Valley. During a trial at Chillon in September 1348 of Jews said to have poisoned wells at Neustadt, one Balavignus, a doctor, was tortured into confessing that Jacob, the rabbi of Toledo, had sent him by hand of a Jewish boy a leather pouch filled with red and black powder, with orders to empty it into the wells of Thonon. Copies of this and other confessions racked from Jews were sent to neighbouring cities of Switzerland and the upper Rhine. On 21 September 1348 the municipality of Zurich voted never again to let Jews into the city. In Basle, all the Jews were shut into wooden buildings and burnt alive. In November 1348 the wave of persecution washed down the Rhine, reaching a climax at Strasbourg, with its large Jewish community.

Pope Clement VI condemned the massacres, pointing out that the Jews were also the victims of the plague they were accused of spreading. Lowlier clerics wanted a scapegoat, as we see from the chronicle of Herman Gigas, a German Franciscan friar, who begins calmly enough, then whips himself into an anti-Semitic frenzy:

> In 1347 there was such a great pestilence and mortality throughout all the world, that in the opinion of well-informed men, scarcely a tenth of mankind survived. Some say that it was brought about by the corruption of the air; others that the Jews had planned to wipe out all the Christians with poison and had poisoned wells and springs everywhere. And many Jews confessed as much under torture; that they had bred spiders and toads in pots and pans, and had obtained poison from overseas . . . God the lord of vengance has not suffered the malice of the Jews to go unpunished. Throughout Germany in all but a few places, they were burnt. For fear of that punishment, many accepted baptism and were spared. This action was taken against the Jews in 1349 and it still continues unabated, for in a number of regions many people, noble and humble, have laid plans against them and their defenders which they will never abandon until the whole Jewish race has been destroyed.

Another German cleric, Heinrich Truchess von Diessenhoven, spells out how these plans were put into effect:

> But now let us follow the killings individually. First Jews were killed or burnt in Solden, then in Zofingen they were seized and some put [i.e., broken] on the wheel, then in Stuttgart they were all burnt. During December they were burnt and killed in the feast of St Nicholas, and on 20 December in Horw they were burnt in a pit. And when the wood and straw had been consumed, some Jews, both young and old, still remained half alive. The stronger of them snatched up cudgels and stones and dashed out the brains of those trying to creep out of the fire, and thus compelled those who wanted to escape the fire to descend to hell.*

---

* Both quoted in *The Black Death*, Manchester Medieval Sources Series, 1994, translated and edited by Rosemary Horrox.

This murderous hatred of the Jews was not confined to fanatical priests or ignorant German peasants. The French poet Guillaume de Machaut gave full expression to such prejudice in one of his poems about the Black Death, *Jugement du Roy de Navarre*:

> Judeé la honnie
> La Maulvaise, le desloyal,
> Que bien net et aime tout mal
> Qui tant donne d'or et d'argent
> Et promis a crestienne gent
> Que puis, riviere et fonteines
> Qui estoient clare et seines
> En plusieurs lieus empoissonèrent

Since Chaucer was an admirer of Machaut, and indeed borrowed other lines from this very poem, we must assume that he knew, if he did not share, Machaut's belief that during the Black Death the Jews 'poisoned wells, rivers and fountains which had been pure and healthy'. It is therefore pleasant to find that Boccaccio, another foreign poet whom Chaucer admired, was philo-Semitic. Italy in the mid-fourteenth century, as in the mid-twentieth, stood as an enclave of tolerance in a Europe maddened by racial hatred. Boccaccio's account of the plague is free from any suggestion that it was caused by the Jews poisoning Florence's wells. Indeed, I have found no record of anti-Semitic outbursts in Italy during the years 1348 to 1350. The propensity of the Jews to make a living by money-lending or usury was unremarkable in a nation of shrewd and even unscrupulous bankers such as the Lombards, the Florentines and the Venetians. Indeed the Venetian Jews in the Middle Ages enjoyed a favoured status, being permitted to set up loan banks, to trade with the East and to practise medicine – which may not seem weighty concessions to us but were tolerant by the standards of the age. The equal right of Jews and Christians under Venetian laws was well summed up by Shakespeare's merchant Antonio in *The Merchant of Venice*:

> The Duke cannot deny the course of law:
> For the commodity that strangers have
> With us in Venice, if it be denied,
> Will much impeach the justice of his state;

Since that the trade and profit of the city
Consisteth of all nations.

When the nine young women and three young men of Boccaccio's *Decameron* have left Florence and settled into their refuge up in the hills of Tuscany, they start to tell the stories which will amuse them over the next ten days. On the very first day, the second and third stories, both told by women, have a wise and virtuous Jew as hero. The first of these, about Abraham, who had wanted to be a Christian, has become so popular that it is now part of our common folklore and is often repeated in garbled form by those who have never heard of Boccaccio.

Abraham is a rich Jew in Paris who is thinking of turning Christian but first wants to travel to Rome to visit the Vatican, presumably before the papacy had moved to Avignon. When his French friend Jehannot hears this, he is thrown into gloom 'for if he goes to the court of Rome and sees what foul and wicked lives the clergy lead, not only will he not become a Christian, but if he had already turned Christian, he would become a Jew again, without fail'.

In spite of Jehannot's protestations, the Jew went to Rome and 'cautiously began to observe the behaviour of the Pope, the cardinals and the other Church dignitaries, and all the courtiers. Being a very perceptive person, he discovered, by adding the evidence of his own eyes to information given him by others, that practically all of them from the highest to the lowest were flagrantly given to the sin of lust, not only of the natural variety, but also of the sodomitic, without the slightest display of shame or remorse, to the extent that the power of prostitutes and young men to obtain the most enormous favours was virtually unlimited.'

When Abraham returned to Paris he told Jehannot what he had seen and gave his opinion that 'your pontiff, and all of the others too, are doing their level best to reduce the Christian religion to nought and drive it from the face of the earth. But since it is evident,' went on Abraham, 'that their attempts are unavailing and that your religion continues to grow in popularity and become more splendid and illustrious, I can only conclude that, being a more holy and genuine religion than any of the others, it deservedly has the Holy Ghost as its foundation and support. So whereas earlier I stood firm and unyielding against your entreaties and refused to turn Christian, I now tell you quite plainly that nothing in the world could prevent me from becoming a Christian.'

Boccaccio's story contributed to the later belief of Protestants and Deists that the Church of Rome was given over to wickedness and unnatural sexual practices; witness Gibbon's remark on the trial of Pope John XXII: 'Among the lesser crimes with which the Vicar of Christ was charged were rape, murder, piracy, sodomy and incest.'

The second story told on the first day of Boccaccio's *Decameron* is a plea for the toleration of Muslims as well as Jews, and might be thought relevant to the Middle East even today. It relates how Saladin, whose worth was so great that it raised him from humble beginnings to the sultanate of Egypt, was short of cash after spending his wealth on wars and acts of munificence. He remembered a Jew, Melchizedek, who ran a money-lending business in Alexandria. He invited Melchizedek to his palace, made him welcome, then asked the following loaded question: 'O man of excellent worth, many men have told me of your great wisdom and your superior knowledge of the ways of God; hence I would be glad if you would tell me which of the three laws, the Jewish, the Saracen or the Christian, you deem to be truly authentic.' The Jew understood that Saladin was trying to trick him into a quarrel, so instead of giving an answer he responded with a parable: 'A worthy man did not know how to divide his fortune among his three sons. He therefore announced that he would bequeath it all to the possessor of his most valuable and beautiful ring. Whichever son was found to have his ring would be heir to the title and fortune. The father then gave his ring to a master craftsman to make two replicas so exact that he himself could not tell them apart. After the father's death, each of the three sons produced an identical ring to claim the title and fortune. But since no one could tell the rings apart, the question of the inheritance remained unanswered. And the same goes for the three laws which God the father gave to his people,' Melchizedek concluded. He then offered Saladin the loan. The sultan later paid him back in full, in addition to which he showered magnificent gifts upon him, made him a lifelong friend and maintained him at court in a state of importance and honour.

Boccaccio's even-handed attitude to the three religions was as rare in fourteenth-century Europe as it is in the Middle East to this day. In a crusading age, his lack of animosity towards the Muslims was still more remarkable than his friendliness to the Jews.

The Italian unwillingness to join in pogroms against the Jews was demonstrated again six centuries later, when all Europe was dominated by Nazi Germany. The Italian dictator Benito Mussolini who came to power in the 1920s did not share the racist views of his counterpart Adolf Hitler; indeed, Jews became prominent in the Italian Fascist Party and even on the general staff of Mussolini's army. When the Italians sided with Hitler in the Second World War, they were allotted spheres of command in Axis-occupied France, Greece and Yugoslavia, but nowhere did they institute measures against the Jews.

Even in 1942, when Hitler ordered Mussolini to enforce the 'final solution' in Italian-occupied countries, the armed forces flatly refused to comply. This attitude sometimes shocked the quisling regimes. When the military governor of the Italian zone of France would not agree to round up Jews for deportation to Poland, the French fascist Pierre Laval was baffled. 'If these were Italian Jews,' he said, 'I could understand your attitude, but they're French Jews.' The senior Italian general in Yugoslavia, Mario Roatta, refused to hand over Jews to the Independent State of Croatia, to be sent to Jasenovac concentration camp 'with the well-known consequences'. The German ambassador to the Independent State of Croatia, Siegfried Kasche, complained that about five hundred Jews were living at Karlovac, some of them letting rooms to Italian officers, so that the Croats were 'unable to carry out measures against Jewry'.

A German officer was shocked to find that in Dubrovnik 'the relationship between Italian officers, Jews and Serbs is an absolutely undeniable fact. Italian officers are often seen with Jewish women in the Gradska Café.'* During the trial of Adolf Eichmann in Israel in 1960, many survivors of Hitler's 'final solution' praised the Italians who had provided false documents, ignored their orders, bent the rules and in hundreds of other ways helped the Jews to escape. The Danes as well had behaved with honour, but as Hannah Arendt observed in *Eichmann in Jerusalem*: 'What in Denmark was the result of an authentically political sense . . . was in Italy the outcome of the almost automatic humanity of an old and cultured people.'

Chaucer's attitude to Jews is, however, more open to debate. The Prioress relates a tale of a small boy murdered by the Jews and thrown

---

* See Jonathan Steinberg's *All or Nothing*, 1990.

into a sewer. Although it is set in Asia, Chaucer links it with the legend of Little Hugh of Lincoln, who was said to be a victim of a ritual murder. Indeed, it is possible that the *Prioress's Tale* was written to be recited during a visit to Lincoln by Richard II.

The *Prioress's Tale* is not overtly connected with the anti-Semitic outbursts on the Continent during the Black Death, because in England there had been no pogroms or stories of poisoned wells, if only because the Jews had been hanged or expelled by Edward I. The tale is shocking not because it reflects the attitudes of the fourteenth century, but because it foreshadows Hitler and his 'Final Solution'. It has become as much an embarrassment to lovers of Chaucer's poetry as *Die Meistersinger* is to lovers of Wagner's opera. And just like Wagner's anti-Semitic work, Chaucer's is hard to explain away.

The *Prioress's Tale* is set in an Asian city, whose ruler maintains a Jewish quarter, or Jewry, for 'usury and lucre of felony', perhaps a reference to the earlier English kings who tolerated the Jews in return for loans. Near the Jewry is a school for Christian children, among them

> A litel clerk but seven year of age
> That day by day to schoole went alone;
> And eek also, whereso he saw the image
> Of Cristes moder, had he in usage,
> As him was taught, to kneel adoun, and say
> His *Ave Mary*, as he goeth his way.

Satan arouses the Jewry against this insult to their laws:

> Our firste foe, the serpent Sathanas,
> That hath in Jewes hert his waspes nest,
> Upswelled and sayde: 'Oh Hebrew people, allas!
> Is this a thing to you that is honest,
> That such a boy shall walken as he list
> In your despyt, and synge of such sentence
> Which is against your lawes reverence?'

The Jews ambush the child, cut his throat and cast the body in a cesspit:

I say that in a pitte they him threw,
Wher as the Jewes purgen their entraile.
O cursed folk! O Herodes al new
What may your evil entente you availe?
Morther will out, certeyn it will nought faile . . .

Sure enough the crime is discovered when the child continues singing from the sewage pit.

This gemme of chastitee, this emeralde,
And eke of martirdom the ruby bright,
Where he with throte y-carven lay upright,
He *Alma redemptoris* gan to synge
So loud that al the place began to ringe.

The Christians call for the provost of the town:

He came anon withoute tarrying,
And praised Christ, that is of heven kyng,
And eek His moder, honour of mankynde,
And after the Jewes did he bynde.

Without apparently any trial, the provost condemns all those Jews who knew of the murder to 'torment and shameful death':

Therefore with wilde hors he did them drawe,
And after that he hung them by the lawe.

The Prioress ends her tale with a reminder that such murder can occur nearer home:

O yonge Hugh of Lyncoln; slayn also
With cursed Jews as it is notable,
For it is but a litel while ago,
Pray eke for us . . .

For hundreds of years after its publication, the *Prioress's Tale* was not regarded as shocking by lovers of Chaucer. True, Wordsworth spoke of its 'fierce bigotry', but Hazlitt considered it 'simple and heroic to the last degree'. In the early nineteeth century anti-Semitism was a feature of even radical, left-wing opinion, exemplified by Hazlitt, Cobbett, Dickens, the *Manchester Guardian* and the revived *Spectator*. To understand how attitudes have changed, we need only look at these comments on the *Prioress's Tale* by Grace Hadow, one of the wisest and wittiest of Chaucer critics, writing in 1914:

> Nothing better illustrates the simplicity and sincerity of Chaucer's religious feeling than the tale of little St Hugh. The story of the Christian child decoyed away and murdered by the Jews was commonly believed in the Middle Ages. Indeed it is said that more than one anti-Semitic outbreak in Russia during the past forty years has been provoked by the relation of similar tales, and we have just seen the conclusion of a 'Blood-ritual' case of the kind. The fierce racial and religious hatred which underlies belief in the possibility of such a thing, is in itself sufficiently terrible, and the story affords ample opportunity for the expression of animosity towards these 'cursed folk of Herodes al newe', but Chaucer's religion would appear to consist less in the denunciation of the Church's enemies than in affection for her saints.

Such a comfortable interpretation of the *Prioress's Tale* was no longer tenable after Hitler came to power, and *Der Sturmer* in 1934 devoted a whole issue to Jewish ritual murder, illustrated by pictures of rabbis sucking the blood of Christian children. It was time for Chaucerians to re-examine the text. One of the best of these reappraisals is R. J. Schoeck's essay 'Chaucer's Prioress: Mercy and Tender Heart'.* Schoeck begins by confronting the idea advanced by Grace Hadow and others that the tale is more concerned with praising the saints of the Church than denouncing its enemies. 'Can the reader close his eyes to the unmistakable reality of the anti-Jewish theme and concern himself only with the literary form?' Schoeck acknowledges that other critics have found some irony in the portrayal of the Prioress. He goes further: 'The interpretation which I am about to suggest is that in the *Tale* which Chaucer assigned to the Prioress, the widely circulated legend of ritual murder is held up for implicit condemnation as vicious and hypocritical.'

---

* *Chaucer Criticism Volume I: The Canterbury Tales*, edited by Richard J. Schoeck and Jerome Taylor, Notre Dame, Indiana, 1960.

To support his argument, Schoeck points out that the blood libel and other accusations against the Jews had been repeatedly denounced by the papacy, as was well known in the fourteenth century: 'At the end of the thirteenth and during the fourteenth century, the charges of ritual murder became more frequent, yet the popes had proclaimed the Truth and set up an ideal against which these excesses and tortures and false charges should have been seen for what they were.'

True enough, and yet these accusations were made and widely believed not just in the Middle Ages but into the nineteenth and even twentieth centuries. Nor have anti-Semitic Christians been convinced by Schoeck's equally cogent argument that the Christian Bible is largely written by and about Jews: 'The attentive reader may well be struck by the irony of having an anti-Semitic legend prefaced by a prayer that is rich in images from the Old Testament. The Prioress invokes Christ . . . then she calls Mary "O moder mayde! O mayde moder free!/O bush unburnt, burning in Moses sight." '

Unfortunately, the obvious fact that Jesus Christ was a Jew born of the Jewish Mary has never prevented Christians calling the Jews the killers of God. Schoeck admits that the irony might be more apparent to the sophisticates of the court than to the more narrow-minded and insular, but nevertheless holds that the Canterbury pilgrims would have detected the hypocrisy of the Prioress as of the Pardoner and the Friar.

Frankly I doubt whether Chaucer's irony, even if he intended it, would have been observed by sophisticates at the court any more than by the stupidest of the Canterbury pilgrims. As any journalist knows, the use of irony is as dangerous in a broadsheet or weekly paper as in a mass-circulation tabloid. Most readers will take it quite literally. Subtle ironist though he was, even Chaucer tended to drop hints in advance when one of his characters such as the Friar or the Pardoner is about to condemn himself from his own mouth.

Again it has been suggested that the bigotry of the Prioress is satirized by her confessor, the Nun's Priest, in his tale of Chaunticleer and Pertelote, the cock and his hen. It is true that the *Nun's Priest's Tale* represents everything that was wise and good in the fourteenth-century Church; however, her priest does not challenge the Prioress's attitude to the Jews. Indeed, one part of the *Nun's Priest's Tale*, concerning a murder, not only repeats but endorses her savage thoughts on crime and punishment. 'Murder will out,' says Chaucer again before showing how some accused men were tortured and racked, 'pyned and engyned'.

Since there is no indication in the *Prioress's Tale* that Chaucer disagreed with its sentiments, attempts have been made to show that his character sketch in the *General Prologue* lays her open to hatred, ridicule and contempt. Certainly he exposes her affectations, her lapdogs, her French from the school of Stratford-atte-Bowe and her brooch with the inscription *Amor vincit omnia* (Love conquers all). She is the first in a long line of comically maddening women in English literature, notably in the works of Jane Austen, Dickens and P. G. Wodehouse. The Prioress can be seen as vain, charming, simpering, sentimental, manipulative or helpless. Whether the reader wants to kiss or to kick her is purely a matter of taste.

To Chaucer's contemporaries, as to modern critics, the comedy of the Prioress lies in the contrast between her vows and her worldly longings. Nuns in the fourteenth century were forbidden to wear adornments, keep pets or go on pilgrimages – at least not in mixed company. Much of the phraseology in her pen portrait comes from medieval romance, especially when she is said to be 'simple and coy'. The nineteenth-century scholar Professor Lowes pointed out that her very name Eglantyne was 'exquisitely incongruous' since it was often used in romantic tales, far removed from the life of a nun. Her sparkling eyes, her small soft mouth and broad forehead were all attributes of sexual attraction.

Many have pointed out that the Prioress was the sort of woman who wept over a dead mouse or a whipped dog but not over the human suffering all around her. Schoeck notes that 'her manners are carefully those of polite society, and to the attentive fourteenth-century listener there was subtle but effective irony in Chaucer's evocation, for the manners described are taken from a famous account in *Le Roman de la Rose* of what wiles a woman is to use to attract and hold her lover.' When I first heard this derivation of the account of the Prioress's table manners, I had not read *Le Roman de la Rose* and thought it was only a poem of love and chivalry. Only later did I discover that this passage comes from a speech by the whore La Vieille on how a tart should pick up a client and empty his pockets. To show how closely the Prioress is based on La Vieille, I append the original lines from the *General Prologue* and Ellis's verse translation of *Le Roman de la Rose*:

At mete wel y-taught was she in all;
She let no morsel from her lippes falle,
Ne wet her fyngres in her sauce deepe.
Wel coude she carie a morsel, and wel keepe,
That never drope upon hire breste should be.
For all her thoughte was set on curtesie.
Hir overlippe wyped she so clene
That in hir cuppe was no ferthyng sene
Of greese, whan she drunken hadde withinne.

Here are the etiquette hints of La Vieille translated by Ellis from *Le Roman de la Rose:*

'Tis well she take especial care
That in the sauce her fingers neer
She dip beyond the joint, nor soil
Her lips with garlic, sops or oil
Nor heap up gobbets and then charge
Her mouth with pieces overlarge
And only with a finger point
Should touch the piece she'd fain anoint
With sauce, white, yellow-brown or
    green
And lift it towards her mouth between
Finger and thumb with care and skill
That she no sauce or morsel spill . . .
                           Then her cup
She should so gracefully lift up
Towards her mouth that not a gout
By any chance did fall about . . .

Nor should she set

Lips to her cup while food is yet
Within her mouth . . .
And first should she
Her upper lip wipe delicately
Lest, having drunk, a grease-formed groat
Were seen upon the wine to float.

Although the English *Romaunt of the Rose*, translated by Chaucer and others, does not contain the parts of the poem about La Vieille, the original French was known at least by reputation to well-read Englishmen and women of the time. They would surely have seen the irony of a prioress taking advice on table manners from a procuress who preached free love and had shocked all France with her talk about castration and 'the wars of the cunnus'.

We can therefore take it as certain that Chaucer regarded the Prioress with mockery, if not contempt. I would like to think that he disapproved of the tale which he assigned to her. Unfortunately I cannot do so. For one thing, the *Prioress's Tale* is one of his most beautiful poems, and he must have been proud of it. We do not know whether he wrote it for the Prioress, or even for the *Canterbury Tales* at all. It could have been ordered for Richard II's visit to Lincoln, where 'Little Hugh' was widely revered as a martyr. Reluctantly, I have come to accept that Chaucer believed in the blood libel just as Machaut believed that the Jews in France were poisoning wells.

5

The Black Death:
Why it was Soon Forgotten

CONTEMPORARIES AGREE THAT THE plague first appeared in England in June 1348 at Melcombe, near Weymouth in Dorset, to which it was probably brought by ship from Calais. However, it could have come at around the same time to some of the other ports in contact with mainland Europe, for isolation had never provided Britain with a *cordon sanitaire*. 'The south-east of England,' writes one economic historian, 'lay at the great crossroads where the trade routes from Scandinavia, the Baltic, the North Sea, the Atlantic coast and the Mediterranean all met, as well as the great riverways of the Rhine, the Meuse, the Scheldt and the Seine.'* The pestilence spread within weeks to London, East Anglia and the English army in Northumberland, tempting the Scots to invade while their foes were ill. The Scots won a battle, then caught the disease themselves, and fled back over the border to infect their fellow countrymen.

Since the Black Death's progress was reported mostly by monks and other clerics, we are best informed on how it affected their own communities and profession, although these were probably typical of the country at large. Philip Ziegler tells us that the Black Death quickly spread from Melcombe to most of the parishes of Dorset, creating the need for a hundred new vicars and other clergymen. The town of Poole was especially hit, and a tongue of land called the 'Baite' was purchased by the councillors as a burial ground. At nearby Bridport the plague did not interfere with the local industry of making rope for the navy (and later the public hangman; hence the term 'Bridport dagger' for a noose), but extra bailiffs had to be found to cope with the

---

* E. A. Kosminsky, *Studies in the Agrarian History of England*, 1950.

emergency. In January 1349 Ralph of Shrewsbury, the Bishop of Bath and Wells, issued a pastoral letter on how to cope with the crisis in the West Country:

> The contagious pestilence of the present day, which is spreading far and wide, has left many parish churches and other livings in our diocese without parson or priest to care for their parishioners. Since no priests can be found who are willing, whether out of zeal and devotion or in exchange for a stipend, to take on the parochial care of these places, nor to visit the sick and to administer to them the sacraments of the Church (perhaps for fear of infection and contagion), we understand that many people are dying without the sacrament of penance.

Bishop Shrewsbury then lets it be known to the faithful that if they are on the point of death and cannot secure the services of a priest, they should make confessions to each other 'as is permitted in the teaching of the apostles, whether to a layman, *or if no man is present, then even to a woman*' (my italics).

The chronicler Knighton, a canon of Leicester, who had gloated over the deaths of friars in Avignon and Marseilles, was saddened by the result of the plague in his native England: 'There is everywhere such a dearth of priests that many churches are left without the divine offices of mass, matins, vespers, sacraments and sacramentals. One could scarcely get a chaplain to serve a church for less than ten marks. [A mark was about two-thirds of a pound.] And whereas before the pestilence, when there were plenty of priests, anyone could get a chaplain for five or even four marks, or for two marks and his board, at this time there was hardly a soul who would accept a vicarage.'

One of the first historians of the Black Death, Cardinal F. A. Gasquet, blamed its toll for a decline of standards in the priesthood and therefore the rise of Protestantism. He explained that, after the first onslaught of the plague and its several recurrences, 'many ignorant people, typically widowers, applied to take holy orders without the neccessary training'. He relates how 'the illustrious William of Wykeham, Bishop of Winchester in June 1385', caused Sir Roger Deanne, Rector of St Michael in Jewry Street, to swear that he would learn in twelve months the articles of the faith, the Ten Commandments, the sacraments of the Church and also the form of 'baptising' – in short the bare essentials of the job.

Cardinal Gasquet points out that Wykeham himself, who had been secretary to the king as well as the architect of the rebuilt Windsor Castle, entered the priesthood only after a second wave of the Black Death in 1361. On becoming Bishop of Winchester, he began a second career as Lord Chancellor and the founder of New College Oxford, as well as Winchester College which still bears his motto 'Manners Maketh Man'. The Black Death devastated Oxford University, the source of most of the priests in England. Richard Fitzralph, who had been the Chancellor before 1348, recalled that 'in his time' there had been 30,000 students compared to a mere 6,000 in 1358, but he blamed the decline not so much on the plague as on the machination of friars who lured students away by ignoble methods.

The friars themselves blamed the Black Death for their failings and unpopularity as we learn from the *Annales Minorum,* the annals of the Franciscan Minorite Order:

> The evil wrought great destruction to the holy houses of religion, carrying off the masters of discipline and those with most experience. From this time the monastic orders, and in particular the mendicants, began to grow tepid and negligent, both in that piety and in that learning in which they had up to this time flourished. Then our illustrious members being carried off, the rigours of discipline being relaxed by these calamities could not be revived by the untrained youths who were taken to fill the empty houses.

The Black Death took its toll along Chaucer's road to Canterbury. A monk, William of Dene, tells us what happened at Rochester in 1349: 'The Bishop of Rochester, who maintained only a small household, lost four priests, five esquires, ten attendants, seven young clerics and six pages, so that no one was left to attend him in any capacity. At Malling he consecrated two abbesses but both died almost immediately, leaving only four established nuns and four novices. To our grief, the plague carried off so vast a multitude of people of both sexes that nobody could be found who would bear the corpses to the grave. Men and women carried their own children on their shoulders to the church and threw them into a common pit. From these pits such an appalling stench was given off that scarcely anyone dared to walk beside the cemeteries.'

William of Dene reports at Rochester some early symptoms of the rebellious spirit which would erupt there during the Peasants' Revolt of 1381: 'There was so marked a deficiency of labourers and workmen of every kind at this period that more than a third of the land in the whole realm was left idle. All the labourers, whether skilled or unskilled, were so carried away by the spirit of revolt that neither King, nor law, nor justice could restrain them.'

William shows that the labour shortage and consequent breakdown of feudal obligations affected the Church estates as much as the secular magnates. During the whole of that winter and the following spring, the Bishop of Rochester remained at Trottiscliffe, near Sevenoaks, bewailing the terrible changes which had overcome the world. 'In every manor of his diocese, buildings were falling into decay and there was hardly one manor which returned as much as £100. In the monastery of Rochester supplies ran short and the brethren had great difficulty in getting enough to eat; to such a point that they were obliged either to grind their own bread or to go without. The prior however, ate everything of the best.'

The priory and convent of Christ Church Canterbury suffered only four deaths during 1348–9, perhaps because the cathedral precinct was clean and free of rats. During that same brief period, three archbishops of Canterbury perished in quick succession, having unwisely chosen to stay in London. Pilgrims continued to visit Becket's shrine but not in such vast numbers as went to Rome in 1350. Nor did the English pilgrims indulge in the penitential excesses which had shocked Pope Clement VI at Avignon. No flagellants were to be seen in England; nor did the populace harm the remaining Jews. There were no recorded scenes of unusual drunkenness and debauchery, such as Boccaccio witnessed in Florence. Although many preachers attributed the disease to the various vices of the age, the one they apparently singled out was men's indecent clothing, or what we would now call drag, which seems to have come into fashion before the return of the Black Death in 1362:

In that and the previous year, the whole of England was thrown into madness and excitement by a rage for bodily adornments. The fashion was first for full doublets cut short to the loins; and for a long garment reaching to the ankles, not opening to the front as is proper for men, but laced up the side to the armhole in the style of women's clothes, so that from the back the wearers look more like women than men.

This garment has an apt name, being called 'gown' in the vernacular
. . . from 'goony', which ought to be pronounced 'wounyg' – that is to
say 'wide open to mockery' . . . They also possess shoes with pointed
toes, as long as a finger, which are called Crackows . . . They are bored
by prayer. Because the people squander the gifts of God, it is only to be
expected that the Lord's vengeance will follow.

Professor May McKisack estimates that perhaps half the clergy fell
victim to the plague and a third of the population as a whole.
However, she insists that the plague of 1348–9 'seems to have caused
neither general panic, flight from the most badly affected areas, nor
more than very temporary dislocation of the wool trade. The shortage
of manpower may have encouraged the use of labour-saving devices
such as the fulling mill. It has even been suggested that the death of so
many monks, the chief transcribers of books, may have hastened the
development of the printing press by Gutenberg in Germany and by
Caxton in England.'

Although during the plague year of 1665 Charles II and his court
fled to the safety of Oxford, Edward III stayed in his capital during
1348–50. Indeed he rebuked the mayor about the filth being thrown
out of the houses: 'The streets and lanes through which people had to
pass were foul with human faeces and the air of the city poisonous to
the great danger of men passing, especially in this time of infectious
disease.' It is true that in January 1349 Edward prorogued Parliament
just before it was due to assemble on the grounds that 'the plague of
deadly pestilence daily increased in severity', but this was probably
just an excuse to avoid a confrontation when he already had a
guarantee of two years' subsidy.

'One of the most striking features of the Black Death in England,'
writes Ziegler, 'attested to in the court rolls of innumerable manors
and those borough records that are still available, is the way in which
communal life survived.' He suggests that the calm with which the
British faced the Black Death, as they did the Blitz of the 1940s, might
have been due to their self-disciplined and phlegmatic nature.

The publication of Ziegler's book and the realization that life in
England did not suffer a total breakdown in 1348–50 prompted
several revisionist studies by historians of medical science. In his
History of the Bubonic Plague in England (1970) J. F. D. Shrewsbury
argues that the 'Great Pestilence', as he calls it, cannot have been as

lethal as historians believed. He points to the absence of deserted villages, in order to argue for a mortality rate of as little as 20 per cent of the population:

> Had the 'Great Pestilence' caused anything like the devastating mortality in England and Wales ascribed to it by so many writers about the 'Black Death', the royal archives would surely have been full of petitions to the King for relief of taxation and for grants in aid. The paucity of the recorded royal pardons and grants suggests that the alleged mortality of the 'Black Death' exists only in the imagination of its subscribers.

Another revisionist historian, the epidemiologist Graham Twigg, suggests in *The Black Death: A Biological Reappraisal* that another disease, perhaps anthrax, was involved. This theory found guarded support from David Herlihy in *The Black Death and the Transformation of the West*: 'Anthrax can produce the characteristic swellings which might be mistaken for buboes and it can also come in pulmonary and pneumonic form. But historically it has never struck human populations in epidemic proportions.'

One of the strangest features of the English as opposed to the continental response to the Black Death was the scarcity of references to it in literature or even in folklore. There was no English Boccaccio to describe the plague in London; no Petrarch to express the sorrow of losing a loved one; not even a Machaut to berate the greed and idleness of the labouring class. Even the little girls' skipping song, which was once said to date to the time of the Black Death, is now more often attributed to the plague of 1665:

> Ring a ring of roses
> A pocketful of posies
> Atishoo! Atishoo!
> We all fall down.

The ring of roses was the red band of spots on the victim's body; the pocketful of posies were herbs to get rid of the stench of death; the sneeze was one of the symptoms of the disease from which the sneezer soon dropped dead.

Siegfried Wenzel, the author of a scholarly essay on 'Pestilence in

Middle English Literature',* begins with the rueful admission: 'Apart from the chronicles and medical or astrological treatises, the literature of the period contains surprisingly few references, and the few that do occur are usually remarks in passing.' Wenzel has discovered that Chaucer in the *Canterbury Tales* uses the word pestilence nine times; but on three occasions it merely means the very last degree of some moral evil, and three other passages use it in the form of a curse, such as the Wife of Bath's closing remark on skinflint husbands: 'And olde and angry niggardes of dispence/God sende hem soone verray pestilence!'

If the pestilence is seldom directly mentioned, the memory of the Black Death is frequently seen in Chaucer's poetry, just as the memory of two world wars remained with Englishmen down to the end of the twentieth century. For example, the sermon already quoted on outrageous clothes is brought to mind by the *Parson's Tale* which is really a sermon in prose on the seven deadly sins. However, Chaucer does not condemn men who dress like women but those who dress to show off their masculinity.

The Parson first denounces the wearing of very long gowns which trailed in the mire, when the extra material could have been used to clothe the poor.† The Parson then turns his attention to lewd apparel:

> Upon the oother side, to speken of the horrible disordinat scantnesse of clothyng as been thise kutted sloppes or haynselyns [loose outer coats, or short jackets] that thurgh hir shortnesse ne covere nat the shameful membres of man, to wikked entente.
>
> Allas, somme of hem shewen the boce [bulge] of hir shap, and the horrible swollen membres, that semeth ike the maladie of hirnia, in the wrappnge of hir hoses. And eek the buttokes of hem faren [behave] as it were the hyndre part of a she-ape in the fulle of the moone.

Chaucer's Parson then goes on to attack the 'outrageous array of wommen' whose faces may be chaste but who advertise through their attire their lechery and pride.

---

* From *The Black Death: The Impact of the Fourteenth-century Plague*; papers of the Eleventh Annual Conference of the Centre for Medieval and Renaissance Studies, New York, 1982.
† Similar criticisms greeted the Paris 'New Look' for women's skirts after the Second World War, when clothes were still rationed in England and France.

The Parson is shown in the *General Prologue* as one of those priests who during the Black Death stayed with their flock rather than going to London to take a well-paid job from a chantry bequest by praying for the soul of some wealthy victim of the plague. In contrast to the honest Parson, the Doctor of Physic appears in the *General Prologue* as one of those who enriched themselves from the Black Death without being able to offer its victims a cure or even relief from pain. Like Boccaccio in the *Decameron*, Chaucer makes fun of the way that doctors claimed to have studied the classics of medical science, while depending more on astrology, quackery and superstition. Once again, David Wright beautifully captures the satire:

> With us there was a doctor, a physician;
> Nowhere in all the world was one to match him
> Where medicine was concerned, or surgery;
> Being well grounded in astrology
> He'd watch his patient with the utmost care
> Until he'd found a favourable hour,
> By means of astrology, to give treatment.
> Skilled to pick out the astrologic moment
> For charms and talismans to aid the patient,
> He knew the cause of every malady,
> If it were 'hot' or 'cold' or 'moist' or 'dry',
> And where it came from, and from which humour.
> He was a really fine practitioner.
> Knowing the cause, and having found its root,
> He'd soon give the sick man an antidote.
> Ever at hand he had apothecaries
> To send him syrups, drugs and remedies,
> For each put money in the other's pocket –
> Theirs was no newly founded partnership.
> Well-read was he in Aesculapius
> In Dioscorides, and in Rufus,
> Ancient Hippocrates, Hali, and Galen,
> Avicenna, Rhazes and Serapion,
> Averroës, Damascenus, Constantine,
> Bernard, and Gilbertus, and Gaddesden.
> In his own diet he was temperate,
> For it was nothing if not moderate,

Though most nutritious and digestible,
He didn't do much reading in the Bible.
He was dressed all in Persian blue and scarlet
Lined with taffeta and fine sarsenet.
And yet was very chary of expense.
He put by all he earned from pestilence;
In medicine gold is the best cordial,
So it was gold that he loved best of all.

The nearest that Chaucer comes to describing the Black Death in England, as Boccaccio did in Florence, is the wonderful *Pardoner's Tale*. The tale is supposedly set in Flanders at a time of social unrest when the young spend their leisure in 'riot, hasard, brothels and taverns', giving the Pardoner a chance to preach against drunkenness. He then introduces the three villains of his tale, who will end up killing each other for ill-gotten gold. The opening scene in the tavern captures the atmosphere of dread and desperation which went with the sound of the bells tolling the plague victims:

These rioters, these three, of which I tell,
Long before prime had rongen any bell,
Were set them in a tavern for to drink;
And as they sat, they heard a belle clink
Before a corpse was carried to the grave;
That oon of them gan calle unto his knave,
'Go out,' quoth he, 'and axe readily
What corpse is that, that passes here foreby:
And look that thou report his name wel.'
'Sir' quoth he 'but that needeth never a del;
It was me told ere ye came here two hours;
He was, pardy, an old fellaw of youres,
And suddenly he was i-slayn to night;
For-dronk as he sat on his bench upright,
There came a privy thief, men clepen Deth,
That in this contree al the people slayeth;
And with his spere he smote his heart a-two,
And went his way without wordes mo.
He hath a thousand slayn this pestilence.'

The three villains resolve in their drunkenness to confront Death:

> 'Yea, Goodis armes!' quoth this rioter,
> 'Is it such peril with him for to meet? . . .
> Hearken, fellows, we three be stout and good;
> Let each of us hold up his hand to other,
> And each of us become the other's brother,
> And we will slay this false traitour death;
> He shall be slayne that so many slayeth,
> By Goddis dignitee, ere it be night.'

If Chaucer did not himself lose any dear ones to plague, he wrote a touching elegy for Blanche, the first wife of his patron, John of Gaunt, who died in a recurrence of the Black Death in about 1368. The *Book of the Duchess* was probably written to be read out on the anniversary of Blanche's death to recall her charm and to comfort her widower, who appears in the guise of a Black Knight.

The *Book of the Duchess* is influenced by Guillaume de Lorris, Froissart and Machaut, yet has a freshness which is both very English and very Chaucerian. In the first dozen lines there is not a word that derives from French rather than Anglo-Saxon. Even the most conventional passages are lit by flashes of original brilliance. Whereas every poet of the day found himself wandering in a forest, Chaucer alone meets

> A whelp that fauned me as I stood
> That had y-followed and coude no good,
> Hit com and creep to me as lowe
> Right as hit hadde me y-knowe
> Hild down his heed and joyned his eres
> And layde down al smothe his heres . . .

Chaucer notices with delight:

> . . . many squirelles that sete
> Ful hye upon the trees and ete
> And in hir maner made festes

Few heroines in medieval poetry have Blanche's vigour and charm:

> I saw her daunce so comlily
> Carole and singe so swetely
> And look so debonairly,
> So goodly speke and so friendly,
> That certes I trow that nevermore
> Nas seyn so blisful a tresore
> Therewith her liste so wel to live
> That dulness was of hir a-drad.

Unlike the usual heroines of medieval chivalry, who wanted their lovers to suffer for their sake, Blanche did not set her knight impossible tasks like walking bare-headed through the desert and sailing through the Gulf of Quarnaro. She sees no sense in sending a man

> . . . into Walayke
> To Pruyse and in-to Tartarye
> To Alisaundre ne in-to Turkye
> And bidde him faste, anoon that be
> Go hoodless to the drye sea
> And come home by the Carrenare . . .

Blanche looks you straight in the face with her big, grey eyes: 'Debonair, goode, gladde, and sadde.'

The widowed Black Knight recalls her readiness to forgive and forget; perhaps more apparent now she is dead than when she lived.

> When I had wrong and she the right
> She wolde alwey so godely
> For-geve me so debonarly
> In alle my youthe in alle chaunce
> She took me in her governaunce.

So affectionate is the character sketch of Blanche that one imagines Chaucer to be in love with her himself, which would not have been improper by the rules of chivalry. However, from this description, Blanche was not the type of married woman who would enjoy making a young poet sigh for her.

The *Book of the Duchess* reminds us that grief over the death of an individual is always more powerful than general lamentation over a plague or a war. It also reminds us that married love could be as strong in the fourteenth century as in any other age. So I believe was the love of children, as one sees from this treatise on the ideal child-nurse or nanny by Chaucer's contemporary, Bartholomeas:

> She is like as the mother, glad if the child be glad and heavy if the child be sorry . . . She taketh the child up if it fall and giveth it suck; if it weep she kisseth it and lulleth it still; and gathereth the limbs and bindeth them together and doth clean it and wash it when it is defiled. And for it cannot speak, the nurse lispeth and soundeth the same words to teach more easily the child . . . and she cheweth meat in her mouth, and makes it ready to the toothless child, and so she feedeth the child when it is hungered, and pleaseth the child with whispering and songs when it shall sleep and swathest it in sweet clothes and righteth and stretcheth out its limbs, and bindeth them together with cradlebands to keep and save the child that it have no miscrooked limbs. She batheth it and anointeth it with good ointments.

Chaucer's love of children is especially apparent where he has added to or adapted stories by other writers. The Monk, in his tale of disasters brought by a change in fortune, relates the story from Dante's *Inferno*, Canto XXXIII, of how Count Hugo of Pisa was locked in a tower with his sons and starved. While Dante concentrates on the terror and pity of the father who watches his children suffer until he is driven by madness to eat them, Chaucer directs our sympathy to the children:

> The eldest scarcely fyf year was of age;
> Allas, Fortune, it was great cruelte
> Suche briddes for to put in such a cage!

Chaucer gives us a heart-rending impression of the little three-year-old looking up and asking

> Father, why do you wepe?
> When will the gayler bring in our potage?
> Is there no morsel bread that ye do kepe?
> I am so hungry that I may nat slepe . . .

before lying down in his father's lap and dying.

Although Chaucer's version lacks the tragic intensity and horror of Dante's original, and indeed verges on sentimentality, it shows the weight he gives to the feelings of children. This is apparent in the *Man of Law's Tale*, adapted from Nicholas Trivet's story of how Constance journeyed from Syria to Northumberland in a small boat. She is driven by the malice of her mother-in-law to put out to sea again, this time with a baby boy. In a passage which Chaucer has added to Trivet's original, Constance is shown getting into the boat:

> Hir litel child lay weeping in her arm,
> And knelyng piteously to him she sayde:
> 'Pees, little son, I will do thee no harm.'
> With that hir kerchief drew she off her head
> And over his little eyen she it layde,
> And in her arm she lulleth it well fast,
> And unto heaven her eyen up she cast.

The Black Death has proved as mysterious to historians as it was to men at the time. Scientists still cannot agree on the origin of the epidemic, the means by which it was spread, or even if it really was a plague or some other lethal disease such as anthrax. Moreover, the inexplicable and random onset of the disaster means that the fourteenth century does not fit into theories of historical progress – religious, ideological, economic or social. It has proved as uncomfortable to Marxists and neo-Darwinists as it was to believers in a benevolent Deity.

In the twentieth century an American historian, Barbara W. Tuchman, made the Black Death the starting point of *A Distant Mirror: The Calamitous Fourteenth Century*. Her foreword begins:

> The genesis of this book was a desire to find out what were the effects on society of the most lethal disaster of recorded history – that is to say, of the Black Death of 1348–1350, which killed an estimated one third of the population living between India and Iceland. Given the possibilities of our own time, the reason for my interest is obvious . . . Although my initial question has escaped an answer, the interest of the period itself – 'a violent, tormented, bewildered, suffering and disintegrating age – . . .' was compelling, and, as it seemed to me, consoling in a period of similar disarray. If our last decade or two of collapsing

assumptions has been a period of unusual discomfort, it is reassuring to know that the human species has lived through worse before.

Since *A Distant Mirror* was published in 1977, we must assume that 'the last decade or two of collapsing assumptions' means that period of the Cold War and nuclear confrontation which almost led to catastrophe in the Cuban missiles crisis of 1962. The settlement of the crisis, and later the end of Communism in Europe, decreased, if it did not entirely remove, the threat of a nuclear war which now in the twenty-first century seems more likely to come from Asia. In any case Barbara Tuchman compared the aftermath of the Black Death not to the aftermath of nuclear war but to the 'discomfort' of living in fear of nuclear war.

As Barbara Tuchman says, the effects of the Black Death were not clear-cut because the fourteenth century 'suffered so many "strange and great perils and adversities" (in the words of a contemporary) that its disorders cannot be traced to any one cause; they were the hoofprints of more than the four horsemen of St John's vision, which had now become seven – plague, war, taxes, brigandage, bad government, insurrection, and schism in the Church. All but plague itself arose from conditions that existed prior to the Black Death and continued after the period of plague was over.'

Yet in *A Distant Mirror* Barbara Tuchman failed to make her lesson from history convincing. For a start, there is no real analogy between an epidemic which wiped out a third of the people of Europe, and a nuclear holocaust which never actually took place.

We should also beware of accepting her view that the Black Death darkened the lives of those who, like Chaucer, survived it. Not everyone in that 'calamitous' fourteenth century lived in dread of the four (or seven) horsemen of the Apocalypse, any more than Europeans lived out the twentieth century in the shadow of two world wars or the crimes of Hitler and Stalin.

When I first read *A Distant Mirror* describing a fourteenth century plunged into gloom by war, bigotry, superstition and above all by the Black Death, I kept reminding myself that this was also the age of Geoffrey Chaucer, the sunniest of poets. It is true that Barbara Tuchman wrote her book around the life of the French knight Enguerrand de Coucy, and that she focused attention on France, which suffered much more than England from war, brigandage, pogroms and other horrors beside the plague. Indeed, one of her first mentions of Chaucer comes in a chapter on housing conditions in Paris and whether the crowding of bedrooms encouraged sexual promiscuity. She reminds us that the two Cambridge students in Chaucer's *Reeve's Tale* 'were conveniently enabled to enjoy the favours of the Miller's wife and daughter because they were put to bed in the same room with the family'.

Nevertheless, England was not cut off from the rest of Europe during the fourteenth century. It suffered the Black Death as badly as anywhere on the Continent; a Peasants' Revolt in which London was sacked and the Archbishop of Canterbury murdered; wars in Scotland and Ireland; and Wyclif's challenge to the Church of Rome. So why did England and its first great poet not succumb to the gloom in this 'calamitous fourteenth century'? Soon after reading *A Distant Mirror*, I picked up G. K. Chesterton's *Chaucer*, published in 1932, and found he was asking the same question, fifty years before Barbara Tuchman's book was written:

Those strangely fanatical historians, who would darken the whole medieval landscape, have to give up Chaucer in despair, because he is obviously not despairing. His mere voice hailing us from a distance has the abruptness of a startling whistle or halloo; a blast blowing away all their artificially concocted atmosphere of gas and gloom. It is as if we opened the door of an ogre's oven, in which we were told that everybody was being roasted alive, and heard a clear, cheery but educated voice remarking that it was a fine day. It is manifestly and mortally impossible that anybody should write or think as Geoffrey Chaucer wrote and thought, in a world so narrow and insane as that which the anti-medievalists describe . . . we know the gentleness of his controversial manner, the way in which he feels confident that a light touch will tell. We know his soaring hilarity and high spirits; never stronger than in his old age and comparative poverty, when he began to sing of the April day when men took the road of Kent to Canterbury. We know that this did not come out of dark and twisted superstition or a debased social slavery; and it only remains for us to ask from what it did come.

To Chesterton, Chaucer's good humour came from his faith, or theology as he prefers to call it, and this is a cue for a theological argument. Chesterton did not agree with Barbara Tuchman that the Black Death had undermined religious belief and opened the way for what she calls 'modern man', but he did maintain it damaged the Roman Catholic Church. Taking his line from Cardinal Gasquet, Chesterton argues:

> The great medieval civilization had already been wounded, mortally wounded, by two great griefs, the first material and the other moral. The first was the Black Death, which turned Christendom into a house of mourning and had dreadful results of every kind; the worst being that priests became so few, and bad priests had so easily become priests that the whole great Christian philosophy and morality was brought into contempt.*

Chesterton's argument that the Black Death wounded the Catholic Church does not, however, explain why it made so little impression on everyday life in England and above all on Chaucer's poetry. My own view is that epidemics such as the Black Death have little lasting effect on the great majority of survivors. I would argue this from a study of two later epidemics, the Great Plague of 1665 and the Spanish influenza of 1918.

In his *Journal of the Plague Year*, Daniel Defoe relates how 100,000 or so died by the end of the year. Yet in spite of the *Journal*'s sombre tone, one gets the impression that London life continued much as normal during the Great Plague as it had done during the Black Death. The impression is reinforced by the diaries of John Evelyn and Samuel Pepys, who carried on working and wenching respectively. At the end of the *Journal*, Defoe compares the Londoners to the children of Israel 'after their being delivered from the host of Pharaoh, when they passed the Red Sea and looked back, and saw the Egyptian overwhelmed in the water, viz, that they sang His praise but they soon forgot His works'.

The Spanish influenza took a far greater toll of human beings but soon it too was almost completely forgotten. The American Professor Alfred W. Crosby ends his fascinating book on the

---

* The other 'great grief' Chesterton mentions was the failure of the crusades, which I discuss in the chapter on Chaucer's Knight.

epidemic* with an Afterword, called 'An inquiry into the peculiarities of human memory', which goes far to answering the question on the Black Death and Chaucer.

> The important and almost incomprehensible fact about Spanish influenza is that it killed millions upon millions of people in a year or less. Nothing else – no infection, no war, no famine – has ever killed so many in as short a period. And yet it has never inspired awe, not in 1918 and not since, not among the citizens of any particular land and not among the citizens of the United States. This inaptitude for wonder and fear cannot be attributed to a lack of information.

The government and people of the United States tried to ignore the epidemic when it was raging in 1918, and forgot it soon afterwards. 'Perhaps the most notable peculiarity of the influenza epidemic,' reflected the *New York Times* in November 1918, when the city had lost 9,000 to it in the previous two weeks, 'is the fact that it has been attended by no traces of panic or even excitement.'

With the end of the First World War, the influenza pandemic faded from the American history books and popular memory. More significant still to the study of Chaucer is the phenomenon noted by Crosby: 'Among those Americans who let the pandemic slip their minds were those supposedly hypersensitive young people who were to write the greatest masterpieces of American literature.' Among those writers of the 'lost generation' mentioned by Crosby were John Dos Passos, who himself crossed the Atlantic in a troopship stricken with influenza but mentioned it only once in his novels; Scott Fitzgerald, who missed seeing the First World War because his troopship was cancelled for fear of an epidemic; William Faulkner, whose Royal Air Force unit in Canada was devastated by Spanish flu, but who did not bring it into his novels; and Ernest Hemingway, whose girlfriend, the nurse of *A Farewell to Arms*, was posted away from him to look after influenza patients.

The only authors to dwell on the Spanish flu were Thomas Wolfe, who described his brother's death in *Look Homeward, Angel*, and Katherine Anne Porter, who wrote of her own tragic experience in the novella *Pale Horse, Pale Rider*.

America's Forgotten Pandemic, The Influenza of 1918, Cambridge, 1998.

Most significantly, though, there is no mention of Spanish influenza in Barbara Tuchman's *A Distant Mirror*, which purports to examine how plague affected the fourteenth-century world. Barbara Tuchman seems to be unaware that she herself, as a child, survived such an epidemic. Nor did Chaucer, as a mature man, have cause to reflect on the plague which had terrified London during his childhood.

It seems that we instinctively know the difference between a natural disaster such as plague and man-made evil such as war. This is why the British have forgotten the epidemic of 1918 but still remember the dead of the First World War on Poppy Day, and even visit the battlefield of the Somme.

6

Chaucer as Schoolboy and Soldier

THE EARLIEST DOCUMENT OF Chaucer's life is a household account book from June 1356 to April 1359, kept for Elizabeth de Burgh, Countess of Ulster and wife of Lionel, one of the sons of Edward III, who had taken on the boy as a junior page. It records the purchase in April 1357 for Galfrido Chaucer of a short jacket, a pair of red and black hose and a pair of shoes, as well as a Christmas gift of 2s 6d. It is also established that while he served in this royal household, Geoffrey travelled with them to Windsor, Liverpool and Yorkshire. His home was in Westminster Palace and it is thought that he probably slept on the floor of the still surviving Great Hall. This magnificent building, which dates from 1100, was written off by architects in the seventeenth and eighteenth centuries as a derelict Gothic pile, yet it survived the fire of 1843, as it did Hitler's incendiary bombs in 1940–41.*

The question of how and where Chaucer received his education has been exhaustively studied by scholars such as Professor Derek Pearsall in *The Life of Geoffrey Chaucer*. He almost certainly attended a grammar or Latin school in the neighbourhood of the family home on Thames Street, perhaps at the almoners' school of St Paul's Cathedral, the Dominican Black Friars (near the present tube station, bridge and pub of that name) or at one of the bishops' palaces on the river.

There is no evidence that he attended Oxford or Cambridge University, one of the Inns of Court or any other institution which might like to claim him. Since Oxford and Cambridge are the scenes of his two bawdiest poems, the *Miller's* and the *Reeve's Tales*, he cannot have

---

* It was in Westminster Hall that the greatest Englishman of the twentieth century, Winston Churchill, lay in state in January 1965 as more than 300,000 mourners shuffled by to pay their respects.

held these towns in awe, though he obviously had a soft spot for his Clerk of Oxenford. Nor does his portrait of the Sergeant of Law as idle, pompous and greedy suggest much respect for the legal profession. The idea that Chaucer might have attended the Inner Temple is based on a court report, now vanished, which Thomas Speight claimed to have seen in the seventeenth century, on how the poet was fined for assaulting a Franciscan in Fleet Street. Certainly Chaucer was critical of Franciscans such as the Friar and the Pardoner of the *Canterbury Tales*, but I cannot imagine him as a violent brawler. The story sounds like Protestant propaganda, dreamed up by Speight to depict Chaucer as an enemy of popish agents, whether fourteenth-century Franciscans or seventeenth-century Jesuits. Nor does the fact that Chaucer drank in Fleet Street suggest that he must have worked at the Inner Temple, any more than five centuries later it would have meant that he worked for a newspaper. More probably he was just a literary man who enjoyed Fleet Street pubs, the first of a line which included Johnson, Goldsmith, Lamb, Tennyson, Thackeray, Dickens, Belloc and Chesterton.

While we do not know where Chaucer was taught, we know that he studied Latin, for this was mandatory for boys and even some favoured girls such as Héloïse, the pupil of Abelard, and Chaucer's Prioress. A child like Geoffrey from a merchant's family would have begun by learning the alphabet from a tabella of wood or horn, then learnt to read and write in English the Hail Mary, the Our Father, the Creed and the Ten Commandments. He would then have studied the same and more in Latin, like the widow's 'little clergeon', or schoolchild, in the *Prioress's Tale*, who learns from the antiphoner, or book of antiphonal hymns, and then coaxes a schoolmate to explain their meaning:

> This litel child, his little book lernynge,
> As he sat in the scole at his prymer
> He *Alma redemptoris* herde synge,
> As children lerned hire antiphoner;
> And as he dorste, he drough hym ner and ner,
> And herkened ay the wordes and the note,
> Til he the first vers koude al by rote.
> Nought wiste he what this Latyn was to seye,
> For he so yonge and tendre was of age.

But on a day his felawe gan he preye
To expounden hym this song in his langage
Or telle him why this song was in usage;
This preyde he hym to construe and declare
Ful often time upon his knowes [knees] bare.
His felawe, which that elder was than he,
Answerede hym thus: 'This song, I have herde seye,
Was maked of our blisful Lady free,
Hir to salute, and eek hire for to preye
To been our help and succour when we deye.
I kan no more expound in this mateere.
I lerne song; I kan but smal grammeere.'

Whether at school or as a page at court, Chaucer acquired the rudimentary classical education evident in his poetry as in the prose translation of Boethius. Unlike Shakespeare, of whom it was jokingly said that he knew 'small Latin, and less Greek', Chaucer never even studied the older language, which was unknown to medieval men as scholarly as Dante. And although he probably read the simpler Latin authors such as Caesar in the original, he used a French crib for difficult poets such as Virgil.

Even his prose translation of Boethius was probably based on the French of Jean de Meun, or the English gloss of Nicholas Trivet, whose Anglo-Norman history was also the source of the *Man of Law's Tale*. According to Professor Pearsall, Chaucer's renderings of the metrical passages from Boethius are 'crabbed, literal, and awkward and show evidence of some labour in the working out and accurate communication of the sense of the Latin'.

Whatever his struggles with the Latin language, Chaucer clearly delighted in the literature of the classical age, whether he read it in the original or in cribs and translations. The Clerk of Oxenford, the Canterbury pilgrim with whom he most clearly identified, was still without benefice or worldly position:

For he would rather have at his beddes hed
Twenty bookes, clothed in black and red,
Of Aristotil, and his philosophie . . .
Yet had he but a litel gold in cofre;
But al that he might gete, and his frendes sent,

On bookes and his lernyng he it spent,
And busily gan for the soules pray
Of them that gaf him money to scolay.
Of studie took he most cure and most heede.
Not one word spak he more than was need.

If the Clerk of Oxenford chose Aristotle – probably in a Latin translation – for his preferred bedside reading, Chaucer himself was happiest with the more light-hearted Ovid, whose witty and scandalous verses shocked Caesar Augustus and whose conduct got him sent into exile on the Black Sea in modern Romania. From the start of the era of an established Christian Church, Ovid enjoyed the same kind of reputation with Europeans in general that French novels later enjoyed with Victorian Englishmen. Just as Ovid took his myths and legends from the Greek poets before him, so he inspired a multitude of later poets including Boethius, Dante, Boccaccio, Petrarch, Guillaume de Lorris and Jean de Meun, down to Chaucer, and after him Shakespeare, Milton and Keats, not to mention countless artists and sculptors.

It was the seventeenth-century poet laureate John Dryden, one of the first to attempt a modern version of Chaucer, who first saw his affinity with Ovid: 'Both of them were well-bred, well-natured, amorous and libertine, at least in their writings, it may be also in their lives.' It is easy to see why Dryden sympathized with the libertine spirit he found in Ovid and claimed to find in Chaucer as well. As a Roman Catholic, Dryden revolted against the Puritan ethos which had prevailed under the Commonwealth and seemed to be making a comeback under the dour Dutchman, William of Orange. Like Ovid, he was a satirist whose verses gave such offence to his targets that he was once beaten almost to death by hired thugs outside the Lamb and Flag, a still flourishing public house in Covent Garden.

In his interesting *Chaucer and Ovid*, John M. Fyler declares that 'Chaucer, like most late medieval and Renaissance poets, owes more to Ovid than any other classical author: the *Metamorphoses* offers a particularly handy source of stories and the most wide-ranging compendium of information about the gods and heroes. Its central concern, the pathos and comedy of love, is the avowed topic of the elegiac poems. Through them Ovid became the Freud of the Middle Ages.' It might be fairer to Ovid to compare these graceful poems – *Ars*

Amatoria, Amores, Remedia Amoris and *Heroides* – to the *Kama Sutra*, Japanese pillow books or popular guides to the joys of sex, than to pyschological treatises by the now discredited Sigmund Freud.

During its first millennium, the Christian Church tried to expunge all memory of the sexual licence and pagan gods of the former Roman empire. In both respects, the works of Ovid offered a tempting glimpse into a forbidden garden of delights, an alternative Eden. With the start of the second millennium and the idea of courtly love, the amorous poems of Ovid afforded rules of etiquette for the lords and ladies who practised the ritual adultery of King Arthur's round table or the court at Poitiers of Queen Eleanor of Aquitaine.

As E. J. Kenney writes in his introduction to *Ovid: The Love Poems*, the poet insisted that respectable freeborn girls and married women were out of bounds to the predatory male, but goes on to add: 'In a society in which married women notoriously intrigued with freedom and in a language in which *vir* meant indifferently "lover" or "husband", not many readers were likely to take this seriously, any more than Ovid, a wit and sceptic, can have done.' He refers to and repeats this passage in his defence of *Ars Amatoria*, pointing out that Rome offered too many opportunities and incentives to lovely women to stoop to folly for a mere book to make much practical difference. 'All perfectly true, but not calculated to appease an emperor who was touchy on the subject of public morals, who had attempted to discourage adultery by legislation, and whose private life was not above reproach.'

In some of his views on sexual morals, Ovid agreed with the teachings of the medieval Church. He regarded homosexuals with disdain and pity rather than condemnation but he was strongly against those women who practised abortion from vanity, to avoid getting stretch marks:

Let ripe fruit fall by nature; let
Grow on; life's no slight prize for small delay,
Why poison unborn children, why take weapons
To probe the womb and delve the life away
No tigress in Armenian dens would do it,
Her cubs aren't murdered by a lioness
But gentle girls do that, though not unpunished
Killing their womb's young life they often die

Die, and they're on the pyre with hair dishevelled
And 'serve them right' say all those standing by.

Ovid's *Amores* (I. 8) introduces the harlot Dipsas (or female dipso) who reappears in *Le Roman de la Rose* as La Vieille:

There's an old hag, an old hag name of Dipsas
Her name speaks for itself, she's never sober
Enough to see Aurora's rosy glow.

Ovid's Dipsas advises a young whore to go with a rich man or even a freed slave rather than with 'great Homer' or any other poet, just as La Vieille says that 'a poor man, even if it's Ovid or Homer, won't be worth two goblets'.

So closely did medieval men identify with Ovid, that when Maître Elie translated the *Ars Amatoria* into French he changed the hints on where to pick up women from ancient Rome to thirteenth-century Paris, from the Colosseum and hippodrome to St Germain-des-Prés and the parvis of Notre Dame Cathedral.

Chaucer acknowledged the *Ars Amatoria* and *Amores* when he wrote of 'Ovide, Venus's clerk' but he borrowed much more from *Metamorphoses*, a ragbag collection of Greek mythology and Latin folklore, loosely joined by the theme of transformation. Animals, men and women turn into other creatures or into trees, stones and heavenly bodies. Here he found the story of Phaeton, whose sisters changed into poplars, of Cadmus and the serpent's teeth, of trans-sexual Salmacis and Hermaphrodite, Echo and Narcissus, the rape of Proserpine, of Cyane changed to a pool, a boy to a newt, Aesculapius to an owl, and Arethusa into a fountain.

All the legends of Europe are to be found in *Metamorphoses*, from the rape of Europe herself to the stories of Daphnis and Chloe and of Orpheus in the Underworld. It provided the Roman empire and the medieval world with the wonder and fantasy of modern science-fiction tales of the natural and supernatural world, *Star Wars*, unidentified flying objects, lost arks and holy grails.

Ovid's *House of Rumour*, from the *Metamorphoses*, inspired one of Chaucer's wittiest poems – *The House of Fame* – in which the poet is carried off in the claws of an argumentative eagle. Nor did Chaucer appear to worry about the theological implications of *Metamor-*

phoses, which worried the fourteenth-century clergy as much as the sexual morals of *Ars Amatoria* and *Amores*. Indeed, the Church had promoted a French gloss called *Ovide Moralisé* which tried to explain such problems as the resemblance between the Flood in *Metamorphoses* and the one in Genesis. It also explains that Actaeon, the hunter who is changed into a stag and killed by his own pack of hounds, has been punished for overindulgence in a sport which the Church considered a luxury.

John Fyler suggests that Chaucer probably used *Ovide Moralisé* as a crib but did not bother about its theology, since he often omitted the transformations, like that of Actaeon into a stag, which raised theological problems. 'Indeed,' says Fyler, 'the omissions indicate his lack of interest in what for us seem the dominant qualities of the poem; its exploration of pyschopathology and the supernatural; its attendant vividness, and often grotesqueness of imagery.'

Nevertheless, Chaucer plundered *Metamorphoses* for the *House of Fame*, the *Legend of Good Women* and the *Book of the Duchess*, as well as for several of the *Canterbury Tales*. Indeed, he makes fun of his own copious borrowings from Ovid, in the opening words of the Man of Law, who has just been asked to speak by the Host (here in the David Wright translation):

'Good host,' said he, '*depardieux*, I assent;
For I've no thought of breaking my engagement.
A promise is a debt; I'll gladly pay it;
I can't say any fairer. And, by rights,
He who lays down the law ought not to break
The law himself, but rather to obey it;
So goes the code. But none the less I'm sure
I don't know any first-rate tale that Chaucer,
For all his little skill in rhyme and metre,
Has not – in language such as he can master –
Told long ago, as many are aware;
If he's not told them in one book, dear sir,
It is because he's told them in another.
For he has told of lovers of all kinds,
And more than Ovid mentions, or you'll find
In his *Epistles*, which are very old.
Why should I tell what's been already told?

In youth he wrote of Ceix and Halcyon;
Since when he's celebrated every one
Of those noble ladies, and their loves as well.
And anyone can look out, if he will,
His huge tome called *The Legend of Good Women*
And read about the wounds so wide and gaping,
Of Babylonian Thisbe, and Lucrece;
The sword of Dido, dying for Aeneas;
Of Phyllis, hanging herself from a tree . . .
The barren island standing in the sea;
And of Leander drowning for Hero;
The tears of lovely Helen, and the woe
Of Cressida; and yours too, Laodamia;
And of your cruelty too, Queen Medea,
Your little children hanging by the neck
Because your Jason proved himself a jilt.
Alcestis, Hypermestra, Penelope,
How highly Chaucer praised your womanhood!'

The Man of Law sourly comments that he cannot hope to compete
with Chaucer and those

'Muses that people call Pierides
– If you have read the *Metamorphoses*
Of Ovid, then you'll know just what I mean –
But nevertheless I don't give a bean
If what I offer, coming in his wake,
Seems like baked haws, the plainest of plain fare;
I'll speak in prose; it's up to him to make
The poetry . . .'

Chaucer's admission, or even pride, that he had lifted ideas from
Ovid and other poets may sound surprising to modern authors who
like to insist that the plots and characters in their novels spring purely
from their own imaginations. Even Dickens was loath to admit
that some of his books owed much to earlier authors: for example,
Oliver Twist to Defoe's *Colonel Jack*. As Chesterton rightly says of
Chaucer:

There is no shadow of shame in being a traditionalist, or as some might say, a plagiarist . . . he is positively full of warm appreciation and admiration of his models . . . He was a great poet of gratitude; he was grateful to God; but he was also grateful to Gower. He was grateful to the everlasting *Romance of the Rose*, he was still more grateful to Ovid and grateful to Virgil and grateful to Petrarch and Boccaccio. He is always eager to show us over his little library and tell us where all his tales come from. He is prouder of having read the books than of having written the poems.

Perhaps later in life Chaucer came to read and admire Ovid's predecessor Virgil, who had kept on better terms with the reigning Caesar Augustus. Dante so revered Virgil that he chose him as his guide to Hell at the opening of the *Divina Commedia*. Indeed, some scholars suggest that Chaucer first studied Virgil after his visits to Italy in the 1370s. It was from Virgil rather than Ovid that Chaucer absorbed the legends surrounding the fall of Troy, especially the Wooden Horse and the escape of Aeneas. In his poem *The House of Fame*, Chaucer invokes the line from the *Aeneid*, 'Arma virumque cano' (Of arms and the man I sing), which for many of us is all the Latin we can remember except for 'Timeo Danaos et dona ferentes' (I fear the Greeks, even bearing gifts). The poet in the *House of Fame* dreams that he finds himself in the Temple of Venus, mother of Aeneas, whose painting he sees on the wall:

> . . . Naked fletynge in a see,
> And also on her bed, pardee,
> Hir rose garlond whit and red . . .
> But as I romed up and down,
> I found that on a wall ther was
> Thus written on a table of bras:
> 'I wol now synge, if I can,
> The armes and also the man
> That first cam, through his destinee,
> Fugitif of Troy contree . . .'

Chaucer retells from Virgil the story of how the Greek traitor Sinon, with his perjury and lying

. . . Made the hors brought into Troye
Through which Troyens loste al their joye.
And after this was grave, alas,
How Ilion assailed was
And wonne, and King Priam yslayn . . .
And next that sawgh I how Venus,
Whan that she sawgh the castel brende,
Down from the heven gan descende,
And bad her son Eneas flee . . .

It was Virgil who transferred the legend of Troy from the Greek to the Latin world by making Aeneas the father of the Roman race and therefore the ancestor of Caesar Augustus.

By Chaucer's time, a legend had taken hold that Aeneas or his descendants went on to establish Trojan kingdoms in northern Europe: hence the city Troyes in France and the proposal to rename London Troynovant or New Troy. The latter idea was based on the theories of Geoffrey of Monmouth, the twelfth-century antiquarian who claimed that our island, originally known as Albion, was invaded by Felix Brutus, descendant of Aeneas, in 116 BC. Although Chaucer does not appear to have had much faith in the legend, unlike his friend and fellow poet John Gower, he inclined to the Trojan side against the Greeks. It was not until the teaching of Greek entered school curricula that Homer's view of the Trojan War began to prevail in England.

For medieval Englishmen the long Trojan War, with its quarrel between two kindred peoples, its sieges and personal combat, must have seemed like a prophecy of what came to be called the Hundred Years' War, in which Chaucer himself was an insignificant soldier.

While we still cannot be sure of the date of Chaucer's birth, we know that he first joined the army in 1359. Our information on both points comes from another ambiguous document in Martin M. Crow, *Chaucer Life Records.*

On 15 October 1386 Chaucer was called before the High Court of Chivalry, sitting in the refectory of Westminster Abbey, in the dispute between Sir Richard Scrope and Sir Robert Grosvenor, as to the right to bear certain heraldic arms, namely *azure a bend or.* Chaucer testified that he saw the said coat of arms borne by Sir Richard and by Sir Henry Scrope, Richard's cousin, when he was himself in arms before the town of Retters (Rethel, near Reims). In reply to questions, Chaucer said it was common knowledge that these were the Scrope arms. As to the counter-claim by Sir Robert Grosvenor, Chaucer told the court that when he was recently walking down Friday Street, he had noticed an inn sign with the Scrope coat of arms outside an herbergerie, or outdoor tavern, and had been surprised to be told that these were the arms of Sir Robert Grosvenor, a knight of the county of Cheshire. 'It is amusing to reflect,' wrote Chesterton in the 1930s, 'that some day the apocalyptic newspaper files with their huge headlines about the first man who flew around the world, or the American professor who thinks we can send wireless waves to Mars, will all seem to our descendants dreary triviality; and that nobody will ever look at the long-lost records, except to find a paragraph in a corner in which Mr T. S. Eliot gave evidence about a motor-car collision.'

The court records for 1386 go on to describe the poet in legal French and Roman numerals as 'Geffray Chaucier XL ans et plus armeez par XXvii'. The vagueness of 'forty years or more' makes it hard to be sure what age Chaucer was when he was first 'armed'. Those who prefer to believe he was born in 1342 or 1343 point to the youthfulness of medieval squires, while those who opt for the round number of 1340 point to the evidence of many squires in their twenties. There is even a question mark over the meaning of 'armeez'. Professor Pearsall defines the term as 'commissioned to bear arms in the King's service', whereas Chesterton sees it as evidence of admission into 'the system of chivalry', interpreting 'arms' in the heraldic sense. Professor Pearsall also sees the report as proof of Chaucer's renown in upper-class London and 'evident pride in his status with his society (his friends Sir Peter Buckton, Sir John Clanvowe and Sir Lewis Clifford gave testimony four days later)'.

Meanwhile Chaucer's evidence at the Scrope case goes to confirm that he served in King Edward's invading army in France in 1359, joined in the siege of Reims and was captured at Rethel, after which, so another document tells us, he was ransomed for the sum of £16.

When Chaucer was 'armeez' in 1359, the campaign in France had changed from an exercise in chivalry to something more like a war of attrition. The Black Death of 1348–50 had not brought about a peace or even a truce between the combatants.

The first test of chivalry in the war on land came in 1351 when thirty knights of France and England met in personal combat in Brittany. It began with a challenge issued by Robert de Beaumanoir, a Breton nobleman on the French side, to one of his peers who had taken the English side. Thirty knights from each nation met on a field of battle where they belaboured each other with swords, bear-spears and axes till four on the French side and two on the English were killed, and a respite was called. Exhausted and bleeding, Beaumanoir asked for a drink, to receive the memorable answer: 'Drink thy blood, Beaumanoir, and thy thirst will go.' The fight was resumed and continued until all sixty participants were badly wounded. The 'Combat of the Thirty' may be the origin of the pitched battle which comes at the end of the *Knight's Tale*. Whatever Chaucer's intention, most modern readers tend to agree with the critic Terry Jones in finding it hard to take the passage seriously.

The oath taken by French Knights of the Star (their equivalent of the Garter) not to retreat more than four sarpents, or 600 yards, in battle proved equally costly of life at another engagement in Brittany in 1352 when a party of Frenchmen was ambushed, surrounded and massacred. Meanwhile, Edward the Black Prince launched an expedition from Bordeaux into the Languedoc with a thousand knights, squires and other men-at-arms, two thousand longbowmen and large numbers of Welsh irregulars, who specialized in robbing and cutting the throats of the knights who had been unhorsed and lay unable to move from the weight of their armour.

The Black Prince and his Welshmen were no doubt the models for Shakespeare's Henry V and the comic Fluellen before the Battle of Agincourt. Their army set off from Bordeaux to Narbonne and back, burning and plundering all through the beautiful valley of the Armagnac. It was an exercise in political terror, aimed at preventing people from ever again wavering in their allegiance to England. Not surprisingly, the people of the Languedoc came to detest the very name of the Black Prince.

'Harrying and wasting the country,' Prince Edward wrote home to the Bishop of Winchester, 'we burned Plaisance and other fine towns and all the lands around.' After looting all valuables, they burned or demolished barns, haystacks, mills, vineyards, fruit trees and bridges. The prince's raiding party plundered Carcassonne for three days without attacking the citadel, which still survives as one of the jewels of France's tourist industry, 'and the whole of that day remained for burning of the said city'. The Black Prince is remembered in Aquitaine as General Sherman is in Georgia.

As the Black Prince no doubt intended, the devastation of Gascony provoked King Jean to march south-west to confront the English army at Poitiers. Before the armies met on the outskirts of Poitiers, they were joined by the Cardinal of Périgord, representing the Pope, who hoped to avert a war between two great princes of Christendom. The cardinal rode up hurriedly to the King of France and made the following overture, as reported by Froissart. 'My very dear lord, you have with you here the whole cream of your kingdom's nobility, pitted against what in comparison is a mere handful of the English. If you could overcome them without a fight by accepting their surrender, it would redound more to your honour and advantage than if you risked this large and splendid army in battle. I therefore beg you humbly in the name of God to let me ride over to the Prince and persuade him of the great peril he is in.' The king assented, and the Cardinal rode across to the Prince of Wales with this proposition. 'I am sure, my son, that if you had seen the King of France's army and formed a correct idea of its size, you would allow me to try to arrange terms between you, if it is at all possible.' The prince agreed to listen to any reasonable proposal which did not affect the honour of himself and his men. According to Froissart it was the French who refused a peace and brought on themselves the disaster of Poitiers.

Among the knights on either side who took advantage of the truce to inspect their opponents' position was Sir John Chandos. Just as Sir John had ridden around observing the French, so one of the French marshals, Sir Jean de Clermont, had gone out reconnoitring the English. In doing this, it so happened that their paths crossed and that some strong words and very ugly insults were exchanged. I will tell you why. These knights who were young and in love – for that must certainly have been the explanation – were both wearing on their left arms the same emblem of a lady in blue embroidered in a sunbeam. They always wore this on their outer garment, whether they were in armour or not. Sir Jean de Clermont was by no means pleased to see his emblem on Sir John Chandos and he pulled up dead in front of him and said: 'I have been wanting to meet you, Chandos. Since when have you taken to wearing my emblem?' 'And you, mine?' said Sir John. 'It is just as much mine as yours.' 'I deny that,' said Sir Jean de Clermont, 'and if there were not a truce between us, I would show you here and now that you have no right to wear it.' 'Ha,' replied Sir John, 'tomorrow morning you will find me more than ready to prove by a show of arms that it belongs to me as much as to you.'

Froissart's account of the Battle of Poitiers prepares the mind for the view advanced by Terry Jones in *Chaucer's Knight*. Froissart tells how the French made a cavalry charge down a narrow lane with no proper protection for their horses' flanks: 'All on horseback they entered the road which had the thick hedge on either side. No sooner were they engaged in it than the archers began to shoot murderously from both flanks, knocking down horses and piercing everything before them with their long barbed arrows. The injured and terrified horses refused to go on. They swerved or turned back, or else fell beneath their riders, who could neither use their weapons nor get up again.'

The massacre of the horses in a sunken road prevented the marshals of France from reaching the Prince of Wales, but the English battered their way to the French King Jean, whose capture, as in a chess game, ended the Battle of Poitiers. Nor does Froissart conceal the greedy motives of those engaged in the final stage of the combat:

As soon as the two marshals, the Earls of Warwick and Suffolk, had come back, the Prince [of Wales] asked them if they had any news of the King of France. They said no, nothing definite. They thought he must have been either killed or captured, since he had certainly not left the battlefield. The Prince had turned anxiously to the Earl of Warwick and Sir Reginald Cobham and said: 'Please go out again and ride about until you have found out the true position.' The two commanders mounted their horses and rode them up a hillock from which they had a view all round. They saw a great mob of men-at-arms on foot moving very slowly towards them. In the midst of it was the King of France, in grave danger, for the English and Gascons had got hold of him, having snatched him away from Sir Denis de Morbecque (who had first accepted the King's surrender). The strongest were shouting: 'I took him, he's mine!' The King, who understood their eagerness to get possession of him, attempted to end this dangerous situation by saying: 'Sirs, sirs, take me in a gentlemanly way, and my son with me, to my cousin the Prince, and stop this brawling over my capture. I am a King, and great enough to make each one of you rich.' These words satisfied them for a moment, but soon the brawling broke out again, and they came to blows at every step they took. With the King and his youngest son Philip, seventeen counts were taken prisoner.

According to Froissart, the captured knights and squires found the English and the Gascons very accommodating and many of them bought their liberty there and then, or were freed simply on their promise to surrender themselves at Bordeaux by Christmas or to deliver the payment there – perhaps a clue to the way that the squire Geoffrey Chaucer was treated when he in turn was captured three years later. Froissart tells us that all those English who took part at Poitiers under the prince 'became rich in honour and possessions not only because of the ransoms but also thanks to the gold and silver which they captured. They found gold and silver bolts and precious jewels in chests crammed full of them. The French had come to the battle splendidly provided like men who felt certain in advance of victory.'

That evening the Prince of Wales gave a supper for the King of France and most of the captured counts and barons. He himself served in all humility both at the king's table and at the others. He insisted that he was not yet worthy to sit with so brave and noble a man as the king had shown himself to be that day.

The courtesies shown at the Battle of Poitiers may have delighted Froissart and generations of English readers but they enraged the stern republican Michelet, writing late in the nineteenth century, when England and France were again rivals for power:

In this war of chivalry waged by the courteous arms of the noblemen of France and England, there was in the end only one enemy, one victim of all the miseries of war: this was the peasant. Before the war he had been squeezed to provide the finery of the noblemen, to pay for their beautiful weapons, their enamelled escutcheons, the rich banners carried at Crécy and Poitiers. And afterwards who paid the ransoms? Once more the peasant.

The prisoners who had been released on parole returned to their lands to gather the sums they had agreed to pay on the battlefield, often without any bargaining. The property of the peasant did not require a complicated inventory: some bony livestock and harness, a wagon, a cart, a few metal implements and personal effects. What more could you take from the poor devil except his own skin? Obviously he had something hidden and so he was worked upon to say where it was, using both fire and the sword.

The demand for ransom money which followed the Battle of Poitiers provoked angry resistance both from the Paris bourgeoisie and the labouring class in the countryside. The former united behind a merchant, Etienne Marcel, who has come to be seen by the French left wing as a harbinger of the 1789 revolution. The peasants in desperation resorted to burning and looting the nearest château and manor. They accepted with grim amusement the nickname bestowed on them of Jacques Bonhomme (James Goodfellow), giving rise to the term Jacquerie for the rising in general. Unlike the Peasants' Revolt in England in 1381, the Jacquerie was deliberately cruel, as even Michelet acknowledges: 'They not only cut the throats of the great seigneurs but took pains to destroy the family, killing the heirs and raping the women.' It was a foretaste of the eighteenth-century horror which Dickens describes in *A Tale of Two Cities*. To add to the horror of the Jacquerie, France at this time began to be infested by the Compagnies or Sands of Freebooting mercenaries who detached themselves from the royal armies to make a living by plunder. As we shall see, Terry Jones believes that Chaucer's Knight was one of these mercenaries.

As another result of Poitiers, the theatre of battle moved from Normandy and the Languedoc to central and north-eastern France where Chaucer himself would join in the fray, for the young Chaucer took part in Edward III's invasion in 1359.

Edward III began the invasion because of his failure to capitalize on the victory at Poitiers. When the French baulked at the terms of a settlement reached in 1358, Edward responded by pushing for even harder terms. In March 1359, when the truce was about to expire, and King Jean of France was desperate for release from captivity, he ceded to Edward most of his kingdom from Calais to the Pyrenees and promised an extra ransom payment of four million gold ecus, payable in instalments and guaranteed by the handing over of forty royal or noble hostages.

Not surprisingly, these terms were unacceptable to Jean's eldest son, the Dauphin Charles, his counsellors and the three estates of the realm, who were France's feeble equivalent of the English

Parliament. Those delegates who braved the Compagnies and the Jacquerie to attend a meeting in Paris in May 1359 called the treaty intolerable and resolved to renew war with England. A few brave spirits tried to raise the money and ships to carry the war to England and maybe release King Jean from captivity. The meagre result of their efforts was seen in the following year, 1360, when French raiders burnt the Sussex ports of Winchelsea and Rye. But in 1359 the choice of a battlefield lay with the English, the stronger side, who therefore set off from the Channel ports towards Reims and Paris. On his first military expedition to France, in October that year, Chaucer served as a squire of a junior knight, like the Squire in the *General Prologue* of the *Canterbury Tales* on a *chyvauchie* or cavalry expedition 'In Flanders, in Artoys and Pycardie':

> A lover and a lusty bacheler
> With lokkes curled as if they lay in press.
> Of twenty years of age he was, I gesse.

Chaucer probably followed the route of the Canterbury pilgrims on this first journey to the Continent, for we know from the records of one of the Clarence party that they returned to London next year via Calais, Deal, Boughton, Ospringe, Sittingbourne, Dartford and Rochester – in fact the itinerary of the Squire and the rest of the pilgrims in Chaucer's poem.

We cannot tell from accounts of the battle in Chaucer's poetry how much fighting he saw in the siege of Reims, or how he regarded war and chivalry. As with Chaucer's views on religion, women, Jews or alcohol, readers and critics have tended to seize on references which confirm their personal prejudices. Those like Chesterton who approved of chivalry and especially crusading (one of his own best poems celebrates victory over the Turks at Lepanto) emphasize passages which convey the heat and clamour of battle:

> Ther stomblen stedes stronge and down goth all
> He rolleth under foot as doth a ball
> He founeth [thrusts] on his feet with a truncheon
> And he him hurleth with his horse adown.

Those who laugh at the thought of grown men whacking each other with axes and truncheons have seized on one passage in the *Knight's Tale* which seems to suggest that the combatants were wading about in a lake of gore:

> Up to the ankle fought they in their blood
> And in this wise I let them fighting dwell
> And first I will of Theseus you tell . . .

Yet as Professor Pearsall reminds us, Palamon and Arcite are not up to their ankles in a field that is all ankle-deep in blood, but their chasses or metal shoes were filled with blood up to the ankle.

The most exciting action scene in Chaucer is the already quoted naval Battle of Actium, which introduces cannon at least a thousand years too early. If my own guess is right, that Chaucer was an unmilitary and even timid man, I think we should study the gruesome account of Cupid's darts in the *Romaunt of the Rose*. In Chaucer's version, the God of Love is not the conventional chubby boy, like Eros in Piccadilly, but the longbowman who struck terror in every medieval soldier:

> The God of Love, with bowe bent,
> That all day set hadde his talent
> To pursuen and to spien me,
> Was standing by a fige-tree . . .
> He took an arrow full sharply whet,
> And in his bow when it was set,
> He straight up to his ear drough
> The strongbow that was so tough
> And shet at me so wondir smert
> That through myn eye unto myn hert
> The takel [arrowhead] smote, and deep it went . . .
> But certes, the arrow that in me stood
> Of me ne drew no drop of blood . . .
> Then took I with my handis tweie
> The arrow, and full fast out it plied
> And in the pulling sore I sighed.
> So at the last the shaft of tree
> I drough out with the feathers three.

But yet the hooked head, ywis,
The which that Beaute called is,
Gan so deep in min herte pass
That I it mighte not arace [uproot] . . .
But ever the head was left behind
For ought I coulde pull or wynde . . .

Am I over-squeamish in finding that Chaucer dwells on the horror of getting an arrow in the eye, let alone pulling it out again by the shaft? Unlike Guillaume de Lorris who wrote the French original, Chaucer had probably seen the victims of arrow wounds. Like any soldier in any war, he must often have wondered how he himself would behave if the worst happened. Certainly, in 1359, Chaucer took part in one of the major campaigns of the Hundred Years' War. He saw at first hand the horror inflicted by ravaging armies, whether of noblemen or peasant Jacques; he got an idea at Reims of the state of mind of both the defenders and the besiegers of a city, which he would use in *Troilus and Criseyde*.

The French were determined to hold on to Reims, which was founded by Charlemagne and later became a favourite place for coronations, like Winchester in England. Indeed, Edward III may have wanted to have himself crowned King of France at Reims, had he managed to capture the city.

The defenders of Reims in 1359 not only strengthened the city walls but pressed into military service its two most famous poets, whom Chaucer came to admire: Guillaume de Machaut and Eustache Deschamps.

In the preface to a collection of Machaut's works, published in 1910, the editor says that the poet was born about 1382 and had spent his early life as a soldier in Germany, Poland and Lithuania, probably with the Teutonic Knights. Machaut had served as a clerk and poet in residence to the kings of Bohemia, whose family also ruled the neighbouring duchy of Burgundy. More recently, Machaut had attached himself to Pierre I of Lusignan, the King of Cyprus, who was trailing around western Europe hoping to win support for a new crusade in the Middle East, which eventually conquered Alexandria. Machaut duly hailed his triumph in his poem *La Prise d'Alexandrie* which incidentally celebrates his patron's father, that blind King of Bohemia who rode to his death at Crécy.

Since 1337, Machaut had held a canonry at Reims, and it may have been at the cathedral that he developed his talents as a composer of music, for which he is now better known in France than as a poet. After the débâcle at Poitiers in 1356, which Machaut blamed on England's superiority in numbers (although the reverse was true), he lived in Reims in what his 1910 editor describes as a state of semi-retirement: 'It is probable that our poet was beginning to feel the weight of age. He suffered from a gouty affliction of which he complained on several occasions, and which his vagabond life had no doubt helped to aggravate.'

Machaut, however, claims to have joined the defence of Reims. 'One organized the military preparations. I myself had to mount guard on the ramparts.' In spite of this, and his gout, he survived until 1377.

When Machaut died, his friend and protégé Eustache Deschamps published a 'Ballade de la mort de Machault', in which he hailed the old man as a 'poète', the first known application of this term to an author in the vernacular rather than Latin. In a note to this Ballade in Poésies morales et historiques de Eustache Deschamps the anonymous editor explains: 'Guillaume de Machaut, poet and musician, born about 1282, was the compatriot, patron and friend of E. D. The adventurous and almost romanesque life of Machaut, who at an advanced age inspired a vibrant passion in Agnes de Navarre, wife of Phoebus, Count of Foix, has preserved his name from oblivion better than the eighty thousand verses he has left to posterity, the same amount as his faithful disciple Eustache Deschamps.' This anonymous editor elsewhere complains of having to read such a mass of verse in order to write an essay of introduction to Deschamps. This nineteenth-century critic clearly regarded the study of medieval literature as a disagreeable chore. He does not mention that Phoebus, Count of Foix, whose wife was supposed to be in love with Machaut, was also the patron and friend of another elderly poet, Sir John Froissart.

Eustache Deschamps almost certainly fought at Reims, either standing on the ramparts, or riding on forays against the English besiegers, perhaps even at Rethel, where Chaucer was taken prisoner. Deschamps was about Chaucer's age (born c. 1340) and had already started on a career as a lawyer, clergyman, courtier and soldier, in which last profession he rose to be equerry (écuyer) and military bailiff (huissier d'armes) to King Charles and Charles VI. From the anonymous editor of his Poésies we learn that Deschamps served in the wars against the Flemish and English, but did not do well from it, unlike other officers: '*Il n'y s'enrichait pas comme d'autres capitaines.*' Moreover, as Deschamps never ceased to remind his king and the readers of his poetry, he had lost his family estate near Vertus to the marauding English. His most memorable poem is his 'Ballade of the Domain of Eustache', 'brulé par les Anglais':

> *Dehors Vertus ay maison gracieus*
> *Ou j'avoye pour long temps demouré*
> *Ou pluseurs ont mene vie joyeus*
> *Maison des champs l'ont plusieurs appelle*
> *Mais, Dieu merci, toute pleine de ble*
> *Or les ongles le feu boute dedans*
> *Deux milles frans m'a leur guerre cousté*
> *J'aray des or a nome Brule des Champs.*

> Outside Vertus stands a gracious house
> Where I had lived for a long time
> And where many others led happy lives
> House-of-the-fields it was often called
> But full of corn, thanks be to God.
> Now the English have put it to the torch
> Two thousand francs their war has cost me.
> From now on I'm known as Burnt-out of the Fields.

The loss of his farm and two thousand francs appear to have made Deschamps an embittered and grumpy old man, contemptuous of the young generation (see his 'Ballade on the Decadence of Chivalry') and cynical about women. Although as a judge at Reims he had the power to hand out savage sentences, he called in verse for ever more capital punishment: one of his refrains goes '*Prenez, pendez et ce sera bien fait*'. ('Arrest, hang and all will be well.') He enjoyed complaining in verse about the discomforts of travel such as fleas, sea-sickness and disgusting foreign food. Above all he ranted against the English invaders, calling them monkeys with long tails.

In several poems, Deschamps broods on the origins of the English race who had devastated his country and burnt down his farm. In his '*Ballade des divers noms d'Angleterre*', he explains that England, the western isle, was first called Albion, from *albus*, the Latin for white, because of the line of chalk cliffs standing high over the Channel. The name Britain came from the Duke Brutus of Troy, after the fall of that city, who slew the giants who lived in the island and called it after himself. Long afterwards it was renamed England by the Saxons, for Angela was the name of the daughter of the powerful Saxon duke who conquered the island and put the Britons to the sword.

Which, if any, of Deschamps's theories is true is still a matter of argument among philologists and historians; however, the ballad shows that even the combatants in the war between England and France were brooding about the difference between the two nations.

7

Romance of the Rose

ONE OF THE FEW public accolades to Chaucer during his lifetime was the *'Ballade a Chaucier'* by Eustache Deschamps, who praised him not for his own original poetry but for his English translation of *Le Roman de la Rose*, a poem by two French authors of the thirteenth century:

> *O Socrates, plains de philosophie*
> *Seneque en meurs et Anglux en pratique*
> *Ovides grans en la poeterie*
> *Bries en parler, sages en rethorique*
> *Aigles treshaulz, qui par la theorique*
> *Enlumine le regne d'Eneas*
> *L'Isle aux Geans, ceuls de Bruth, et qui as*
> *Semé les fleurs et planté le rosier*
> *Aux ignorans de la langue pandras*
> *Grant translateur, noble Geffroy Chaucier.*

O Socrates, full of wisdom, Seneca in morals and Aulus in practice, great Ovid in your poetry, brief in speech, wise in versifying, most lofty eagle who, by your philosophy, illuminates the kingdom of Aeneas, the island of Giants – those whom Brutus destroyed – and who has sown the flowers of poetry and planted the rose tree, you will spread light to those ignorant of French, great translator, noble Geoffrey Chaucer.

One may detect in this ballad early hints of a misunderstanding between the French and English that has little to do with the Hundred Years' War. The description of Chaucer as *'bries en parler'* could simply mean he was taciturn and reserved, like the Clerk in the

Canterbury Tales who prefers his book to the bonhomie of the other pilgrims. Or was Chaucer the prototype for the Gallic caricature of an Englishman, a tight-lipped Major Thompson, without the umbrella and bowler hat?

The ballad to Chaucer says he is well employed in bringing to Albion the glories of the 'Romance of the Rose', which all Frenchmen then believed to be the summit of poetic achievement. Another contemporary, Laurent de Premierfait, even suggested that Dante's *Divina Commedia* was inspired by reading the *Roman* during a visit to Paris. A nineteenth-century French savant* suggested that all Chaucer's work was derived from French poets and troubadours. Certainly *Le Roman de la Rose* was the biggest single influence on Chaucer's style, imagery and plots, affecting his early court poems, the tragic *Troilus and Criseyde* and the satire of the *Canterbury Tales*.

As Deschamps knew when he wrote his ballad, it was not the literary worth of the *Roman* that made it so popular with the English public and prompted Chaucer to join in its translation. It was rather the public quarrel and scandal in Paris which gave the poem the status in English eyes of the first French dirty book. Such was its fame among readers of French that thirty original manuscripts of the *Roman* are still preserved in the British Library. But fluent French readers in England were growing rare during the lifetime of Chaucer: English was taking over at court, in Parliament, in legal proceedings and in the pulpits of churches, as we can tell from the sermons in the *Canterbury Tales*. Even the Bible in English was made available in Wyclif's version. French was becoming an accomplishment instead of a habit or a necessity, as is shown by the will of a Kent man, James de Peckham, who died in the same year as Chaucer. In a codicil of 1400, he made a bequest of his sheep and oxen and asked his executors to distribute 'all my books in French to those who know how to use them'.

The dispute over the *Roman de la Rose*, which had been rumbling away since the poem first appeared in the thirteenth century, broke out again in Chaucer's lifetime when the Chancellor of Paris University said he would like to burn every copy he could find. Then a feminist poet, Christine de Pisan, called the poem 'a handbook for

---

* *Etude sur G. Chaucer considéré comme imitateur des trouvères*, Etienne Gustave Sandras, 1859.

lechers . . . a cunning trap to deceive a foolish demoiselle'. Christine was in turn compared by one of the *Roman's* supporters to 'that Greek prostitute who dared to write against Theophrastus'. Much of the fury revolved around the use of such rude words as *coilles* for testicles and *con* (or the Latin *cunnus*) for the female genitalia.

Of course the prurient English public wanted to read the *Roman*, if only to say that they could not understand what all the fuss was about. The idea that sex was more exciting in France has persisted down to recent times, as I recall from the poster advertisement for a Hollywood film – 'Whatever it is French women have, Madame Bovary had more of it' – or the story I heard in Lancashire about a coal miner who one year went for his holiday to Paris rather than Blackpool. To the questions of his inquisitive friends, he merely answered: 'I'll tell you one thing about Paris: fooking's only in its infancy in Wigan.'

It was in this spirit during the 1370s that the English wanted to read the *Romaunt of the Rose*, translated by Geoffrey Chaucer and others unknown, although in fact it included none of the dirty bits which had offended Christine de Pisan and the Chancellor of Paris. Textual scholars believe that Chaucer himself wrote only about a third (or fragment A) of the *Romaunt*, which in turn translated only a third of the 20,000 lines of the French original. But the whole of the *Romaunt* is always included in Chaucer's collected works, and during his lifetime Chaucer accepted the blame as well as the credit for the translation. Indeed, he went out of his way to remind his readers of his connection with what one modern publisher called 'the rollicking Romance of the Rose'.

For example, in one of his courtly poems, the *Legend of Good Women*, which may have been written at the behest of Richard II's Queen Isabella, Chaucer describes how the Poet approaches the God of Love, one of the allegorical characters of the *Roman de la Rose*, and is given a frosty reception:

> What dost thou here
> In my presence and so boldly,
> For it were better worthy, truly
> A worm to comen in my sight than thou . . .
> Thou art my mortal foe and me werreyest [warrest on me]
> And of my olde servauntes thou missayest [speakest ill]
> And hindderest them with thy translation
> And lettest [preventest] folk to have devotion

To serve me and holdest it folly
To serve love. Thou maist it not denye
For in pleyn text, without need of glose
Thou hast translated the Romaunce of the Rose.

These words of the God of Love are a cue to provide my own 'glose', or gloss, to the *Roman de la Rose* and to the word 'glose' itself, which keeps cropping up in this chapter, not least because of its useful rhyme with 'rose'.

A gloss (in Latin *glossatio*) – meaning 'a search for the moral or philosophical as opposed to the literal sense of texts' – was the chief concern of medieval scholars and pedagogues, as can be seen from the countless glosses of the Bible, Boethius, the classical poets and the early Christian fathers. The medieval writing of glosses almost exactly corresponds to the modern study of texts by academic scholars of various rival schools, such as Marxists, Freudians, Jungians, feminists, deconstructionists, annalists and post-modernists, all of them now equipped with computer technology. As in the Middle Ages, some modern theorists of the 'glose' began their careers in Paris but have followers in the English-, German- and Spanish-speaking worlds. Just as the '*Querelle*' over *Le Roman de la Rose* erupted in Paris during the Middle Ages, it was again in Paris after the university rising of 1968 that the poem was once more glossed, or 'deconstructed', in order to find its sociological 'subtext' or 'hidden agenda'.

In my own examination of *Le Roman de la Rose*, I shall try to confine myself to explaining who were the two poets who wrote it, why it caused such offence, and how it affected the thought and writing of Chaucer.

The fact that *Le Roman de la Rose* was started by one poet, Guillaume de Lorris, around 1337 and finished by another, Jean de Meun, almost fifty years later, has fascinated generations of literary critics and even divided them into Guillaume or Jean supporters. Although medieval readers, including Chaucer, do not appear to have cared about the divided authorship, Guillaume and Jean were different enough to have left their separate influences on Chaucer's thinking and poetry: the first romantic and courtly, the second crude and sardonic.

Guillaume de Lorris tells us that he was 'twenty year of age' when he started to write the *Roman* as a present for his lady love. He came from near Orléans (as did his successor Jean de Meun) and he may have served at the court of Louis IX, St Louis, who tended to choose his household from that part of his kingdom. Guillaume was steeped in the poetry and chivalric lore of the twelfth-century troubadours who attended the 'courts of love' presided over by Eleanor of Aquitaine at Poitiers. He was well versed in the legends of Arthur and his Knights, and had studied the Latin author Ovid on the art of love (*Ars Amatoria*) and Macrobius on the theory of dreams. Indeed, the story of the *Roman* appears to Amant the lover as a dream, which Chaucer translates as 'sweveninge'.

> *Aucungs gens dient qu'en songes*
> *n'a se fables non et menconges . . .*
> Many men sayn that in sweveninges
> Ther nys but fables and lesynges;
> But men may same swevenes sen
> Which hardely [certainly] that false ne ben,
> But afterward ben apparaunt.
> This may I draw to warraunt
> An author that hight Macrobes . . .

Chaucer again cites Macrobius in his *Nun's Priest's Tale*, when Chaunticleer dreams he is carried away in the jaws of a fox.

Guillaume's Lover dreams of setting forth on a May morning into the countryside, 'the briddes for to hear', as in many of Chaucer's invocations of spring, not least the immortal *General Prologue* to the *Canterbury Tales*. In his fragment A of the *Romaunt*, Chaucer struggles to put into English the birds, trees and flowers listed in Guillaume's *Roman*, not always with total success. '*Alpes*', apparently bullfinches, are left as *alpes*, while 'wodewales' or woodpeckers are numbered among the song birds. The solitary and reclusive nightingale is seen to fly in a 'great route' or flock, like a starling.

Since Chaucer repeated Guillaume's lists of flora and fauna in some of his own poems, such as the *Book of the Duchess*, we have to accept the judgement of Etienne Sandras, the French nineteenth-century critic, that the poet 'who sensed the beauties of nature and knew how to describe them, was often content to be the copyist of G. de

Lorris'. Indeed, in the *Book of the Duchess*, Chaucer uses the *Roman* itself as part of the decoration of his poet's bedchamber:

> And all the walles with colours fine
> Were painted, bothe texte and glose,
> Of all the Romance of the Rose.

Guillaume's Lover approaches the Garden of Delight to which he is given admission by Idleness, a seductive woman. There he sees handsome couples dancing and flirting in the open air, without restraint or embarrassment:

> For who spake of them evil or well
> They were ashamed never a dell [not a bit]
> But men might see them kiss therein
> As it two yonge doves were . . .

Guillaume's Lover passes through a forest abounding in 'roes, does and squirrels full great plenty' and then through an orchard with trees

> Such as men nutmegs call
> That sweet of savour been withal
> Here youths and their lemans [mistresses]
> Stroll through leafy groves where
> Grass sprung up as thicke set
> And soft as any velvet
> On which men might their lemans lay
> As on a featherbed to play.

Such lines are a reminder that even in Guillaume's innocent first part of the *Roman de la Rose*, the Garden of Delight is a place of sexual licence, as it appears again in Chaucer's *Merchant's Tale* when the old husband January is cuckolded by his young wife May and her lover in the branches of a tree over his head. Chaucer reminds us there that Priapus was the god of gardens:

> . . . So fair a garden wot I nowhere noon.
> For out of doubt I verily suppose
> That he that wrote the Romance of the Rose

Ne could of it the beauty well devise,
Ne Priapus ne might not well suffice,
Though he be god of gardyns, for to tell
The beaute of the garden, and the well
That stood under a laurel evergreen . . .

If Guillaume looked on the garden as the playground of Priapus, the phallic god, or a classical Arcadia, it was also the biblical Eden from which Adam and Eve were expelled. To C. S. Lewis, the author of *Allegory of Love*, Guillaume's garden represented the court of chivalry. To many of us it recalls the gardens which Alice finds in her journeys through the looking-glass and in Wonderland. Like Guillaume's Lover she begins her adventure in a dream and encounters strange and even alarming characters. Guillaume's Lover passes ponds

In which there no frogges were
And fair in shadow was every well . . .

He stops under a tree which

. . . in France men call a pyn
But since the time of King Pepyn,
Ne grew there tree in manne's sight
So fair, or so well woxe [grown] in height.

A sign announces to passers-by that this was the well where Narcissus drowned as he peered at his own reflection, at which point Guillaume retells the story. The Lover in turn peers into the pool of water and sees a rose bush, crowned with red roses, each with its *botoun* (modern French *bouton*) or bud, which Chaucer translates as 'knoppe', like the German *Knopf*. The Lover chooses and plucks a stalk as firm as a rush, on which stood a knoppe so upright that it bent neither to one side nor the other.

Even in Guillaume's decorous part of the poem, the red rose and its bud quite obviously represent a woman's genitalia. Like the story of Lancelot which aroused Dante's Paolo and Francesca, the imagery of the rose was just as erotic to medieval readers, especially women, as the explicit crudity of a pornographic novel or film today.*

In Guillaume's poem, the Lover's plucking of the rosebud is followed by his expulsion from the Garden of Delight and the imprisonment of the gate-keeper, Idleness, by the malevolent warders and wardresses Hate, Disdain, Envy and Wicked-Tongue. Here Guillaume gives a foretaste of the sexual and religious satire which characterizes the part of the poem written by Jean de Meun. The figure of Hate is shown as a 'Mynoresse', or sister, of the Minorite Order of St Clare, the female branch of the Franciscan Order. She is remarkable for her wrath, ire and 'onde' or envy:

> An angry wight, a chideresse
> And full of guile and fell courage [evil heart]
> Frounced [wrinkled] foul was her visage
> And grinning for dispiteous rage
> Her nose snorted up for tene
> Her head full writhen [wrapped] was, ywis,
> Full grimly with a great towayle [towel]

This ferocious, turbaned lady may be a caricature but nevertheless rings true of a certain kind of Mother Superior. Guillaume's onslaught suggests that the Franciscans were growing unpopular soon after they first arrived in France and before they became notorious for the wealth and abuse of power which Jean attacked in the second half of the thirteenth century.

One of the enemies facing the Lover is Malebouche (literally Bad-mouth – in English 'Wicked-Tongue') who is always portrayed as followed by Norman 'soldiers', or mercenaries, because they fight for a 'solde' or wage. The Normans are 'janglers' or gossips, and they in turn go around with a band of musicians who play discordantly on their viols and 'hornpipes' of Cornwall. These references to the Normans and to Cornwall, a place in Brittany as well as in Britain, suggest that Guillaume was fully alive to regional differences and dislikes. This is evident when he says that Wicked-Tongue's anger sits, or suits, his ancestry:

---

* In *Citizen Kane*, Orson Welles's film about the newspaper magnate William Randolph Hearst, much play is made of the significance that Kane attached to the word 'Rosebud'. Apparently this was the term which Hearst and his mistress used for her private parts.

He was so full of cursed rage
It sat him well of his lineage.
For him an Irish woman bare.
His Tungue was filed sharp and square,
Poignant and right carving
And right bitter in speaking.

According to the rules of chivalry laid down by Guillaume in the *Roman de la Rose*,* the Lover should avoid all '*pensées de bassesse*' (low thoughts), he should take care of his dress, be modest and measured in his speech, develop his natural talents, be gay and playful in manner, and never speak ill of women, and above all love his lady with a faithful and undivided heart.

Besides laying down these general principles, the God of Love instructs the Lover in the practical code of conduct; for instance, on not being seen to enter or leave his lady's apartment, a necessary precaution against jealous husbands and gossiping neighbours. Chaucer's Troilus is careful to follow this rule for, although his Criseyde is a widow, she does not want her affair made public.

As can be seen from the extracts below, Chaucer borrows from the advice given to the Lover in the *Romaunt of the Rose* to describe the young Squire in the *General Prologue* to the *Canterbury Tales*. Here is some of Cupid's advice:

Maintain thyself after thy rent
Of robe and eke of garnement . . .
And look always that they be shape
What garment that thou shalt make : . .
Comb thine heed right jolily
Also to you it longeth ay
To harp and gitterne, daunce and play
For if he can well foot and dance
It may him greatly do advance

Here is the Squire in the Everyman edition of the *Tales*:

---

* See the introduction to the edition published by Felix Lecoy, Paris, 1976.

... A lover and a lusty bacheler
With lokkes curled as if they lay in presse
Of twenty year he was of age I gesse ...
Embroidered was he, as it were a mead.
Al ful of fresshe floures, white and red.
Syngynge he was, or fluting, al the day;
He was as fresh as is the month of May.
Short was his gowne, with sleeves long and wyde.
Wel could he sitte on hors, and faire ryde.
He coude songes make and wel endite,
Joust and eke daunce, and wel portray and write.
So much he loved, that by nightertale
He slept nomore than doth a nightingale.

Sleeplessness was a constant affliction of Guillaume's Lover, as of
many of Chaucer's lovers. It accounts for one of the liveliest passages
of the *Romaunt*, as well as the first use in English of the phrase 'castles
in Spain' (though not in the sense we know today):

For when thou wenest for to slepe,
So ful of peyne shalt thou crepe,
Start in thy bed about full wide,
And turn ful ofte on every side
Now downward groff [face down] and now upright,
And walowe in woe the longe night
Thine armys shalt thou sprede a-bred [apart]
As man in werre were forwerryed [beaten in war]
Than shal thee come a remembraunce
Of her shape and her semblaunce,
Whereto none other may be pere [equal]
And wite thou wel, withoute were [without doubt],
That thee shal seem some time that night
That thou hast her that is so bright
Naked between thine armes there,
All sothfastnesse [reality] as though it were.
There shalt make castles then in Spayne
And dreme of love, all but in vayne,
And thee delighten of right nought ...

The Oxford critic and theologian C. S. Lewis praised Guillaume's treatment of 'falling in love', not imagining that his own affair with a woman dying of cancer would one day become a touching film. Others might think Guillaume's Lover is more in the grip of fantasy and infatuation as he lies on his bed imagining castles in Spain.

Although Chaucer's fragment A of the *Romaunt of the Rose* is hard to distinguish from those of the other contributors, one finds hints of his individual touch in the translation from the French. Like Shakespeare in *Henry V*, two centuries later, Chaucer made gentle play with the difference between the French and English languages:

> Such sweet song was them among
> That me thought it no briddis song,
> But it was wonder like to be
> Song of mermaydens of the sea,
> That, for their singing is so clere,
> Though we mermaydens clepe hem here
> In English, as is our usaunce,
> Men clepe hem syrens in France.

Chaucer may or may not be responsible for two significant mistranslations which found their way into English through the *Romaunt of the Rose*. The first of these is the rendering of the adjective *papelard* 'smarmy' (apparently from *paper*, meaning to guzzle and *lard*, meaning bacon) as 'poope-holy' or 'pope-holy', a word for hypocrite which soon became popular with religious reformers. Similarly, one may question the already mentioned portrait of Wicked-Tongue:

> . . . He was so full of cursed rage,
> It sat him well of his lineage,
> For him an Irish woman bare . . .

The original French says merely that he was *'fiuz [fils] dune vielle irese'*. According to the glossary of the edition published by Felix Lecoy *irese* means *coléreuse, méchante, acharné*, in fact 'irate' rather than 'Irish'. Perhaps the translator thought it came to the same thing.

Guillaume de Lorris broke off writing the *Roman de la Rose* abruptly, at line 4429, perhaps because he was ill or dead, but it was forty years before Jean de Meun began his continuation. The passage of time is further announced by Jean's references to the triumphs of Charles of Anjou in Italy and the scandals involving the friars at Paris University in the 1250s.

Sociologist and Marxist critics have claimed to see a distinction between the aristocratic courtly Guillaume and the 'bourgeois' bumptious Jean, who represented the interests of an emergent capitalist class. Certainly Jean despised the idea of love as anything more than the physical act, so that what had begun as the quest for a rosebud ends in brutal rape. Whereas Guillaume was above all a poet, Jean was an intellectual and satirist, who turned the *Roman* into a vehicle for polemic.

Like Chaucer a century later, Jean de Meun was a devotee of Boethius, and he filled the *Roman* with ideas from the *Consolation of Philosophy*. It was probably from the *Roman* that Chaucer got his first knowledge of Boethius, as he did of Plato, Socrates, Cicero, Suetonius, Horace, Ovid and Abelard, the twelfth-century scholar and lover of Héloïse.

While Jean preserves the story and some of the allegorical figures of Guillaume's poem, he turns it into a vehicle for his own opinions, usually voiced by Lady Reason, a character modelled on Philosophy in Boethius, and perhaps on the Blessed Virgin Mary. The attitudes and opinions which Jean disliked are personified by grotesques such as La Vieille, a prostitute, Jaloux, a cuckold, and Faussemblant, a villainous friar.

Although La Vieille and Jaloux scarcely appear in the *Romaunt of the Rose*, Chaucer used the original French to create his most wonderful character, the Wife of Bath, of whom he says in the *Prologue* (Everyman Edition):

> Her kerchiefs weren all ful fyne of grounde;
> I durste swer they weigheden ten pound
> That on a Sunday were upon her head.
> Her hosen were of fyn scarlet red,
> Ful streyt y-tyed, and shoes ful moyst and newe . . .

Jill Mann, in her entertaining *Chaucer and Medieval Estates Satire*, traces these lines to passages in the *Roman* when Le Jaloux berates his wife:

Vos portez qui vaut c(ent) livres
d'or et d' argent sur vostre teste
Et tant estait vos re chauciez
Que la robe sovent hauciez
Pour montrer vos piez aus ribauz

You wear on your head what is equivalent to £100 worth of gold and silver and you wear such light shoes that you often raise your dress to show your feet to debauchees.

Jean de Meun's La Vieille is both a greedy old whore and a pioneering feminist. She is full of comic advice on how to empty a man's pockets before allowing him sexual favours, but also expounds some twenty-first-century theories of women's liberation. Women are born free, she says, but have had to abandon their freedom for monogamy. Marriage was instituted to put down concupiscence and crimes of passion and to help in the rearing of children. But Nature urges women to regain their freedom, whatever the strife this causes. 'Read Horace,' urges La Vieille. Even before Helen of Troy, there were many battles fought over the *con*. There will be many more, because Nature is stronger than upbringing. Horses, cows and sheep all mate indiscriminately. People ought to behave the same way. La Vieille proclaims a sexual free-for-all, looking ahead to Paris in 1789 or 1968:

Toutes pour tous et tous pour toutes
Chacune pour chacun commune

Hundreds of years after Jean de Meun was dead, the ideas he put in the mouth of an aged whore were re-invented and popularized by Rousseau, Marx, Freud, Wilhelm Reich and the neo-Darwinists, who tell us that we are animals, and free to behave like animals.

Although Jean de Meun made fun of extravagant feminist theories, he refused to join in crude abuse of women. The misogynist Jaloux is caricatured as a mean-minded brute and wife-beater like Jankin, the Wife of Bath's fourth husband, who deafens her with a blow to the ear.

Chaucer's discussion of sex in the *Canterbury Tales* is subtler and funnier than Jean de Meun's, but it was from the *Roman de la Rose* that Chaucer gained his knowledge and understanding of the feminist debate, which was just as developed in the thirteenth as in the twenty-first century. Jean de Meun's section of the *Roman de la Rose* is also the basis of Chaucer's portraits of the villainous Pardoner, Friar and Summoner, as well as the self-indulgent Monk and the Jew-baiting Prioress. Although Jean wrote in the heat of an argument in thirteenth-century France, specifically over a quarrel at Paris University, his satire was still more apposite when it appeared in an English translation almost a hundred years later. His attack on the friars, which takes up 3,500 lines of the *Romaunt of the Rose*, came out when John Wyclif at Oxford was making a general attack on Church abuses, especially among the mendicant orders. Chaucer's *Romaunt of the Rose* and his use of it in the *Canterbury Tales* helped to prepare the minds of Englishmen for the coming quarrel with Rome and the Reformation. Both are essential in trying to answer the hypothetical question of whether by nature Chaucer belonged to the Church of Rome or of Canterbury.

This ranting monologue in the *Romaunt* begins when Cupid, the God of Love, enlists Fals-Semblant into his expedition to regain the Garden of Delight and with it the rosebud:

> 'Fals-Semblant,' quoth Love, 'in this wise
> I take thee here to my servise
> My king of harlots [rascals] shalt thou be'

When Fals-Semblant is recruited into the service of the God of Love, and is asked to describe his profession to the assembled company:

> Withouten wordes more, right than
> Fals-Semblant his sermon began
> And said them thus in audience
> 'Barons, take heed of my sentence'

He then begins a catalogue of his crimes and deceptions. Chaucer used much the same opening to the prologue of the *Pardoner's Tale*:

> 'Lordyngs,' quoth he, 'in churches when I preach
> I peyne me to have a loude speech,
> And ring it out, as clear as doth a bell,
> For I know all by rote which that I tell.
> My theme is always ones, and ever was;

Radix malorum est cupiditas . . .
Thus can I preach against the same vice
Which that I use, and that is avarice.'

Although the Pardoner has the effrontery of Fals-Semblant, he works in a different racket – the selling of phoney relics – and differs from him in other important respects. The Pardoner will squeeze even the poorest to get his accustomed food and drink:

Though it were given by the priest's page,
Or by the poorest widow in a village,
While that her children starve for famine . . .

Fals-Semblant, on the other hand, considers it not worth his while to bother with poor and unimportant people:

I love better the acquaintance
Ten times, of the King of France
Than of a poor man of mild mood
Though that his soul be also good
For when I see beggars quaking
Naked on middens all stinking
For hunger cry and eke for care
I meddle not in their welfare
They are so poor and full of pyne
They might not once give me to dine
But a rich, sick usurer
Would I visit and draw near
Him would I comfort and rehete [console]
For I hope of him gold to get

And although the Pardoner says in his prologue that he intends to have 'a jolly wench in every town', it is clear from the *General Prologue* that Chaucer has written him off as a homosexual or nothing at all:

A voice he had as small as any goat.
No beard had he, nor never beard should have
As smooth it was as it were late i-shave
I trow he were a gelding or a mare . . .

Fals-Semblant in the *Romaunt of the Rose* is always accompanied by his 'loteby' or mistress, Forced Abstinence, who may be a nun or a beguine (a devout laywoman):

> And with me followeth my loteby
> To don me solas and company
> That hight Dame Abstinence-Streyned.

Towards the end of the English translation, the God of Love tells how Fals-Semblant and his paramour debate whether to put on disguise to visit the gossip Wicked-Tongue:

> Now will I tell the countenance
> Of Fals-Semblant and Abstynance
> That ben to Wikkid-Tunge went
> But first they held their parlement
> Whether it to done were
> To maken them be knowen there
> Or elles walken forth disgised
> But at the last they devised
> That they would go in Tapinage [with covered face]
> As it were in a pilgrimage
> Like good and holy folk unfeigned
> And Dame Abstinence-Streyned
> Took a robe of Kamelyne [wool mixed with silk]
> And gan to clothe as a beguine
> A large coverchief of thread
> She wrapped all about her head.
> But she forgot not her salter
> On which she told her beads.
> But she bought them never a del,
> For they were given her, I wot wel,
> God wot, of a full holy friar
> That said he was her father dear,
> To whom she had more often went
> Than any friar of his convent
> And he visited her also
> And many a sermon said her so,
> He nolde lette for man on lyve
> That he ne wolde her ofte shrive

[He would not let any man alive
Prevent his often shriving her of her sins]
And with so great devocioun
They made her confession
That they had often, for the nonce
Two heades in one hood at once

In his physical description of Abstinence-Streyned, the God of Love
praises her body, but otherwise compares her with the pale horse and
rider of the Apocalypse, the traditional bringers of pestilence:

Of fayre shape I devise her thee
But pale of face somtime was she
That false traitouresse untrue
Was like that sallowe horse of hue
That in the Apocalypse is shewed
That signifyeth folk beshrewed
That ben al ful of trecherie
And pale through hypocrisie
For on that horse no colour is
But only dead and pale, y wis

Fals-Semblant equips himself for his pilgrimage with a Bible around
his neck, a crutch called Treason on which to rest his limbs, and by
slipping into the sleeve of his coat

A razour sharp and well-biting
That was forged in a forge
Which that men clepen coupe-gorge

The cut-throat razor in a pilgrim's sleeve may have inspired Chaucer's
vision of civil war and anarchy in the *Knight's Tale*:

Ther saw I first the dark imagining
Of felony and all the compassyng;
The cruel wrath, as any furnace red;
The pickpurs, and eke the pale Dread;
The smyler with the knife under his cloke:
The stables burning with the blake smoke;
The treason of the murtheryng in the bed . . .

8

Chaucer in Florence

AFTER SEVERAL MILITARY AND diplomatic missions to France, Flanders and Spain,* Chaucer enjoyed the great good fortune of visiting Italy, centre of Europe's ancient civilization and now of its renaissance into the modern age. He was the first of a long line of English poets, including Milton, Byron, Shelley, Keats and the Brownings, who were able to blossom under the influence of the sun and the Mediterranean temperament. As a disciple of Virgil, Ovid and Boethius, Chaucer was well aware of how Christian civilization grew from the pagan past, as was evident from the Roman remains at Canterbury. The Roman inheritance was still more apparent on the Italian peninsula, the geographical heart of the empire, where ancient and modern life went on in the same buildings and institutions. The island republic of Venice had survived since imperial times with no intervening rule by barbarian conquerors. In Florence the Temple of Mars, the Roman war god and patron of the city, had become a church in honour of John the Baptist, the city's new patron saint. Some Florentines maintain that the Marzocco, or heraldic lion, which stood guard over the Ponte Vecchio until it was swept away by a flood in 1333, had also been carved as a statue of Mars. The statue had overlooked the scene of the clan murder in 1215 which started the feud of Guelfs and Ghibellines.

More than the ruined stones remained of Rome's imperial legacy. The principles of Roman law were upheld by most of the states in the Italian peninsula. The empire itself was revived by Charlemagne when he had himself crowned by the Pope in AD 800. Although most Holy

---

* As recently as 1955, a researcher in the royal archives of Navarre at Pamplona discovered a safe conduct issued to 'Geffrog de Chauserre, escuier englois' to cover the period from 22 February to Pentecost (24 May) 1366; see Pearsall *The Life of Geoffrey Chaucer*, p. 51.

Roman emperors since had been Germans or other north Europeans, they all aspired to dominate Italy. The fearsome Barbarossa had started the subjugation of Lombardy by catapulting the children of the besieged Cremonans against the city walls. Henry IV had failed to browbeat the Pope and ended up on his knees in the snow at Canossa. Later Hohenstaufens, notably Frederick II, 'Stupor Mundi' or the wonder of the world, ruled from Naples or Palermo, before they were overthrown by the French Angevins. As late as the fourteenth century there were Ghibelline or pro-imperial parties in most of the city states of Italy, the forerunners of those who wanted a federal, centralized Europe in the tradition of Charlemagne. There were also the fore-runners of other modern ideologies such as fascism, democracy and socialism, exemplified by the 'Clogs' and the 'Worms of the earth'. Florence even produced the first left-wing terror, in which citizens were encouraged to denounce their counter-revolutionary friends, neighbours and relatives.

The power of the papacy had been weakened at the start of the fourteenth century by its physical transference from Rome to Avignon. Although many Romans clamoured for the return of the institution which gave them wealth and importance, most of the cardinals felt safer and better off in their handsome new palace beside the Rhône under the aegis of the kings of France.

Many Italian city states were also against the papacy's return to Rome. The Doges of Venice recalled how one of their emissaries had been made to kneel all day at the foot of the Pope's throne for failing to demonstrate proper humility. The Visconti brothers, the rulers of Lombardy, were violently anti-papal, if not anti-clerical. The Ghibel-lines of Tuscany were opposed to the papacy, if only because the Guelfs were its friends. There was also within the Italian Church the beginning of a European-wide heretical movement, here called Patar-ene, which followed the Manichaean tendency of the Bogomils, the Albigensians and the Cathars. These early 'protestants' were later to find a hero and martyr in the friar Savonarola of Florence.

The involvement of the French kings on the side of the Avignon papacy meant that Italy was caught up in the Hundred Years' War, attracting both French and English mercenaries, or *condottieri*, as they were locally called. Of these the most hated and feared were the Breton knights in the service of France, and Sir John Hawkwood's White Company in the pay of Edward III, the origin of the saying that an

Italianized Englishman is the devil incarnate (*Inglese italianato, diavolo incarnato*).

Besides being the cockpit of Europe's political, religious and dynastic quarrels, Italy was the economic hub of the Continent, as it had been under the ancient Roman empire. Venice and Genoa dominated the trade of the eastern and western Mediterranean respectively. Lombardy and Tuscany were the most advanced centres of banking and also of manufacture, comparable with Lancashire in the Industrial Revolution, the Ruhr a century later, or 'Silicon Valley' in California today.

Above all, Florence was the world's most exciting cultural centre, as later, and in different ways, were Paris, London, Berlin, New York, Los Angeles, Prague and Barcelona. The scholars of Naples, Palermo and Bologna vied with those of Paris, Oxford and Cambridge in keeping alive the study of Latin, to which they were adding Greek, Hebrew and Arabic. Meanwhile the study of ancient art and learning contributed to the blossoming of a modern synthesis known to us as the Renaissance. This age saw the revival of the dome in architecture, the male nude in sculpture, the first genuine opera (Jacopo Peri's *Dafne*), the public library, the invention of perspective in painting, and the revival of public poetry readings, all these in Florence alone. The same city and century produced the first masters of Italian Renaissance art in Cimabue, Giotto, Uccello and Brunelleschi, who also designed the dome of the cathedral.

Although most of us think of the Italian genius as expressing itself first of all in the visual arts and later in music, Italy during the Middle Ages led the rest of Europe in literature, both poetry and prose. Vernacular Italian became acceptable as a literary language while English and French were still considered vulgar alternatives to Latin. The three greatest poets of the age – Dante Alighieri (1265–1321), Francesco Petrarca, or Petrarch (1304–74) and Giovanni Boccaccio (1313–75) – were not only admired and imitated by Chaucer but may have encouraged him to write in English, rather than French.

Chaucer first went to Italy on a trade mission to Genoa, whose merchants wanted a seaport in England. The records show that on 1 December 1372 he received an advance on expenses of one hundred marks (£66 13s 4d) and that on his return in May 1373 he sent in receipts to show he had also visited Florence. Chaucer's expenses claim does not prove he had been to Florence or anywhere else in Italy, but in those days public servants at least had to offer evidence of the money they said they had spent. In contrast, at the end of the twentieth century, the members of the European Parliament voted by two to one to abolish the need for them to produce receipts for expenses claimed on EC business.

The normally cautious biographer Derek Pearsall seems to accept the old story, popularized by Chesterton, that Chaucer was chosen for this assignment because of his knowledge of Italian 'which he had probably picked up as a boy from the merchants with whom his father and his step-cousins, the Herons, had had business'. This conjures up a delightful picture of the young Chaucer at study among the wine vats on Thames Street. In fact there is not a shred of evidence that Chaucer spoke Italian before, or even after, his first visit to Genoa and Florence.

King Edward III must have had his doubts about Chaucer's language qualifications, for he appointed to the same commission two native Genoese resident in England. They were John de Mari (Giovanni del Mare) who had formerly been an agent for recruiting Genoese crossbowmen (now less valuable since the development of the English longbow) and Sir James de Provan (Jacopo Provano), an agent for hiring ships.

It is probable that Chaucer and his commission travelled by ship to Genoa, as war made it unsafe that year to ride overland through France and across the Alps. From Iris Origo's superb *The Merchant of Prato: Daily Life in a Medieval Italian City*, based on the archives of the Datini family, we learn that most of the vessels sailing from Thames ports had English ship-masters, though a few were Venetian or Genoese. Those sailing from Southampton were Genoese-owned, with Genoese ship-masters, though sometimes an Englishman, as in one example quoted by Iris Origo: 'This is to inform you,' wrote the firm of the Mannini brothers from London on 6 August 1392, 'that we have chartered, together with Nicolo di Luca and Francesco di Giovanni, one third of a ship made by one of the greatest knights in this land. His name is Sir Thomas di Presi [Duplessis] and he has an English Master, who is a valiant seaman. And the said ship will be accompanied by 50 good men, furnished with arms and crossbows, and will be in Southampton on the 8th of November.'

The hiring of crossbowmen was necessary to guard the ship against pirates from North Africa, Spain and the rival sea-republics of Venice, Pisa and Genoa. The *guerra di corsa* (war of the journey), in which merchantmen were seized and the cargo and crew held to ransom, was so well established that the profession of 'corsair' no longer carried a stigma. Even Sir Thomas Duplessis and his 'English Master, who is a valiant seaman' could well have engaged in piracy on the side, like Chaucer's Shipman, who commonly sent his captives 'home by sea' – that is, threw them overboard.

The corsairs would have especially prized the cargoes of ships sailing from England to Pisa and Genoa. The finest and most expensive Italian cloths were made of English wool, mostly from the Cotswolds (*Ghondisqualdo* in Italian) – especially from Northleach (*Norlecchio*), Burford (*Boriforte*), Cirencester (*Sirisestri*) and Winchester (*Guincestri*). The main Tuscan wool merchants in London – the Guinigi, Mannini, Alberti and Caccini – sent their buyers around England to collect wool from the monastic houses and individual farmers, or to purchase it from the local woolmen. Iris Origo quotes a letter to Datini from his London agents, acknowledging one of his orders:

> You say you have written to Venice to remit us 1,000 ducats with which, in the name of God and of profit, you wish us to buy Cotswold wool. With God always before us, we will carry on your bidding, which we have well understood. In the next few days, our Neri will ride to the Cotswolds and endeavour to purchase a good store for us, and we will tell you when he has come back.

Datini, the merchant of Prato, imported from England not only wool but cloth, which was cheap as well as good quality, since English manufacturers had the advantage over their Flemish and Italian competitors of excellent raw material on the spot, and an export tax on cloth of a mere 2 per cent, against 33 per cent on wool. Moreover, English imports were becoming fashionable in the late fourteenth century, especially Essex cloths (*panni stretti di sex*), Guildford cloth in various colours, and unbleached cloths from the Cotswolds and Winchester.

Chaucer's experience at Genoa would have stood him in good stead for his later job of controller of customs and excise in London. Produce for Italy was an exception to the English law in that all wool exports to the Continent had to pass through the staple or official marketing agency at Calais. Some Tuscan merchants elected to buy from Calais and then ship their purchases home from Sluys, the port of Bruges, but others shipped them direct from England, all the way by sea. The twice-yearly fleet of Venetian galleys sailed straight to Italy from London or from Sluys, touching England at Sandwich, or Dartmouth if it was driven there by a storm. This perhaps explains why in 1373 Chaucer was sent down to Dartmouth to free a Genoese captain who had been arrested there. Some bad experience may have caused him to make 'Dertemouth' the home port of his villainous Shipman.

After discussing trade at Genoa, it was natural for Chaucer and his commission to visit Florence, the greatest commercial city of the interior and principal market for English wool and cloth. Although he clearly relished the cultural life of the city of Dante, Petrarch and Boccaccio, he must have found Florence in a state of crisis and xenophobia, specifically Anglophobia, for it held England responsible for some of its woes.

After the miseries which Florence suffered in the thirteenth century and which Dante described in the *Divina Commedia*, the city's troubles grew even worse in the next of the many disasters, both natural and man-made, which it endured from the 1330s onwards, at least two of which were attributable to the English. The bad times began with the flood of 1333 which swept away the statue of Mars, the city's protector in Roman times. According to the historian Villani, the flood was preceded by a storm that lasted four whole days and nights. Towers tumbled, tiles cascaded into the street, and all the church-bells tolled as men and women, howling for mercy, moved from roof to roof on narrow planks, to the terror of themselves and those watching below. The towers of St John the Baptist were half submerged; but nevertheless the baleful influence of the war god Mars, which Dante saw as a curse of Florence, did not disappear with the statue.

Soon after the flood came new political turmoil between the Guelfs and Ghibellines, with the intervention of foreign mercenaries drawn by the riches which Florence offered to plunderers. One of these was the French adventurer and self-styled Duke of Athens, who made himself the dictator of Florence until he was overthrown in 1343 by a mob which killed and ate one of the duke's lieutenants in the Piazza della Signoria. Such barbarities were common among the splendours of early Renaissance Italy. Political foes were often 'planted' or buried head down in the earth, while the Pisans punished a treacherous general, Ugolino, by shutting him up with his two little sons to starve to death in a tower, as later described by Dante, and by Chaucer in the *Monk's Tale*.

In the same year, 1343, that saw the demise of the Duke of Athens, Florence began to feel the effects of Edward III's defaulting on his debts to the banking houses of Bardi, Peruzzi and Acciaoli. Although the collapse did not become final until 1376, these banks soon lost the reputation that was their stock-in-trade. Throughout Europe, French *lettres de foire* came to acquire the credit once reserved for Italian *lettere di cambio*. The city's resentment against Edward III and the English generally comes across in Villani's *History* and in the *Decameron*.

Also, although it could not be blamed for the Black Death which devastated Florence more than any other great city of Europe in 1348–9, England cannot evade responsibility for the mercenary leader, Sir John Hawkwood, and his White Company who first landed in Italy in 1360 to fight in the service of Pisa against its traditional enemies Genoa and Florence. The Italian city states of that age habitually lured away outside generals to lead their armies, just as today the clubs of the Serie A buy up the managers of rival or even foreign football teams.

In the 1370s Sir John Hawkwood was called from Pisa to join in the war that was raging between the Avignon papacy and the Italian city states. The papal legate in Italy, Cardinal Robert of Geneva, especially wanted to reimpose authority on Rome and defend the integrity of the papal states in the Romagna, the north-central region of the peninsula. Sir John Hawkwood and his White Company fought at different times for the papacy and its two most powerful enemies, the city of Florence and the Visconti of Lombardy.

After going to Lombardy, Hawkwood accepted a bigger offer from the papal side. Cardinal Robert had at first hired Breton mercenaries to crush a revolt in the papal states, but when Cesena on the Adriatic coast protested against the Breton looting, he called in Hawkwood to teach the city a lesson. '*Sangue et sangue*' (blood and more blood), he ordered. Hawkwood obliged by shutting the gates of Cesena and letting his White Company kill 5,000 men, women and children. As befitting an officer in the service of the Pope, Hawkwood allowed some survivors to seek asylum in Rimini, and when he found two soldiers squabbling over a pretty nun, he followed the judgement of Solomon and had the woman cut in half.

When the papacy was remiss in its payment, Hawkwood listened to overtures from the Republic of Florence which now had a Ghibelline and violently anti-papal government. Like a modern football manager, he demanded a transfer fee in cash, a favourable contract and certain fringe benefits – in this case the promise of an equestrian statue. When Hawkwood later transferred his services back to Lombardy, in return for the hand in marriage of one of Bernabo Visconti's daughters (plus a dowry of 10,000 florins), the city of Florence in turn broke its promise by commissioning Uccello to paint the feigned equestrian statue of Sir John in *trompe l'oeil* perspective which still can be seen on the wall of the Duomo. This is sometimes cited as an example of Florentine parsimony, but Mary McCarthy offers a subtler explanation:

> More likely it is an example of that Florentine hatred of private glory which grudged, so long as the Republic lasted, the marble symbol of an enduring fame to an individual citizen or foreign employee of the state. In any case, the original memorial, which was done by Agnolo Gaddi, a late Gothic painter of the school that followed Giotto, must have been in some way unsatisfactory, and Uccello was ordered to do a new one, which was at least intended to create the *illusion* of a three-dimensional tomb. Uccello, with his perspective obsession, gave more attention in the monument to imitating the effects of sculpture than to making a portrait of the dead knight, who appears as a sort of ghostly chessman, greenish pale and melancholy on his greenish pale horse (which was copied, it is thought, from the great bronze horses of the Hellenistic period that the painter had seen on St Mark's balcony in Venice).

Whatever its inspiration, Uccello's Hawkwood survives as the quintessential 'Pale Horse, Pale Rider' of Katherine Anne Porter's novella.

When Chaucer visited Florence in 1373, its three greatest poets were at the height of their fame and popularity. Although Dante had died in Ravenna in 1321, he had been posthumously honoured by the city which had banished him and ordered him to be burnt at the stake if he dared to come home. Francesco Petrarch, whose father had also been exiled from Florence as a Guelf, spent most of his life in Avignon, Pavia, Venice and latterly Padua, but when he became Italy's first poet laureate he was courted by the Florentines to reside among them. The youngest of the three, Giovanni Boccaccio, had made a name for himself as a poet as well as the author of the prose *Decameron*, but he devoted much of his time to explaining and popularizing the work of the other two. Although Petrarch and Boccaccio wrote easily in Latin, and struggled to learn ancient Greek, they followed Dante's example by writing mostly in Italian. Chaucer found himself for the first time in a country where the vernacular was an accepted means of expression in poetry, prose and even the worship of God, as in Dante's *Paradiso* (Canto XXVII):

> *Al Padre, al Figlio, allo Spirito Santo*
> *Comincio gloria tutto il Paradiso*
> *Si che m'inebbriava il dolce canto*
> *Cio ch'io vedev, mi sembrava un riso*
> *Dell'universo: perche mia ebbrezza*
> *Entrava per l'udire e per lo viso.*
> 'To Father, Son and to the Holy Ghost,
> Glory,' all Paradise began to sing
> So that I was drunk with the sweet song.
> What I saw seemed to me to be
> The universe smiling; so my intoxication
> Came both from what I heard and what I saw.

Dante's example must have encouraged Chaucer to use the English language not only for poetry but for biblical and other religious texts, as in the *Parson's Tale*. Paradoxically, the Catholic Dante appeared to justify the argument of Wyclif and later Protestants that worship of God should not be confined to a dead language, Latin.

The Florence of Dante's youth, which he celebrates and scolds in the *Divina Commedia*, was little changed by the time of Chaucer's visit and, astonishingly, can still be seen and enjoyed by a twenty-first-century visitor. The Baptistry where he was given his Christian name, and later officiated as one of the priors or magistrates of the city, remains as popular as Brunelleschi's Duomo. The River Arno continues to break its banks, but never as fatally as the first recorded flood of 1185. At the start of the fourteenth century, the river featured in one of those man-made disasters which Florence regards as a judgement on its wickedness. In 1304, when Dante was in Ravenna, beginning to write the *Inferno*, his fellow citizens decided to mount a pageant or representation of Hell on the decks of a chain of boats beside the Caraia Bridge. It was advertised as a series of *tableaux vivants* of naked souls tormented by devils with pitchforks, or burning in real flames as they pleaded for mercy. So great was the crowd for this spectacle that the bridge collapsed under their weight and hundreds were drowned. 'They wanted to see Hell and got their wish quicker than they expected,' was the verdict of the city.

A sense of the past is strongest of all in the 'ancient circle' of Florence between the Baptistry and the river, whose tourist sights include the Badia, the Bargiello, the Tower of the Donati family and the Casa Dante or Dante museum and reputed birthplace. The 'ancient circle' is lauded by one of Dante's ancestors in Canto XV of the *Paradiso*:

> *Fiorenza dentro della cerchia antica*
> *Ond ella toglie ancora e terza e nona*
> *Si stava in pace sobria e pudica.*
> Florence, within the ancient circle
> From which tierce and nones are still rung,
> Lived in peace, soberly, decently.

At the centre of this 'ancient circle' stands the tiny eleventh-century Church of Santa Margherita where Dante first met Beatrice, the love of his life; where he married another woman, Gemma Donati, and where he watched in dismay as Beatrice married another man. The austere, even puritanical Church of Santa Margherita represents the virtues of the 'ancient circle' which Dante celebrates in Canto XV of *Paradiso*.

> *Non avea catanella, non corona*
> *Non donne contigiate, non cintura*
> *Che fosse a veder piu che la persona*
> *Non faceva nascendo ancor paura*
> *La figlia al padre, che il tempo e la dote*
> *Non fuggian quinci a quindi la misura*
> *Non avea case di famiglia vote;*
> *Non v'era guinto ancor Sardonapolo*

The transept of the martyrdom, Canterbury Cathedral.

The martyrdom of St Thomas of Canterbury, frontispiece of the
Harleian Manuscript 5102.

The Battle of Crécy, with the castle of Broc
in the distance (Froissart).

The Battle of Calais between the English, under
Sir Walter de Manny, and the French (Froissart).

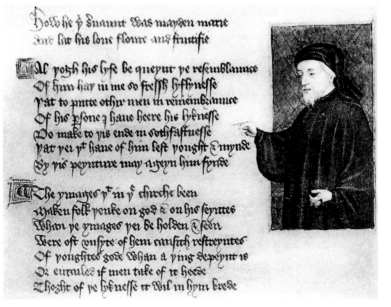

Geoffrey Chaucer, a frontispiece from *Romaunt of the Rose*.

A party of pilgrims.

Illustrations from the Ellesmere Manuscript.

CHAUCER.

THE KNIGHT.

THE WIFE OF BATH.

THE MILLER.

THE SECOND NUN.
(FROM THE ELLESMERE MS.)
[The relater of the Tale of St. Cecilia.]

THE NUN'S PRIEST.
(FROM THE ELLESMERE MS.)
" This sweetè priest, this goodly man Sir John."

Wat Tyler is killed by Walworth during the Peasants' Revolt and King Richard puts himself at the head of the rebels (Froissart).

King Richard and the rebels in the City of London (Froissart).

King Richard resigns his crown and kingdom to the Duke of Lancaster (Froissart).

Henry Duke of Lancaster crowned King of England (Froissart).

There were no golden chains or coronets,
Embroidered gowns nor bands about the middle
Which were more to look at than the person herself.
The daughter did not yet frighten her father
Merely by being born; for then the age
Of marriage and the dowry were both reasonable
There were no houses empty of families;
And Sardanapalus had not arrived . . .

My 1885 edition of the *Divina Commedia* appends an explanatory note to these last lines: 'Small families then as now were characteristic of a profligate and luxurious society.'

Dante's *Divina Commedia* would feature on most well-educated people's list of the masterpieces of literature, and yet it is one of the least read today. The reason for this is perhaps best understood in the Church of Santa Margherita, for Dante was above all a religious writer who tried to interpret his age in terms of the Christian message. His masterpiece can also be seen as a version of the legend of Orpheus and Eurydice, with Dante venturing into the underworld to rejoin his beloved Beatrice. It has also been construed as political satire, in which Dante literally damns to Hell his enemies and persecutors. More recently Dante has been analysed and 'deconstructed' in terms of various isms and ideologies. All such interpretations miss the point that Dante was a committed Christian, concerned with his own and mankind's salvation. Moreover, for all his attacks on individual popes and emperors, Dante remained a Catholic who looked to Rome as the seat of spiritual as well as political power, for although he dreamed of a united Italy, he saw it as part of the Holy Roman Empire.

Dante began his masterpiece when the papacy had already moved to Avignon but before the schism of 1378 resulted in two rival popes. Nor had the papacy had to meet the challenge of critics like Jan Hus in Bohemia and John Wyclif in England. Chaucer was one of the first English poets to read Dante, but also one of the last to share Dante's faith in a Roman and universal Church.

Even in Chaucer's lifetime, the teachings of Wyclif were casting doubt on Dante's beliefs, including Purgatory as a staging post on the way to Heaven, and the scene of the middle section of Dante's poem. Although Wyclif did not reject belief in Purgatory, he and his disciples condemned the custom of rich men leaving money in chantry bequests for priests to sing and pray for their souls in Purgatory. Chaucer praises the Parson who stayed with his country parish:

> He sette not his benefice to hire
> And left his sheep encumbered in the mire
> And ran to London unto Seynte Paules
> To seeken him a chaunterie for souls.

Within two centuries of Chaucer's lifetime, the English Puritans had rejected Dante's idea of Heaven and Hell as well as of Purgatory. Dante believed with Thomas Aquinas that individual Christians were given the power of choice between good and evil and therefore their fate in the afterlife. This idea of Free Will came into conflict with the essential Protestant doctrine of Predestination, and therefore salvation only by God's grace. The vision of human beings doomed to Hell by a wrathful God was present in Wyclif's teaching as in the later Calvinist churches of Geneva, Scotland, New England and the Transvaal.

Chaucer came to Florence only fifty years after Dante's death. Did he realize that he was following in the steps of one of the greatest poets of all time? And if so, why did he not set down in verse or prose his impressions of Florence and its presiding genius? It is a question we often ask with regard to Shakespeare and literary travellers to seventeenth-century London. Perhaps Chaucer knew that Boccaccio was already writing a life and critical study of Dante. Perhaps he did not want to encroach on the territory of his friend and colleague Froissart who was writing the chronicles of the age, although sadly giving more space to deeds of chivalry than to the lives of poets.

It is unreasonable to complain that Chaucer, who left us such entertaining poems, did not write a travelogue of his visits to Italy. It was not the custom in those days for poets to double as journalists. Nevertheless it has to be said that Chaucer's work shows little awareness of the wonders of the Italian Renaissance. As a later clerk of works who helped to rebuild Westminster Abbey and Canterbury Cathedral, he ignored the architectural innovations of the cathedral at Florence. In contrast to modern tourists he paid more attention to the literature than to the art of Florence.

Although Chaucer had been on a trade mission to Genoa, he does not seem to have had the knowledge of shipyards which Dante demonstrated in his account of the Venice Arsenale:

As in the arsenal of the Venetians
In winter they boil up the sticky pitch
To caulk their vessels, which are beginning to leak
Since they are unable to sail them; and instead
One builds the ship anew, and one stops up
The side of a ship which has made many voyages.
Some rivet up the prow, and some the stern;
Others make oars, or twist ropes for new rigging
While one repairs the mainsail or the jib.

Chaucer is oddly silent on the novelty of the Tuscan countryside and its strange flora and fauna: the trilling of the cicadas, the shimmering of the olive trees as their leaves turn in the breeze, and the birds which stop to rest on migration. He continued to write of rabbits and squirrels but not of the southern creatures which Dante describes so beautifully, here in the charming Dorothy Sayers translation:

And just as a lizard with a quick, slick slither
Flicks across the highway from hedge to hedge
Fleeter than a flash in the dog-day weather.

Chaucer does not mention the dog-day weather, nor the bane of life in Florence – mosquitoes – 'which come out at evening when the flies disappear', as Dante observed.

One could quickly compile too a list of the ways Chaucer differed from Dante and therefore did not respond to his poetry. For a start, Chaucer displayed no interest in politics, either the ideological issues or the malicious gossip. Nowhere in Chaucer's work do we get his opinion of Magna Carta, the quarrel of Henry II and Becket, the Peasants' Revolt or the Irish problem. Although Chaucer himself sat in the House of Commons and wrote his satirical poem called *The Parliament of Fowls*, scholars cannot determine which, if any, of these birds correspond to contemporary politicians. Chaucer mocks and abuses the creatures of his imagination such as the Friar and the Pardoner, but never identifiable living people, or even the recent dead. Here Chaucer differs not only from Dante but from later English satirical poets such as Dryden, Pope and Swift.

Although Chaucer was a different kind of poet, he clearly read and admired Dante, and often borrowed his stories, phrases and images. He used Dante's hymn to the Virgin in the *Second Nun's Tale*, and the story of Ugolino in the *Monk's Tale*. On several occasions he credits Dante, perhaps to show off his knowledge of Italian. Even the Wife of Bath says in her tale:

> Wel kan the wise poete of Florence
> That highte Dante, speken in this sentence
> Lo, in swich maner rym is Dantes Tale . . .

Even when Chaucer does not refer to Dante and may not have known he was quoting him, the scholars are eager to point out resemblances or derivations. This is not an exact science because Dante himself used some of the same sources as Chaucer: for instance Virgil, Ovid, Boethius, St Bernard and the Arthurian romances. Moreover, Chaucer's contemporaries such as Machaut, Deschamps and Froissart, from whom he often borrowed, had also read Dante in translation.

Some scholars maintain that Chaucer was so impressed by the *Divina Commedia* that he underwent a religious renewal or was 'born again', as we say these days. I can see no sign of it in the poems Chaucer wrote on his return from Italy. They suggest that he hugely admired Dante but recognized that his own genius lay in humour rather than in matters of Heaven and Hell. This is evident from a passage in which Chaucer turns upside down the famous lines in Dante's *Inferno*, the inscription over the gates of Hell.

> *Per me si va nella citta dolente . . .*
> Through me you go into the city of weeping
> Through me you go into eternal pain
> Through me you go among the lost people.

In the *Parliament of Fowls*, the delightful frolic Chaucer wrote for St Valentine's Day to cheer up the court during the cold dark weeks before the arrival of spring, the poet as usual wanders in dream through a magical landscape until he reaches a gate, on one side of which can be seen the words:

> Through me men gon into that blyssful place
> Of heartes health and deadly woundes cure;

Through me men gon into the welle of grace,
There green and lusty May shall ever endure.
This is the way to all good aventure.
Be glad, thou reader, and thy sorrow off-cast;
All open am I – passe in, and speed thee fast!

On the other side of the gate are written lines of an opposite, dismal nature, more like Dante's 'Abandon hope, all ye who enter here', but it is obvious to the reader that Chaucer favours cheerfulness over gloom. This is evident once more in the *House of Fame*, based on the stories in Virgil and Ovid, about a celestial factory of information and rumour. The great Chaucerian commentator F. N. Robinson wrote that it 'makes so much use of Dante that the poem has been regarded – unjustifiably to be sure – as an imitation of the *Divine Comedy*'. In a note to the Riverside Edition, the modern scholar John M. Fyler adds: 'Even so it is apparent that the *House of Fame* and the *Divine Comedy* have several interests in common and that Chaucer does sustain an ironic counterpoint to Dante's poem.' To me it suggests a light-hearted parody, especially the passage where Chaucer is carried aloft by an eagle.

In Canto IX of the *Purgatorio*, when Dante is spending his first night on the mountain, he dreams he is snatched up by an eagle when in fact he is carried asleep to the gates of Purgatory by St Lucia. Dante himself may have derived the idea from the story of Ganymede, who was taken up by an eagle to be the cup-bearer of Zeus, or from Exodus 19:4: 'I have carried you on an eagle's wings and brought you here to me.' Dante describes the dreams as so frightening that he turns to Virgil, his 'comforter', for reassurance:

At the hour at which the swallow begins
Her sad song at the approach of morning,
Perhaps in recollection of her first misfortunes;
And at which our minds are estranged
More from the flesh and less taken with thoughts,
And have visions which are almost divinations:
In a dream I thought I saw hanging
In the sky above, an eagle with golden feathers,
And wings open as if ready to drop . . .
Then I thought that, when it had circled,

Terrible as lightning, it descended,
And carried me aloft into the fire . . .
So I was startled, as from my face
Sleep fled, and I became pale,
As a man does when fear freezes him . . .
'Have no fear,' my master said to me;
'Be assured, we are in the right place:
Do not shrink, but put out all your strength.'

Chaucer encounters the eagle when he is wandering in the Libyan desert:

Myn eyen to the hevene I caste . . .
Me thoughte I saw an eagle soar
But that it seemed moche more
Than I had any eagle seyn.
But this as sooth as deth, certeyn,
It was of gold and shone so bright
That never saw men such a sight,
But if the heaven had y-wonne
All new of gold another sun;
So shone the eagle's feathers bright
And somewhat downward gan he light.

In Book II of the *House of Fame*, Chaucer returns to this marvellous bird:

The eagle of which I have you told
That shone with feathers as of gold
Which that so hye gan to soar
I gan beholde more and more
To see the beauty and the wonder;
But never was there clap of thunder
Ne that thing that men call fouder [lightning]
That smote sometime a tower to powder
And in his swift comyng brende
That so swithe gan descende
As this fowl when it beheld
That I a-round was in the field.

And with his grimme pawes stronge
Within his sharpe nayles longe
Me fleeing, in a swoop he hente
And with his soars again up wente
Me carrying in his clawes starke
As lightly as I were a larke,
How high I cannot telle you . . .
What with his soars and with my dread
That all my feeling gan to dead . . .

Whereas Dante in his terror had looked for comfort to Virgil, it is the eagle itself which tries to reassure Chaucer, first by rallying him from his fright and then by joking about his weight, as the Host makes fun of the size of Chaucer's waist.

Thus I longe in his clawes lay,
Til at the laste to me he spake
In manne's voice, and seyd 'Awake!
And be not aghast so, for shame!'
And called me tho by my name . . .
And here-withal I gan to stir
And he me in his feet to bear
Till that he felt that I had heat
And felt eke tho myn herte beat.
And tho gan he me to disporte
And with wordes to comforte,
And sayde twice, 'Seynte Marie,
Thou are noyous [troublesome] for to carry.'

Like any good airline pilot, the eagle provides a commentary on the landscape below and even the sky above:

See yonder, lo, the galaxy
Which men clepeth the milky wey
For hit in white, and some parfey
Kallen hyt Watlinge Street.

There is another passage in Chaucer which might be seen as a satire on Dante's journey from Hell up to Paradise. It comes at the start of the prologue to the *Legend of Good Women*, which was a court poem, perhaps written at the behest of Richard II's new wife Anne, and not to be taken entirely seriously:

> A thousand tymes have I heard men telle
> That there is joy in hevene and peyne in helle
> And I accord wel that it ys so;
> But natheles, yet wot I wel also
> That ther is noon dwelling in this countree
> That either hath in heven or helle y-be,
> Ne may of it noon other weyes witen
> But as he hath heard seyd or found it writen.

The fact that Chaucer could joke about Dante's eagle or even the concept of visiting Hell and Heaven does not imply a rejection of Dante's Christian faith. On the contrary, the passages quoted belong to an old tradition of self-deprecatory Christian humour: we have all encountered the kind of parson who jokes about his waistline or makes a coy reference to Hell as 'the other place'. Even in the fourteenth century it was possible to believe in Hell as a state of spiritual deprivation rather than as an actual infernal region of boiling oil and devils with pitchforks.

There is no reason to think that Chaucer suffered the religious doubts which made Dante so alien to succeeding generations. Although Chaucer disliked the sale of indulgences, he nowhere denounced belief in Purgatory. Whatever he thought of Wyclif, as far as we know Chaucer never rejected the Catholic view on Hell and mankind's freedom to choose between good and evil.

To judge by his writings, Chaucer was much more bothered by the question of what became of the souls of the 'virtuous pagans', and here he found comfort in the *Divina Commedia*. In the fourteenth century, only a third of the way through the second millennium, the Christian (or AD) period seemed brief compared to the pagan (or BC) age. Yet most of the literature and history read by medieval men and women concerned men and women who had died without hearing Christ's promise of salvation. Concern for the souls of the 'virtuous pagans' corresponded to the anxiety felt by children after the death of their parents and other loved ones.

One of the reasons why Chaucer and other medieval men loved

Boethius's *Consolation of Philosophy* was the way it linked the classical and the Christian worlds, giving a kind of posthumous holiness to pre-Christian poets and philosophers. Boethius himself was credited with conversion, although there is no mention of Jesus Christ in the *Consolation*.

Dante too was a devotee of Boethius and mentions him among the blessed in Canto X of the *Paradiso*, 'the holy soul who shows anyone who listens attentively how deceitful the world is'. However, it is Virgil whom Dante chooses to be his guide through the *Inferno* and the lower slopes of the mountain in *Purgatorio*. Even before Dante's poem, Virgil had been adopted by the Roman Catholic Church as a kind of honorary Christian. Dante's Virgil says of the souls in the First Circle:

> They have committed no sin, and if they have merits
> That is not enough because they are not baptised
> Which all must be to enter the faith which is yours.
> And, if they lived before the Christian era,
> They did not adore God as he should be adored
> And I am one of those in that position.

Virgil guides Dante through the *Inferno* and as far as Canto XXX of the *Purgatorio*, where Beatrice once more becomes his instructress. Almost at once she rebukes him for inconstancy, rather as Philosophy rebukes Boethius:

> Regally, in her gesture still severe,
> She went on, like a speaker who keeps back
> The sharpest things he has to say till last . . .
> As a mother may seem stern to her child,
> So she appeared to me; because it is a bitter
> Taste that is left by sharpness in pity.

Dante's Beatrice has always appealed to women rather than men readers. She is well aware of the hold she has on Dante through her sexual attraction but cannot resist extending her power by improving his mind and even saving his soul. Readers of P. G. Wodehouse will recognize in Beatrice the prototype of those beautiful but bossy girls who become engaged to Bertie Wooster and try to prepare him for marriage by making him read Spinoza or Schopenhauer. In the same way Beatrice expounds to Dante the theological doctrines of St Thomas Aquinas. As this exposition continues for canto after canto, the reader begins to nod, and it is comforting to discover that Dante does as well.

> And after that, another and another
> And so I wandered from one to the next
> And then my drifting thoughts became a dream.

One can assume that Chaucer also nodded off during the theological lectures in the *Divina Commedia* for he never himself quotes or refers to the works of St Thomas Aquinas. Although he sometimes mentions the sermons of St Gregory or St Bernard, Chaucer leaves metaphysical matters to his comic characters such as the Wife of Bath or the cock and hen, Chaunticleer and Pertelote in the *Nun's Priest's Tale*. Chaucer had a very English distrust of abstract ideas and foreign intellectuals. When he does refer to contemporary schoolmen, it is usually to Englishmen such as Thomas Bradwardine.

9

Chaucer in Lombardy

WHEN SIR JOHN HAWKWOOD went back to Lombardy, he found employers suitable to his talent. The Visconti brothers, Bernabo and Galeazzo, who ruled from the neighbouring cities of Milan and Pavia, were infamous for their greed and cruelty even in fourteenth-century Italy. The wealth of Lombardy, from banking, the wheat of its plains, and from the manufacture of armour, supported the Visconti in their ostentation and luxury, which foreshadowed that of the Borgias in the fifteenth and sixteenth centuries. The behaviour of the 'Vipers of Milan' furnished Barbara Tuchman with some of her ripest material on the decadence of Europe after the Black Death: 'Murder, cruelty, avarice, effective government, alternating with savage despotism, respect for learning and encouragement of the arts, and lusts amounting to sexual mania, characterized one or other of the family. Lucchino, an immediate predecessor, had been murdered by his wife who, after a notable orgy on a river barge, during which she entertained several lovers at once, including the Doge of Venice and her own nephew Galeazzo, decided to eliminate her husband to forestall his same intention with regard to her. The debaucheries of Matteo, eldest brother of Bernabo and Galeazzo, were such that he endangered the regime and was disposed of by his brothers in 1335, the year after their accession.'

The Visconti brothers were infamous for their cruelty as well as their lust. Soon after coming to power they promulgated a Quarentino, or forty-day programme of torture for real or suspected enemies of their rule. It was a catalogue of torment comprising the rack, the wheel, the strappado, flaying, gouging of eyes and amputation of other features, each day of torture followed by one of rest to make the victim suffer the dread of anticipation. The Visconti brought the Quarentino into their foreign policy, which consisted largely of war against the Avignon popes and grabbing the territory of the Papal States. When Bernabo was served with a Bull of excommunication, he forced the papal legate to eat the offending document, including the silken cord and seal of lead. He was reputed to have burnt alive four nuns and roasted a monk to death in a cage. There was no doctrinal motive for his loathing of the papacy. He showed no sympathy to the Manichaean heretics, or 'bougers', who flourished in Milan, as we know from the *Romaunt of the Rose*.

Apart from seizing Bologna and other towns of the Papal States, the Visconti brothers advanced themselves by marrying off their children, and the marriage of one of these may have been the occasion for Chaucer's first visit to Lombardy. Bernabo had seventeen children by Regina, his wife, who was reputedly the only person capable of controlling him in his fits of mad rage. When their daughter, Violante Visconti, was just thirteen in 1368, she was betrothed by proxy to Lionel, Duke of Clarence, a younger son of Edward III, and the first royal lord of Geoffrey Chaucer. On the way to Milan with his entourage, Lionel was lodged and lavishly entertained by the King of France at the Louvre in Paris. Among those attending the feast was Guillaume de Machaut, the poet who wrote a 'romance' for the bride's uncle, Amadeus VI of Savoy, and in return was given enough gold to buy his wife four lengths of cloth of Reims, and a *jaguette* lined with 1,200 squirrel skins. Another French poet, Sir John Froissart, a courtier to Queen Philippa, the bridegroom's mother, went on to attend Lionel's wedding in Milan, as did the poet laureate of Italy, Petrarch, who was already resident in Pavia.

We do not know for certain whether Chaucer was there, but because of the presence of Machaut, Froissart and Petrarch, several historians including Barbara Tuchman assume that Chaucer too joined in celebrating the nuptials of Lionel and Violante. The vulgarity and excess of the wedding feast recalls the age of such Roman emperors as Caligula and Nero. The menu alone is enough to make one bilious. The meats and fish were gilded with a paste of powdered egg, saffron, flour and real gold leaf, and paired in the most incongruous mixtures – for instance crabs with sucking pig, hare with pike, a whole calf with trout, capon with carp in lemon sauce, beef with sturgeon, cheese with eel pie.

This banquet of thirty courses was held outdoors to a concourse of wedding guests including 1,500 soldiers of the White Company who had just been hired for the first time by the Visconti brothers. Perhaps as a consequence of this banquet, the bridegroom, the Duke of Clarence, died soon afterwards, while his bride Violante, now a widow at only thirteen, was married off to a new husband, the Marquis of Montferrat, who supposedly got his sexual excitement from strangling young male servants.

Undeterred by the failure of this English connection, Bernabo Visconti planned a few years later to marry another daughter, Caterina, to Richard of Bordeaux, son of the Black Prince and soon to succeed to the throne as Richard II. This betrothal was one of the purposes of a later mission to Lombardy in which Chaucer certainly took part between May and September 1378 as squire to a senior diplomat, Sir Edward Berkeley. The other was to forge an alliance in Italy while England was engaged in peace negotiations with France. It was one of several journeys undertaken by Chaucer between 1377 and 1381, at least two of them on secret business ('*in secretis negociis domini regis*'). Perhaps fortunately for Richard, he was not fated to have a Visconti as father-in-law, but the mortal sickness of Edward III and of his son, the Black Prince, as well as political and religious dissension at home, gave urgency to the task of making the country stable for his accession.

Since Chaucer was by now a civil servant and family man, he made arrangements for his absence abroad by appointing his colleague Richard Bassett as deputy controller of the wool customs, and granting powers of attorney to his fellow poet John Gower and to another friend Richard Forester, who afterwards took over Chaucer's house in Aldgate. After drawing expenses, Chaucer and Berkeley were formally ordered to carry King Edward's greeting to Bernabo Visconti, Lord of Milan, and to '*nostre cher et foial*' (our dear and faithful) Sir John Hawkwood.

Chaucer's role as conveyor of greetings to one of the cruellest despots and one of the greediest mercenaries of the fourteenth century has puzzled and dismayed some of the poet's admirers. Of course, it is pointed out that Chaucer could no more have criticized his sovereign's choice of allies than a junior diplomat in the twentieth century could have refused a posting to Hitler's Germany or Stalin's Russia. Moreover, for all their crimes, the Visconti brothers were patrons of art and literature, including Petrarch, the first Italian laureate. The libraries of Milan and

Pavia gave Chaucer the chance to read and copy Dante and Boccaccio. Pavia was especially sacred to him as the place where Boethius in the seventh century wrote the *Consolation of Philosophy* in prison, before he was tortured to death by his jailers, in Visconti fashion.

There is ample evidence in his poetry that Chaucer understood the wickedness of the Visconti brothers. In the prologue to the *Legend of Good Women*, Alceste tells the God of Love to be generous and merciful to Chaucer, as all lords should be to their subjects, and 'nat be lyke tyrauntz in Lumbardye'. Chaucer, in the *Monk's Tale*, numbers Bernabo Visconti among the proud and powerful men and women who have been brought low by the turn of Fortune's wheel. He alludes to Bernabo's murder in 1385, at the instigation of his nephew, but characteristically does not comment on how and why he met his death or whether he deserved it:

> Of Melayn grete Barnabo Viscount,
> God of delit and scourge of Lumbardye,
> Why should thin [e] infortune I nought acounte [recount],
> Since in estaat thou clomben were so hye?
> Thy brother sone, that was thy double allye,
> For he thy nephew was and sone-in-law,
> Within his prisoun made thee to dye;
> But none know why or how thou were y-slawe.

One of the nastiest characters in Chaucer, the protagonist of the *Merchant's Tale*, is also from the Visconti domain:

> Whilom ther was dwelling in Lombardy
> A worthy knight that born was of Pavye,
> In which he lyvved in prosperitye;
> And fourty yeer a wyfless man was he,
> And folwed ay his bodily delyt . . .

As mentioned in the chapter on merchants, this 'worthy knight' is a monster of selfishness to his much younger wife, and eventually gets his deserts when she cuckolds him in a tree above his head. However, the critics looking for evidence of Chaucer's attitude to the Visconti brothers have tended to go to the *Clerk's Tale*, which is also set in Lombardy and also concerns a husband's cruelty.

Whether the *Clerk's Tale* of patient Griselda was taken from Petrarch, Boccaccio or one of their several French translators, it has never ceased to enrage its female, and still more its feminist, readers from Chaucer's time to the present day. Indeed, the authors themselves were clearly rather embarrassed by it. The story of Griselda is told by Boccaccio in his tenth tale of the tenth day of the *Decameron*, of which this is his summary:

> The Marquis of Saluzzo, obliged by the entreaties of his subjects to take a wife, follows his personal whims and marries the daughter of a peasant. She bears him two children, and he gives her the impression that he has put them to death. Later on, pretending that she has incurred his displeasure, and that he has remarried, he arranges for his own daughter to return home, and passes her off as his bride, having meanwhile turned his wife out of doors, in no more than the shift that she is wearing. Finding that she endures it all with patience, he cherishes her all the more deeply, brings her back to his house, shows her their children, who have now grown up, and honours her as the marchioness, causing others to honour her likewise.

Petrarch so much admired Boccaccio's story that he wrote his own version of it in Latin. It is this that the Clerk claims to have heard at Padova where Petrarch lived, as did Giovanni di Lignano, a scholar of canon law:

> I wil you telle a tale, which that I
> Lerned at Padowe of a worthy clerk,
> Y-proved by his wordes and his werk.
> He is now ded and nayled in his chest,
> And may God give his soule wel good rest!
> Fraunces Petrark, the laureat poete,
> Highte this clerk, whos retoricke swete
> Illumynd al Ytail of poetrie,
> As Linian did of philosophie,
> Or lawe, or other art particuler;
> But deth, that wol not suffre as dwellen here,
> But as it were a twinckling of an eye,
> Them bothe hath slayn, and alle shall we dye.

Although the Griselda story is told on the Tenth Day of the *Decameron*, devoted to those 'who had performed liberal and munificent deeds', Boccaccio's narrator says that the marquis was remarkable 'not for munificence but senseless brutality' and recommends that nobody should follow his example. Similarly the *Clerk's Tale* is followed by a facetious epilogue called 'Chaucer's Farewell', urging women not to follow Griselda's example, but to behave like shrews and termagants to their husbands, making them jealous and spending their money:

> Ye archewyves, stand ye at defence,
> Since ye be strong, as is a great camel,
> Nor suffer not that men you do offence.
> And slender wyves, cruel in batayle,
> Be eager as a tiger, yond in Inde;
> Ay chatter as a mylle, I you counsaile.
> Dreade them not, do them no reverence,
> For though thy husband armed be in mail,
> The arrows of thy crabbid eloquence
> Shall pierce his breast, and eke his visor frail:
> In jealousy I counsel thou him bind,
> And thou shalt make him cower as doth a quail.
> If thou be fair, when folk be in presence
> Show thou thy visage and thy apparaile;
> If thou be ugly, be free of thine expense . . .

But as so often in Chaucer and Boccaccio, disclaimers like this could be tongue in cheek. Both men were anxious not to offend their women readers, but were sceptical of the attitude of the more aggressive feminists. As both men seem to be hinting, the cruelty of the marquis, Walter, was in part the result of his own 'munificence' in taking a peasant girl as his bride and raising her to a status where she is ill at ease. By trying to please the socialists, he has given offence to the feminists.

However repulsive to modern ideas, the *Clerk's Tale* can be seen as a variant of the old and ever popular legend of Cinderella, or the female equivalent of the labours of Hercules, or countless other legends of a young man's trial by danger and battle. It can also be understood as a satire on royal marriage, as practised in Lombardy in the fourteenth century, or in England much more recently. Chaucer was well aware that when it came to the marriage of a future ruler, considerations of love or even compatibility took second place to the interests of politics and power. Even in fourteenth-century England, the choice of a bride for a royal prince was subject to the approval of the lords, the bishops, the House of Commons and what we would now call public opinion, as voiced by the popular press and the answers to questionnaires. The experience of the Peasants' Revolt in London in 1381 had taught the ruling classes not to ignore the sentiment of the mob.

In the *Clerk's Tale*, Chaucer imagined a Lombardy, or Saluces as he calls it, in which public opinion tells the ruler not only when he should marry and how he should choose a bride, but when he should get a divorce and a younger, prettier wife, for his subjects are always delighted to see 'a newe lady in their town'. The behaviour of Lombard public opinion to Walter, the marquis in the *Clerk's Tale*, is not unlike that of the British press to modern princes and princesses. Prince Edward, the Prince of Wales in the 1920s and 1930s, suffered constant advice on whom he should marry until he fell in love with the unacceptable Mrs Simpson. Forty years later the British popular papers welcomed Prince Charles's marriage to Lady Diana Spencer, although urging her not to promise to honour and obey him. When the marriage started to go wrong, the self-appointed voices of public opinion took sides on deciding who was to blame and, after the death of Diana, lectured the whole royal family on how to behave at her funeral.

The marquis in the *Clerk's Tale* is chided by public opinion because he has not yet married:

> Only that point his peple bar so sore,
> That flocking on a day to him they went,
> And one of them that wisest was of lore . . .
> He to the marquis said as ye shal here . . .
> 'Accept, o lord, now of your gentilesse
> That we with piteous heart to you complaine . . .
> For certes, lord, so wel we loven you
> And al your werk, and ever have done, that we
> Coude not ourselves lightly devisen how
> We mighte live more in felicitee:

Save one thing, lord, if that your wille be
That for to be a weddid man you list
Then were your people in their hearts at rest.
Bow then your neck under that blissful yoke
Of sovereignty not of servise
Which that man clepe spousail or wedlock . . .'

The spokesman of public opinion goes on to suggest that if Walter agrees to marry, they, his people, will choose him a bride from the noblest and highest in Italy:

'Accepte thenne of us the trewe entent
That never yet refused all your hest
And we wil, lord, if that ye will assent,
Choose you a wyf, in short time atte lest,
Born of the gentilest and the highest
Of all this lond, so that it ought to seem
Honour to God and you, as we can deem.'

In response to all these entreaties, which take up most of Part One of the *Clerk's Tale*, Walter the marquis appears to consent but on the conditions that he alone shall choose his bride, and that once he has married her his people will have to abide by his choice. Walter will marry, he tells his people, as soon as ever he may:

'But whereas ye have proffered me today
To choose me a wyf, I will release
That choice and pray you of that proffer cease . . .'

On principle he rejects a wife chosen because of her lineage, or what we would now call her genes:

'For God it wot that childer oft have been
Unlike their worthy elders them before;
Bountee cometh all of God, nought of the strain
Of which they be engendrid and i-bore.
I trust in Godde's bountee and therefore
My mariage, and myn estat and rest

To God I leave . . .
Let me alone in choosing of my wife
That charge upon my back I will endure.
But I you pray and charge upon your life
That what wife that I take, ye me assure
To worship while that her life may endure
In word and work, bothe here and everywhere,
As she an emperoure's daughter were.
And furthermore thus shall ye swear, that ye
Against my choice shall never murmur or strive
For since I shall forgo my liberty
At your request, so may I ever thrive
Where my own heart is set, there will I thrive.
And save you will assent in such manere,
I pray you speak no more of this matere.'

Assuming that the marquis has chosen a bride from 'the highest and gentlest in the land' (the word gentle here meaning noble or genteel), his people prepare a wedding feast of Visconti opulence, so that his palace is 'stuffid with plentee'. But the marquis has long ago noticed and singled out for his bride a humble peasant girl, Griselda, who is as virtuous and diligent as she is beautiful:

No love of pleasure was in her body run;
For ofter of the welle than of the tunne [wine barrel]
She drank . . .
And in great reverence and charitee
Hir old poore father fostered she
And when she spun, sheep in the field she kept
She never yet was idle till she slept.

When she came home in the evening, Griselda boiled the herbs and vegetables she had picked in the field that day. Her life was dominated by what would now be called patriarchal values:

She made her bed full hard and nothing soft
And ay she kept her father's life aloft,
With every obeissance and diligence.

On the day of the wedding, the marquis leads his lords and ladies to meet Griselda, whom he has not yet warned of his plans for her. In fact she is doing her chores in the hope of getting a chance to see the woman whom the marquis has chosen for his bride.

> She sayd: 'I wol with other maidens stand
> That be my fellows, in our door and see
> The marquysesse, and I will take in hand
> To do at home, as soon as it may be
> The labour which that longeth unto me
> And then may I at leysir hir beholde . . .'
> And as she would over the threshold goon
> The marquis came and gave hir for to calle.
> And she set down her water pot anon
> Beside the threshold of this oxe stall
> And down upon her knees she gan to falle
> With sobre countenance she kneeleth stille
> Till she had heard what was her lordes will.

The marquis asks Griselda to take him to her father:

> He by the hand then takith this olde man
> And sayde thus, when he him had aside:
> 'Janicula, I neither may nor can
> Longer the pleasure of my herte hide;
> If that you vouchesafe, what so betide
> Thy daughter will I take ere that I wende
> As for my wife, unto hir live's ende.'

Only at this late stage does the marquis propose to Griselda, and then in a fashion so peremptory that it sounds like an ultimatum.

> 'Grisyld,' he sayde, 'ye shal wel understande
> It liketh to your father and to me
> That I you wedde and eke it may so stande
> As I suppose you will that it so be;
> But these demandes ask I first' quoth he
> 'That since it shall be done in hasty wise
> Will you assent, or wait and you advise?'

Without giving her time to consider his proposal, the marquis explains to Griselda his terms for marriage, which are to do his bidding whether it makes her 'laugh or cry' and not to complain by the slightest word or action.

When Griselda changes into the wedding dress which the marquis has prepared for her, the woman servants are loath even to touch her peasant rags:

> And for that no thing of her olde gear
> She should bring unto his house, he bade
> That women should despoil hir right there
> To which these ladies were not ful glad
> To handle her clothes wherein she was clad.

There is a modern parallel of this scene in Shaw's *Pygmalion* and the musical version *My Fair Lady* when Professor Higgins brings home the Covent Garden flower girl Eliza Doolittle and orders his reluctant housekeeper to supervise bathing her and giving her new clothes. Like Eliza in the modern story, Griselda adapts to her new social status:

> I say, that to this newe marquisesse
> God such favour sent her of his grace
> That it seemed not by any liklynesse
> That she was born and fed in rudenesse
> As in a cote or in an oxe stall,
> But nourisht in an emperourer's halle.

Griselda is taken to heart by the people of Saluces:

> To every wight she waxen is so deere
> And worshipful, that folk where she was born
> And from hir birthe knew her year by year . . .
> They thought she was another creature.
> For thought that ever vertuous was she,
> She was encreased in such excellence
> Of manners good, i-set in high bountee,
> And so discreet, and fair of eloquence,
> So benigne, and so digne of reverence,

And coulde so the peples heart embrace
That each her loveth that looketh in her face.

Although Griselda has proved the marquis's theory that natural virtue
is more important than noble birth, the marquis himself refuses to
acknowledge this, and determines to subject her to further tests of
character by sending away her children and pretending they are dead.
His pretext is that the nobles do not accept her:

'Ye wot yourself how that ye comen here
Into this house, it is nought long ago;
And though to me that ye be leef and deere,
Unto my nobles ye be no thing so.
They seyn, to them it is great shame and woe
For to be subject and be in servage
To thee that born art of a small village.'

The marquis says that this discontent has grown since the birth of their
first child, a daughter, and that therefore:

'I must do with thy daughter for the beste,
Not as I would, but at my people's heste.'

To please this imaginary public opinion, the marquis has their
daughter and later their son taken off to be raised in Bologna. With
added cruelty, he lets Griselda think that the sinister sergeant who
takes the children away is intending to murder them. Although she
accepts her husband's decision, Griselda pleads with the sergeant not
to make the little ones suffer or let their corpses be eaten by scavenging
beasts.

The marquis once more blames public opinion when he submits
Griselda to her harshest test by pretending to exchange her for a
younger wife. He forges a papal Bull permitting him to divorce. He
then explains to Griselda that he is getting rid of her in the interest of
preserving civil peace:

'My people me constraineth for to take
Another wife, and crien day by day;
And eek the pope, rancour for to slake,

Consenteth, and I must it undertake . . .
My newe wife is coming by the way.
Be strong of hert, and voyde anon your place . . .'

In secret, the marquis has arranged for his and Griselda's daughter to be brought from Bologna, in the guise of his new young bride, to the great delight of the people of Saluces:

For she is fairer, as they demen all,
Than is Griseld, and tenderer of age
And more pleasaunt for her high lineage.

The *Clerk's Tale* can be seen as a homily on patience and obedience to the will of God. Chaucer compares Griselda several times to Job and perhaps implicitly to the Virgin Mary who used to be shown in medieval art as spinning and guarding the sheep at the same time. Griselda's sacrifice of her children might be compared to that of Abraham. Yet I believe the moral of the tale lies in the diatribe against silly and impertinent gossip about the love-lives of the great:

O stormy people, unfirm and ever untrue
And indiscret, and changing as a vane
Delyting ever in rumour that is new.
For like the moon aye waxe ye and wane;
Dear at a grote your praise and your disdain.
Your word is false, your service evil provith,
A full great fool is he that you believeth.

10

Wyclif and the Friars

WHILE CHAUCER WAS IN Italy, then torn by a papal schism between Rome and Avignon, another religious crisis came to a head at Oxford. A cantankerous don, John Wyclif (1329–84) challenged the authority of the Roman Catholic Church, advancing views that came to be seen as the start of the later Protestant Reformation. A Church Council at Konstanz in Switzerland in 1415 ordered the Czech preacher Jan Hus to be burnt to death on charges of 'Wyclifism', and Wyclif's remains at Lutterworth in Leicestershire to be disinterred and thrown in the River Swift. Wyclif's writing inspired Martin Luther in Germany and Thomas Cranmer in England, as well as helping to justify Henry VIII's breach with Rome and the dissolution of the monasteries. Then, after Elizabeth's Settlement of the Church in 1559, Wyclif became a figurehead to the Puritans who opposed her. Throughout the seventeenth century Wyclif became a saint to people who did not believe in sainthood, and Lutterworth was a shrine to Dissenters, like Daniel Defoe, who did not approve of pilgrimage.

To the Whig historians of the nineteenth century, the Wyclif affair, along with the Black Death and the Peasants' Revolt, was seen as a milestone on the road from feudal superstition to liberal democracy, but thanks to an academic backlash against the Whig view of history, and the persistent efforts of pro-Catholic writers such as G. K. Chesterton, the career of Wyclif is now regarded as less influential and certainly less admirable than it was before. Nevertheless Wyclif first popularized in England the ideas put into practice by Henry VIII of a breach with the papacy and the dissolution of the monasteries. Wyclif is still more important to understanding the life and works of Geoffrey Chaucer.

When he was first under attack from the Pope and the English hierarchy, Wyclif found a protector in John of Gaunt, the Duke of Lancaster, who was also the patron and friend of Chaucer. Chaucer's *Canterbury Tales* are proof that he shared many of Wyclif's views on the corruption of the Church, the friars and the sale of indulgences. Above all, there are hints in his writing, as in his choice of friends, that Chaucer sympathized with Wyclif's posthumous followers, commonly known as Lollards. It is from his attitude to the Wyclif debate that we have to decide whether Chaucer in a later age would have become a Protestant or remained obedient to the Roman Catholic Church.

Although Wyclif was probably born near Richmond in Yorkshire, and died in his parish at Lutterworth in Leicestershire, he made his career at Oxford University, where he was junior fellow of Merton in 1356, Master of Balliol in 1360, and a doctor of divinity by 1372.

Quite apart from the Wyclif debate, contemporary Oxford figures large in Chaucer's writing and study. Even in his day, Oxford enjoyed a scholarly reputation equal to Paris or Bologna, although it was probably very much smaller in numbers than claimed for it by contemporaries (such as estimates that there were 30,000 students before the Black Death). The great majority were studying for a simple arts degree and living in private halls or lodgings rather than in the colleges such as Oriel, Exeter and Queen's.

The large number of students living in digs in Oxford, and often engaged in part-time employment, contributed to the enmity between 'town and gown'. The main point at issue was the extent of the university Chancellor's power over the townspeople. A statute of 1290 had allowed him jurisdiction in all cases of crime, except homicide and maiming, and over all contests arising when one of the parties was a scholar. In 1328 Edward III granted the Chancellor partial control of the market in bread and ale, and therefore the price of essential food. This, and a slump in the local wool industry, may have sparked off the affair of St Scholastica's Day (10 February 1355) which began as a tavern brawl and developed into a riot, costing many lives.

The other great cause of contention in fourteenth-century Oxford was jealousy between the friars and the secular dons at the university. In England as in France during the thirteenth century, the zeal for learning of the mendicant orders won them rich endowments as well as senior teaching posts.

Just as jealousy of the friars at Paris University inspired much of the malice towards them in Jean de Meun's *Roman de la Rose*, it was an Oxford scholar, Richard Fitzralph, Archbishop of Armagh, who became their principal scourge in the British Isles. He travelled to Avignon in 1357 to complain to the Pope that the friars were enticing boys away from the university, a practice he blamed for Oxford's depopulation during the Black Death.

Both friars and secular clergymen contributed to the fame of Oxford in philosophy and in the sciences of astronomy and mathematics. Among the leading philosophers of medieval England were the Oxford friars Duns Scotus and his successor William of Ockham, whose concept known as Ockham's Razor has come to stand for the incomprehensible arguments of medieval schoolmen, along with the question of how many angels could dance on the head of a pin.

Most of the astronomers who made Oxford a kind of medieval Greenwich were fellows of Merton, like Bishop Thomas Bradwardine (also a controversial theologian), but some of the mendicants also contributed to the science, notably Nicholas of Lynne, a Carmelite who at John of Gaunt's request compiled a calendar of the latitude and longitude of Oxford.

A Treatise on the Astrolabe, which Chaucer wrote for his small son Lewis, is based on the work of Nicholas of Lynne, as are the astronomical observations which come at various points on the pilgrimage to Canterbury:

> By that the Maunciple had his tale endid,
> The sonne from the south line is descendid . . .
> Degrees nine and twenty as in hight.
> Four on the clokke it was, so as I gesse,
> For eleven foote, or litel more or lesse,
> My shadow was at thilk tyme of the yere
> Of which feet as my lengthe parted were
> In sixe feet equal of proporcioun.
> Therewith the moones exaltacioun
> In mena Libra, alway gan ascende.

Whether Chaucer himself followed the latest Oxford disputes on Predestination, the cock and the hen in the *Nun's Priest's Tale* are thoroughly versed in these and the writings of 'the holy doctor

Augustyn, Boece and Bishop Bradwardyn'.

As I have tried to suggest already, the Clerk of Oxenford, as described in the *General Prologue*, is so sympathetic a figure as to appear as Chaucer's *alter ego*, certainly as a model for an Oxford scholar and gentleman:

> A Clerk there was of Oxenford also
> That unto logik had long time i-go
> As lene was his horse as is a rake
> And he was not right fat, I undertake;
> But looked hollow and therto soberly.
> Ful thredbare was his overest cloke to see,
> For he had nought geten him a benefice,
> Nor was so worldly to have high office.

The Host upbraids the scholar, as he does Chaucer himself, for putting his studies before the party spirit:

> 'Sir Clerk of Oxenford,' our hoste seyde,
> 'Ye ride as still and coy as doth a mayde
> All newly spoused, sitting at the board;
> This day I heard not of your mouth a word.
> I trow ye study some disputacioun;
> But Solomon saith, everything hath season.
> For Godd's sake! be thou of better cheer,
> It is no tyme for to study here.'

As in his own encounter with the Host, Chaucer expresses the enmity between the scholar and the philistine, between gown and town. He gets his revenge in the *Miller's Tale* in which an Oxford carpenter is cuckolded by Nicholas, a university student (here in the David Wright version):

> At one time there was living at Oxford
> A rich old gaffer, carpenter by trade,
> Who took in paying guests; and he'd a lodger
> Living with him, a needy hard-up scholar
> Learned in the liberal arts; but all his fancy
> Turned to the study of astrology:

He could work out a few propositions,
And thus calculate answers to questions,
When people came to ask him if the stars
Were auguring dry weather or downpours;
Or he'd forecast what events would befall,
One kind or another – I can't list them all.

In the description that follows, Chaucer cleverly points out the differences as well as resemblances between Nicholas and the 'Clerk of Oxenford', his idealized scholar. Both have books at their bed-head, but Nicholas also has musical instruments, like a modern undergraduate with his compact discs and hi-fi equipment, as well as his computer. Although both men may seem 'shy as a maid', Nicholas is 'fly' or cunning in pursuit of women. Nor is he really as poor as the Clerk of Oxenford, for he earns or sponges the money to have a room to himself and his loud music.

Fly Nicholas was what they called this scholar.
For love *sub rosa*, pleasing, or for pleasure
In bed or out of it, he'd a great knack;
And he was wily too, and close as wax,
Although he looked as demure as a maid.
In the house he lodged in, he'd a room and bed
All to himself, and prettily furnished
With sweet delicious herbs . . .
His *Almagest*, and astrological
Treatises, with his textbooks great and small,
The instruments required for his science,
His astrolabe, and abacus-counters,
Were neatly stacked on shelves beside his bed;
His wardrobe-chest was draped with scarlet frieze.
A splendid psaltery hung overhead,
On which, at night, he'd play sweet melodies,
And fill the room with music till it rang;
'The Angel to the Virgin' he would sing,
And after, 'The King's Tune' would be his choice.
Folk often praised him for his cheerful voice.
And so this genial student spent his time
Living on his friends' money and his own.

In his pursuit of Alison, the carpenter's delicious wife, 'fly' Nicholas has a rival in another university man, young Absolon, a clergyman at a local church, who is just as much of a ladies' man in spite of his pious duties.

> In fantastically fenestrated shoes
> And scarlet stockings, he dressed stylishly.
> He wore a light blue jacket, fitting tightly,
> A mass of fine tagged laces laced it neatly,
> With over it a surplice white and gay
> As blossom blooming on a branch of may.

Absolon supplemented his clerical stipend with odd jobs and legal work to pay for his music and fun in the Oxford pubs.

> Lord save us and bless us, but he was a lad!
> For he could shave and barber, and let blood,
> Draw up a quittance or a conveyance.
> In twenty different styles he'd jig and dance
> But in the Oxford mode, as was the fashion,
> Flinging his legs in every direction;
> He'd play upon a tiny two-stringed fiddle,
> And sometimes he would sing, a loud falsetto;
> And he could play as well on a guitar.
> In the whole town there was no inn or bar
> He'd not enlivened with his company,
> The ones with lively barmaids, naturally.

Whereas Nicholas lived under the same roof as Alison, clerk Absolon yearned at a distance, when she came to church.

> This Absolon, high-spirited and gay,
> Was taking the censer round on that saint's day,
> Censing the women of the parish, when
> He'd take his chance to cast sheep's eyes at them –
> Especially at the carpenter's wife.
> To look on her seemed happiness enough
> She was so neat and sweet and flirtatious.
> Take it from me, if she had been a mouse

And he a cat, he would have pounced at once.
He was so smitten with a love-longing,
This parish clerk, this gallant Absolon,
That when he went round with the collection,
He wouldn't take a penny from the women;
Good manners, so he told them, quite forbade.

At the end of the *Miller's Tale* it is Nicholas who goes to bed with Alison, while Absolon is offered only her backside to kiss, but as in the *Reeve's Tale*, it is a triumph of gown over town. Chaucer gives us another portrait of Wyclif's Oxford in Jankin, the latest man in the life of the Wife of Bath:

My fifth husband – may God bless his soul!
Whom I took on for love, and not for gold,
Was at one time a scholar at Oxford,
But had left college, and come home to board
With my best friend, then living in our town.

The Wife of Bath had met him when her fourth and previous husband was dead and on his way to the churchyard

Followed by the neighbours, all in mourning,
And one among them was the scholar Jankin.
So help me God, when I saw him go past,
Oh what a fine clean pair of legs and feet
Thought I – and so to him I lost my heart.
He was, I think, some twenty winters old,
And I was forty, if the truth be told.
But then I always had an itch for it! . . .
There's little more to say: by the month's ending,
This handsome scholar Jankin, gay and dashing,
Had married me with all due ceremony.
To him I gave all land and property,
Everything that I had inherited.
But later I was very sorry for it –
He wouldn't let me do a thing I wanted!
My God, he once gave my ear such a box
Because I tore a page out of his book,

That from the blow my ear became quite deaf.
I was untameable as a lioness;
My tongue unstoppable and garrulous . . .

When one pauses to consider that Jankin, 'fly' Nicholas and Absolon
were clergymen from the major theological school in England, it is
easy to understand why Oxford was ripe for a puritan reformer such
as Wyclif.

Wyclif himself was a man of wrath and indignation, to judge from
his writings and from his early death of a paralytic stroke brought on
by high blood-pressure. In a later age, Wyclif might have grown
furious over the Middle East, fox-hunting or fluoridation of water, but
since he was an Oxford don in the fourteenth century he directed his
anger into religion.

Most of the theories connected with Wyclif were current in Oxford
when he arrived, and only excited controversy when he carried them
to extremes. The doctrines of Predestination and salvation by grace,
rather than works, which came to be seen as the cornerstone of
Protestantism were taught by St Augustine of Hippo (354–430)
who is now best remembered for his *Confessions*. Although Augustine
and his theology have been embraced by the Roman Catholic Church,
he and St Paul are rightly claimed as kindred spirits by Calvinists
today, whether the Dutch Reformed Churchmen of Pretoria or the
Orangemen of Belfast.

Wyclif's lectures on St Augustine caused no trouble until he touched
on the delicate subject of 'dominion', or the ownership of property
and wealth. Wyclif taught that since everything belonged to God, the
custodianship of property should only be entrusted to the 'elect', or
those predestined to be saved from Hell. But, like Augustine, Wyclif
believed that no human being could know who was or was not saved.
Hence, for the time being, we should wait patiently, even under unjust
rulers.

It followed from this that the king had authority over the civil estate.
But the ecclesiastical estate, because it is called to spiritual service,
should be stripped of all temporal possessions except what was
necessary for food, clothing and shelter. No clergyman should accept
any civil office; the king should remove all unworthy clerics, and all
ecclesiastics from the Pope down should live in poverty like St Peter
and the other apostles.

Wyclif's enemies pointed out at the time that he himself did not turn down civil office or a comfortable benefice at Lutterworth. But then Wyclif's argumentative skills as well as his views made him useful to John of Gaunt and his brother the Black Prince, who in effect ran the country during the illness of their father Edward III. In their efforts to raise more money for the Crown in spite of complaints from the House of Commons, the royal brothers saw Wyclif's theories as an excuse to plunder the Church and in particular the monasteries, as Henry VIII was to do in the sixteenth century. Gaunt also understood the advantage of hiring a clever polemic writer, just as Robert Harley, the first Earl of Oxford, put Swift and Defoe on the government payroll in the eighteenth century. Gaunt sent Wyclif to Bruges on a diplomatic mission, at which he proved far less adept than the more tactful and even-tempered poet, Geoffrey Chaucer. It was probably Gaunt who got Wyclif appointed to Lutterworth.

With the encouragement of John of Gaunt, Wyclif broadened his attack to question the Pope's authority over the English Church. While the papacy was in Avignon and under the sway of the King of France, the Parliament complained that money sent there might be used for the enemy's army. Wyclif was asked by the Crown to frame a formal answer to the question: 'Whether the Realm of England can legitimately, when the necessity for repelling invasion is imminent, withhold the treasure of this realm that it be not sent to foreign parts?'

But Wyclif's attack on the papacy had more to do with the quarrel between the 'regular' clergy, the monks and friars who followed the rules of their order, and the secular clergy responsible to a bishop. The regulars derived their authority from the Pope and came to be seen as agents of a foreign power, just as Communists used to be seen as servants of Moscow. The friars in England, as in France and Italy, were widely seen as seducers of women, dealers in relics and the sale of indulgences, and above all as usurping the power of the parish priests to hear confession and give absolution.

Wyclif went on to preach that confession had no validity unless it was done voluntarily and in public. It was no true sacrament and was quite unnecessary to absolution. He could find only voluntary confession among the Acts of the Apostles. Increasingly Wyclif looked to the Bible as a higher authority than the Pope. He regretted that there was no vernacular Bible except in Anglo-Saxon and French which were becoming almost as remote from the popular tongue as Latin.

Wyclif's increasingly strong sayings and writings were reported back to Pope Gregory XI who made them the subject of a Bull of denunciation. Wyclif was summoned to St Paul's to explain himself before the Bishop of London, William Courtenay. There was an angry confrontation between the bishop and John of Gaunt, who had arrived to support his protégé.

As a hostile biographer, K. B. McFarlane, has pointed out, Wyclif escaped condemnation largely because there was so little heresy in England during the fourteenth century that the papacy never installed an inquisition which might have pressed the charges against him. Whether or not Wyclif was safe from physical persecution, he did not abandon his writing on controversial topics. It was his avowed intention to make the Christian people of England attach more importance to the pulpit than to the sacraments, except that of marriage, which he believed to be necessary for priests as well as for laymen. In this and in his rejection of the supremacy of the Pope, Wyclif was close to the attitude of the Eastern or Orthodox Church which had broken with Rome in the eleventh century. From playing down the importance of the sacraments, Wyclif moved on to question the nature of the sacrament of Communion, in particular the belief that the bread and wine were the actual body and blood of Christ. By casting doubt on transubstantiation, as it is called, Wyclif anticipated the acrimonious religious debate of the seventeenth century which led to civil war in England, Scotland and Ireland.

Wyclif also anticipated most of the attitudes of the seventeenth-century Puritans. He taught that the splendid architecture and gaudy decoration of churches drew people's minds away from their worship. On the question of music in church, Wyclif liked to quote Augustine: 'As oft as the song delighteth me, so oft I acknowledge I trespass grievously.' He disapproved of pilgrimage and could not believe that canonization by Rome created the character of a saint. Rather surprisingly, though, he did not condemn the cult of the Virgin Mary, but wrote a treatise called *Ave Maria* which holds up her life as a model to women.

These were some of the doctrines and attitudes which Wyclif passed on to his little band of followers, who came to be called the Lollards, possibly from a Flemish or dialect word for an idler.

Some of these Lollards were vagrant preachers or 'hedge priests' and seem to have been most numerous in Leicestershire and Herefordshire. But as we shall see in the following chapter, they played no part in the Peasants' Revolt of 1381, although Wyclif was held responsible by many in Parliament and in the hierarchy of the Church. Those who had feared for their lives from the rebels, such as members of Parliament, lawyers and senior ecclesiastics, talked of the Lollard danger as right-wing politicians used to talk of a Communist conspiracy. The monkish chronicler Knighton warned his readers that 'scarcely would there be two men on the road but one of them was a disciple of Wyclif'.

Simon of Sudbury, the Archbishop of Canterbury in 1381, was widely blamed for not having dealt harshly enough with Wyclif several years earlier; Sudbury was one of those murdered by the rebels. When the time came to choose his successor, the obvious man was William Courtenay, the Bishop of London who had summoned Wyclif for questioning at St Paul's in 1377. On that occasion, Courtenay was forced to back down under pressure from Wyclif's friends in court. Now, in 1382, Courtenay, as Archbishop of Canterbury, was hailed as the man to get tough with the Lollards.

The archbishop summoned a council of bishops and theologians to the chapter house of Blackfriars in London to examine the Lollard doctrines. This council included seven bishops, sixteen masters of theology, all of them friars, and another six friars who were bachelors of theology. Not surprisingly, Wyclif condemned it as a council of friars. When the council convened in May 1382, the doctrines contained in a number of propositions were read out 'clearly and distinctly', and the theologians asked to return a few days later and pass formal judgement on them.

When the council returned on 17 May, proceedings were halted by a severe earthquake, which led to panic – not surprisingly, since even the mildest tremors are almost unknown in London or anywhere in the British Isles. Several bishops urged an adjournment but Archbishop Courtenay would not hear of it. According to Joseph Dahmus, the author of *The Prosecution of John Wyclif* and *William Courtenay, Archbishop of Canterbury 1381–1396*, from which this account is taken, Courtenay argued that the earthquake was a good omen. In fact it symbolized the cleansing of the realm of heresy: 'For as air and the spirit of infection are held in the bowels of the earth, and escape by means of an earthquake, though not without great violence, in like manner there are many heresies burned in the hearts of the reprobate of which the kingdom had been cleansed, but not without travail and great effort.'

The idea that an earthquake represented a massive subterranean fart or evacuation must have amused the Wyclifites who enjoyed the medieval legend that the friars resided in Hell, which was also the devil's rectum – a story told in *Le Roman de la Rose*, and repeated by Chaucer in his *Summoner's Tale*:

'Hold up thy tail, thou Satanas,' quod he,
'Schew forth thine ars, and let the friar see
Where is the nest of friars in this place?'
And er than half a furlong way of space,
Right so as bees swarmen out of a hive,
Out of the devil's ers they gonne drive
Twenty thousand friars on a route
And throughout helle swarmed al aboute
And comen again as fast as they may goon,
And in his ers they crepen everichoon.
He clappid his tail agayn and lay full stille.

In spite of the earthquake, the theologians reached agreement that twenty-four of the Lollard propositions were heretical and another six erroneous. Among those condemned as heretical were:

1. That Christ is not present in the altar, identically, truly and really in his own corporeal presence.

7. That God must obey the devil.

8. That if the pope be foreknown [i.e., predestined to Hell] and a wicked man, and in consequence belongs to the devil, he has received no authority over Christ's faithful from anyone, except possibly from the devil.

9. That after Urban VI, no one is to be recognized as pope, but everyone live after the manner of the Greeks [i.e., the eastern orthodox Church] after his own laws.

10. To say it is contrary to sacred scriptures to have temporal possessions.

Among the propositions condemned as erroneous were:

20. That any person who belongs to a religious order is thereby rendered the less capable and fit to observe the commands of God.

22. That members of the clergy who belong to religious orders are not members of the Christian religion.

23. That friars must earn their living by the labour of their hands and not by begging.

24. That anyone who bestows alms on a friar is excommunicated and so is the person who accepts the alms.

It is hardly surprising that a council made up largely of friars should have rejected propositions 20, 22, 23 and 24. It is more surprising that Wyclif should have escaped with his life if he really expressed opinions so clearly heretical as that God must obey the devil, which is the doctrine of the Manichaeans. But as Joseph Dahmus suggests, the propositions may have been a compendium of the kind of views which their enemies attributed to the Lollards.

After the Blackfriars council, Archbishop Courtenay used the threat of a heresy charge to crush Wyclif's supporters at Oxford University but found it harder to deal with the simple Lollards in the countryside, particularly in their strongholds of Leicestershire and the Welsh border. Lollard preachers or 'poor parsons' went on denouncing the papacy, the friars and the 'transubstantiation' of bread and wine at Communion. Work continued on a translation of the Bible which came to be known as Wyclif's, though it was really the work of many hands.

Wyclif's teaching also appealed to an influential group at the court and in the House of Commons, who came to be nicknamed the Lollard Knights. Some were greedy men who wanted to seize the property of the Church in the style of Henry VIII, but others were real religious reformers. The hostile chroniclers Knighton and Walsingham give us the names of ten knights whom they regarded as heretics, such as Sir John Montagu who sheltered Lollard preachers and threw the images out of his chapel. They were forerunners of Sir John Oldcastle who headed a Lollard rebellion in 1417 and was burnt to death as a heretic. The Lollard Knights included friends of Chaucer such as Sir Lewis Clifford and Sir Richard Stury.

Although Archbishop Courtenay's campaign against Wyclif and the Lollards did not amount to persecution or terror, it was enough to make Chaucer more than usually careful, especially since he held office under the Crown. In spite of this, Chaucer's writing on religious matters seems to me heavily weighted in favour of Wyclif's teachings and attitudes.

The very concept as well as the execution of the *Canterbury Tales* might be seen as a satire on pilgrimage, which Wyclif denounced as idolatry and commercial exploitation. Except for the Parson, every one of the men and women in holy orders, as well as their lay accomplices such as the Summoner, are shown as corrupt, selfish, lustful or hypocritical, or all these things at once. The fact that the Friar, the Pardoner, the Summoner and the Prioress are riding to Canterbury 'the hooly blisful martir for to seke' only emphasizes the distance between the Church's theory and practice.

Even before Wyclif began his campaign against pilgrims, the numbers going to Canterbury were in decline. In a sermon on St Thomas's Day 1340, the then archbishop, John Stratford, complained of those who were denigrating the saint. By the end of the century, East Anglian Lollards were chanting derisive songs about 'Thomme of Cankerbury'. Chaucer himself in the *Canterbury Tales* more often mentions Doubting Thomas or Thomas of India than Thomas Becket, and when Alison in the *Miller's Tale* swears by 'Thomas of Kent', it is in a context so obscene that it needs to be read in David Wright's translation:

> It so fell out
> That this Fly Nicholas began one day
> To flirt and play about with this young wife,
> Her husband having gone off to Osney
> (These scholars are so artful, and so sly!)
> And on the quiet caught her by the cunt,
> And said to her, 'Unless I have my way,
> Sweetheart, for love of you I'll surely die.'
> He held her by the haunches hard and tight,
> 'Now let's make love at once,' cried he, 'sweetheart
> Or it's the end of me, so help me God!'
> She bucked and shied like a colt being shod,
> And quickly wrenched away from him her head,
> Saying, 'I'll not kiss you, on my word.
> 'Let go,' she cried, 'now stop it, Nicholas!
> I'll scream for help, I'll rouse the neighbourhood!
> Take your hands off! It's no way to behave!'

But Nicholas began to plead; he made
So good a case, offered himself so often,
That in the end her heart began to soften.
She gave her word, and swore by St Thomas,
That when she saw a chance, she would be his.

The fact that Alison 'swoor her oath by St Thomas of Kent', whose shrine they were on their way to visit, cannot have been lost on the Canterbury pilgrims.

Chaucer agreed with Wyclif that priests should be free to marry, if only to prevent them taking mistresses. This had been a matter of argument since celibacy of the clergy was introduced by the twelfth-century popes; indeed, Henry II invaded Ireland to stop the priests there taking concubines.

Chaucer's Host, Harry Baily, is fond of teasing the clergy about their attraction to women, and why it should not go to waste. He first addresses the Monk, here again in the David Wright version:

'God confound him, I pray, whoever first
Led you to take up the monastic life,
For you'd have been a rare cock with the hens.
If you had freedom, as you have the power,
To copulate as much as you desire,
A fellow like you would have fathered dozens!
For pity's sake, why do you wear the cope?
God damn my soul, but if I were the Pope,
Not only you, but every lusty man,
Tonsure and all, should be allowed a woman;
For otherwise the world is like to perish.
Religion has got hold of all the best;
As for us laymen, we're no more than sprats . . .
No wonder that our wives want to try out
Clerics like you, for you pay Venus' debt . . .'

The Host returns to the theme when he thanks the Nun's Priest for his tale of barnyard fowls:

'Your breeches and your very balls be blessed!
That was a splendid tale of Chanticleer.

But on my word, were you a secular,
Then you'd be a rare cock among the hens! ...
Look at the muscles on this splendid priest!
What a great neck he has, what a broad chest!
And brighter than a sparrowhawk's, those eyes!
What a complexion too! He needs no dyes,
Scarlets from India or from Portugal
To touch it up! Bless you, sir, for your tale!'

Chaucer clearly agreed with Wyclif in regarding the 'regular' clergy, the monks and friars, as more libidinous than the secular or parish priests, and the friars as worse than the monks. The Friar and the Pardoner, who is also a friar, are the two unquestioned villains of the *Canterbury Tales*, and the Parson its only hero among the clergymen. It is true that the Friar's equally loathsome antagonist, the Summoner, is employed by a bishop's court and therefore represents the secular clergy, but then Wyclif detested the English hierarchy almost as much as he did the minions of the papacy. If Archbishop Courtenay had read the *Canterbury Tales*, he would not have liked the *Friar's Tale*, abusing a Summoner, any more than the *Summoner's Tale* of a friar who swindles a poor old lady.

Modern readers who seldom come into contact with the religious orders may wonder why Chaucer portrayed the mendicants as more vicious than the cloistered monks. Apologists for Henry VIII and the dissolution of the monasteries have taught us to think of the monks themselves as idle, greedy and even sinister, while the mendicants are remembered largely by Robin Hood's jovial companion Friar Tuck. Chaucer pokes fun at the Monk and the Prioress but lets them off lightly compared with the mendicants. It is true that the villain of the *Shipman's Tale*, who cheats as well as seduces a merchant's wife, is a monk, but he has won her confidence as a family friend and not, like the friars, by abusing his job of hearing confession.

Chaucer was one of the first English masters of the sermon, which came to be seen as the basis of Protestant worship, as distinct from the Mass, with its emphasis on Holy Communion. Wyclif constantly taught that the proper place of a clergyman was the pulpit, expounding the Bible. When his followers were excluded from their churches, he urged them to preach the Word in the fields and hedgerows. This was the start of the preaching tradition carried on by the seventeenth-century Puritans, the Wesley brothers and more recently by the Presbyterian ministers of Scotland, Northern Ireland and the southern United States.

However, in fourteenth-century England, the sermon was just as important to Wyclif's papal enemies as it was to his Lollard supporters. The friars themselves had learnt from St Francis and St Dominic to become consummate preachers, using the arts of story-telling, humour, mimicry and occasional music to get across their message to a simple congregation. The most famous preacher of the age, the Franciscan San Bernardino of Siena, wanted his listeners to be 'contented and illuminated, not confused'. Like a stand-up comedian, he would tease and engage in badinage with his congregation. He would croak like a frog or crow like a cock (*chichirichi*) to illustrate vanity or pride. Even enemies of the friars such as Jean de Meun or Boccaccio were ready to grant them the gift of the gab.

Chaucer acknowledged this in his *General Prologue* to the *Canterbury Tales*:

> A Frere there was, a wanton and a merry,
> A preacher and a full solemne man.
> In all the orders four is none that can
> So much of dalliance and fair language . . .
> And certainly he had a merry note.
> Well could he singe and pleyen on a flute.

The finest sermons in the *Canterbury Tales* come from members of those religious orders that Wyclif opposed. The *Pardoner's Prologue and Tale* is a histrionic masterpiece, comprising a lecture on drunkenness as well as a crime story. The Prioress and the Second Nun show that cloistered women can preach as well as worldly friars; moreover, their tales are proof that Chaucer remained a devotee of the Blessed Virgin Mary, an issue that later divided Protestants from Catholics.

Most readers would say that the finest sermon is in the *Nun's Priest's Tale*, in which Chaunticleer the barnyard cock represents human pride, lust and vanity. It also touches upon the controversies of Wyclif's Oxford, echoing the Latin words of Wyclif: '*Omnia quae eveniunt de necessitate eveniunt*' (All things that come about come about from necessity).

Protestants who would like to believe that Chaucer was a Wyclifite have looked for support to the 'poore Parson' whose character sketch in the *General Prologue* sets him apart from such affluent hypocrites as the Monk, the Friar, the Pardoner and the Prioress. Moreover, like Wyclif, the Parson took his religion from the Bible:

> He was also a lerned man, a clerk
> That Cristes gospel gladly wolde preach;
> His parishioners devoutly wolde he teach . . .
> Wide was his parish, and houses far asunder,
> But yet he lafte not for rain or thunder,
> In sickness and in mischief to visite
> The farthest in his parish, small and great,
> Upon his feet, and in his hand a staff.
> This noble example unto his sheep he gaf,
> That first he wrought, and after that he taughte,
> Out of the gospel he those wordes caughte . . .
> But Cristes love, and his apostles twelve,
> He taught, and first he followed it himselve.

Early on in the *Canterbury Tales*, the Parson arouses hostility among the other pilgrims. When the Host rudely calls for a story, the Parson reproves him for swearing, a practice frowned on by Wyclif and his followers. The Host then calls him 'Jankin', a derisive term for a priest, and even a 'Loller' or Lollard:

> Our Host answered 'O Jankin, be ye there?
> I smell a Loller in the wind,' quod he . . .
> 'Abyden, for Goddes dign passioun,
> For we shall have a predicacioun [sermon]
> This Lollere will prechen us somewhat.'

The Shipman, who is the next to tell a tale, then joins in accusing the Parson of wanting to spread some heresy, by sowing weeds in the 'clean corn' of the faith.

These exchanges lead one to suppose that the *Parson's Tale* will be a 'dissertacioun' of Wyclif's views, especially when it is known that Chaucer himself had friends among the Lollard Knights. We learn from the chroniclers that as early as 1382 Sir Thomas Latimer, Sir

Richard Stury and Sir Lewis Clifford had forced their tenantry to attend Lollard sermons, and stood by in arms to ensure that the preachers were not molested. In the very year of the *General Prologue*, 1387, these same knights, as well as Sir John Clanvowe, Sir William Neville and Sir John Montagu, supported a written attack on the morals of the friars. This group, who were known as the Hooded Knights (*Milites Capuciati*) because they did not doff their caps on taking Communion, joined with John of Gaunt in 1388 and again in 1390 in signing protests to the Pope about the corruption of the clergy and what they called the heresy of the official Church. All of these men except Montagu were Chaucer's friends, while John of Gaunt was his patron at court.

With friends like these, one might have expected that Chaucer would make the *Parson's Tale* a sermon as brilliant as the *Pardoner's* or the *Nun's Priest's Tale*, but preaching the message of Wyclif. Unfortunately for the readers, the *Parson's Tale* is written in prose, after a brief introduction explaining why he rejects rhyme, fables, jests and 'rum-rum-ruf' or north of England dialect stories:

> Thou getist fable noon i-told for me,
> For Poul that writeth unto Timothe
> Repreveth them that flee from sothfastnesse
> And tellen fables and such wrecchednesse.
> Why should I sowen chaff out of my fist
> When I may sowen wheat, and that the best? . . .
> I will full fain at Cristis reverence
> Do you plesaunce lawful as I can.
> But truste well, I am a southern man
> I can not jest 'rum-rum-ruf' by letter,
> And, Got wot, ryme I holde but littel better . . .

The *Parson's Tale* is not a story or even a sermon so much as a treatise on penance. There is no discernible Lollard teaching or even an exposition of 'Cristes lore and his apostles twelve' but much concerning the seven deadly sins and the formulation of confession, topics sanctioned and even prescribed by the hierarchy, then as now. It is principally interesting for the way Chaucer translates biblical texts from Latin or French into popular English and how this compares with the King James or Authorised Version two centuries later. To take an example:

Of the springing of sins, as Saint Paul saith, in this wise; that right as by man entered first into this world, and through that syne death, right so thilke deth entered into alle men that synneden; and this man was Adam; Of that like Adam took we thilke synne original, for of him fleshly descendit be we alle, and engendrit of vile and corrupt matiere . . .

The Parson comes down especially hard on lust in all its manifestations, in or out of wedlock: 'Lo what sayeth Saint Mathew in the gospel that whoso seeth a woman to coveytise of her lust, he hath done lechery with her in his herte.'

The *Parson's Tale* sounds less like a statement of Wyclif's views than Chaucer's own penance for lustful passages in the other *Canterbury Tales*. The impression is reinforced when Chaucer adds to his most famous work an epilogue 'The Preces de Chauceres', recanting most of his life's work. The poet begs the readers to pray that God will have mercy on him and forgive his sins, namely his 'writings in earthly vanities', in which he includes *Troilus and Criseyde*, the *Book of the Duchess*, the *Legend of Good Women*, and the *Canterbury Tales* itself – in fact everything except his Boethius translation and various homilies and lives of the saints.

There are several explanations of why Chaucer ended his most famous work with the timid *Parson's Tale* and a grovelling recantation. He may never have taken Wyclif seriously or meant the Parson to be a Loller. He may have been feeling remorse for the sins of his youth and anxious to make his peace with the established Church. Or he may have abandoned the Lollards when they were on the run and in danger of persecution.

As Chaucer was writing the *Canterbury Tales*, his friends Sir Richard Stury and Sir Lewis Clifford were wavering in their support of Lollard principles. As late as 1395 they were listed as advocates of the Wyclifite 'Twelve Conclusions' but Stury was forced to recant under royal pressure and soon afterwards died. Clifford in 1402 not only recanted but informed on his associates, and two years later wrote a will denouncing himself as a false traitor to God, unworthy to be called a Christian, even asking to be buried in the furthest corner of the churchyard. We can only surmise that Chaucer too had repented of his opinions. Besides, during the 1390s Chaucer was worried about his job and pension, not to mention his burial in Westminster Abbey, as demonstrated in his poem 'Complaint to His Purse'.

Perhaps we can best understand Chaucer's religion by thinking of him as Anglican, even before the creation of the Church of England. In his attitude to religion, as to politics, war, chivalry, class and marriage, Chaucer was easygoing, ready to hear an opposite view and always quicker to laughter than to rage. He could make fun of the Pardoner and the Friar but he did not hate them. Unlike Swift or George Orwell, he did not suffer from righteous indignation. Had Chaucer been born into the seventeenth century, it is hard to see him taking up arms to defend the Divine Right of Kings or Wyclif's successors, the Cromwellite Puritans. He would let a barnyard fowl argue the case for Predestination, but would not go to the stake for an abstract principle, nor send others to the stake for theirs.

11

The Peasants' Revolt

IT WAS IN 1381 that for the first and last time in its history England came close to a bloody revolution, comparable with France's in 1789 or Russia's in 1917. Although the uprising was not confined to the countryside, it came to be known as the Peasants' Revolt because its aims included an end to feudal obligations. Later the Peasants' Revolt was seen as a Protestant manifestation, presaging King Henry VIII's breach with Rome. The Whig historians of the nineteenth century interpreted the Peasants' Revolt as a stage in the progress towards parliamentary democracy. By the sixth centenary in 1981, the Peasants' Revolt had come to be seen by Marxists as an example to those who still hoped for a Communist Britain. Although Chaucer had witnessed the Peasants' Revolt in two of the most affected regions, Kent and London itself, and clearly referred to it in his poems, he characteristically did not take sides. However, his most political poem, *The Nun's Priest's Tale*, gives us an indication of how he might have regarded socialism, that great obsession of the twentieth century.

Contemporary chroniclers as well as modern historians connected the Peasants' Revolt with the labour shortage caused by the Black Death. As early as 1349 a monk, William Dene of Rochester, complained: 'There was so marked a deficiency of labourers and workmen of every kind at this period that more than a third of the land in the whole realm was let idle. All the labourers, skilled or unskilled, were so carried away by the spirit of revolt that neither King nor law nor justice could restrain them. . .'.

During the next thirty years the Crown and Parliament tried in vain to make the peasants return to their old contracts and feudal obligations. In his *Chronicon*, Henry Knighton tells us that Edward III 'sent notice into all the counties of the realm that reapers and other labourers should not receive more than they used to take under a penalty . . . but the labourers were so arrogant and so hostile that they took no notice of the King's mandate, and if anyone wanted to employ them, he was obliged to pay them whatever they asked, and either to lose his fruit and crops or satisfy at will the labourers' greed and arrogance.' Another hostile chronicler, Sir John Froissart, thought the revolt had its genesis in the 'ease and riches that the common people were possessed of'. In this he anticipated De Tocqueville's theory about the French Revolution: that people grow more rebellious as their condition improves. It is significant the Peasants' Revolt was fiercest in the richest parts of England such as Kent, Essex, Suffolk and London the capital, but scarcely affected the poorer and still strongly feudal north. Nor does it seem to have touched the Lollard strongholds of Leicestershire and the Welsh border.

The immediate cause of the Peasants' Revolt was the government's attempt to pay for the war in France by imposing a poll tax or standard levy on every adult person in the realm. Since Richard II, who had succeeded to the throne on the death of his grandfather, Edward III, in 1377, was still a minor, the poll tax has often been blamed on his guardians and legal counsellors, especially the Treasurer, Robert Hales, and Richard's uncle John of Gaunt, the Duke of Lancaster. However, it was Parliament in the previous year which had thought up the poll tax as a way of shifting the cost of the war from themselves, the ruling class, on to the common people.

The Peasants' Revolt began in the Essex marshes when the Brentford tax commissioner, Thomas Bampton, tried to collect the levy from the three coastal villages of Fobbing, Corringham and Stanford-le-Hope. These three little communities are now more than a mile from the estuary of the Thames, though at Fobbing one can still see the steps running down from a wharf to the old harbour. In Chaucer's time, this stretch of the Essex coast had a reputation for smuggling and piracy, as we might guess from the Merchant's concern about keeping the route safe between the mouth of the Orwell and Holland. The tradition dies hard, for the district is still involved in the shipment of drugs, and recently witnessed a series of murders between rival gangs.

It was into these sinister marshes that Thomas Bampton in 1381 sent his men to collect the poll tax. The instigator or 'prime mover' of the revolt was Thomas, a baker of Fobbing, according to the *Anonimalle Chronicle*. Under his leadership, the people of Fobbing,

Corringham and Stanford-le-Hope assembled to the number of a hundred or more, and told Thomas Bampton to his face that they would not deal with him or give him any money. The monkish chronicler goes on to say that when Bampton ordered arrests to be made, the men of the three villages beheaded two of his clerks, and sacked the house of a local official, drinking three barrels of his wine. Another hostile chronicler, Walsingham, says that the rebels now constituted an army, 'some equipped with rusty swords, some merely axes and others with bows, more reddened with age and smoke than old ivory, while many of their arrows had only one plume'.

The *Anonimalle Chronicle* says that these Essex men were ready to kill all lawyers, jurors and civil servants, though not apparently private landowners. As the revolt spread north into Suffolk and Cambridgeshire, it soon became clear that its driving spirits were disgruntled clergymen and secular townspeople hostile to the established Church. 'For periods of between a weekend and a fortnight,' writes R. B. Dobson in *The Peasants' Revolt of 1381*, 'much of East Anglia was plunged into a state of near anarchy. In June 1381, Norfolk, Suffolk and even Cambridgeshire were on the verge of experiencing a general revolution.'

The Suffolk clergyman John Wrawe was by a long shot the nastiest of the leaders of the rebellion. He first made his appearance at Liston, then moved to Bury St Edmunds, the wealthiest town in the county of Chaucer's ancestors. The merchants and burgesses of Bury had long envied the land and privileges of the abbey there, even burning it down in 1327. 'Destroyed by the townspeople,' says an inscription over the main gate today, 'and rebuilt 1327.'

A mob in Bury, inflamed by Wrawe's oratory, hunted down the prior, 'a worthy and artistic man, surpassing in his musical skill the Thracian Orpheus, the Roman Nero and the British Belgabred', to quote once more from the *Anonimalle Chronicle*. They caught him and cut off his head, as they did to his friend, the judge Sir John Cavendish. The rebels then thought it amusing to mount the heads on poles and use them as puppets, putting the judge's mouth at the ear of the prior, as though saying confession, or making them kiss one another on the lips.

From Bury St Edmunds, Wrawe sent out demands for gold to other rich towns such as Thetford and Sudbury. Rebel forces also moved on Cambridge, whose university aroused the same hatred among the townspeople as the abbey at Bury. On Sunday 16 June 1381, the mayor, bailiffs and burgesses of Cambridge compelled the masters and scholars of the university, under pain of death and destruction of their property, to renounce all kinds of franchise and privilege granted to them by all kings of England 'since the beginning of time'.

Although the town of Cambridge especially hated Corpus Christi College, the act of compulsion must have been aimed at the late Edward III whose college of Trinity had been founded four years earlier. The rabble of Cambridge emerged in their true colours. At the House of the Carmelites, later the site of Queens', they ransacked the chapel and seized the books which were supposed to become the university library. All these were dragged out to the market square and burnt. It was said that an old woman, Marjorie Starre, while hurling books and documents on to the blaze, shouted, 'Away with the learning of clerks! Away with it!'

The conduct of Marjorie Starre no doubt inspired Chaucer's account of the Cambridge town-versus-gown dispute in the *Reeve's Tale*. As we have seen, the Miller had already portrayed the Reeve as the Oxford carpenter who is cuckolded by his undergraduate lodger. The Reeve gets his revenge by making a butt of the Miller who lives at 'Trumpyngtoun nat fer fro Cantebridge', a bullying, swaggering rogue who has married the parson's daughter. The Miller has enriched himself by selling adulterated flour to Cambridge colleges such as King's Hall (or Solar Hall as it was called because of its bay-windowed rooms) which later merged into Trinity. Two undergraduates from Northumberland ask the Warden if they can try to foil the Miller's trickery (here in the David Wright version):

Of course this miller had the monopoly
Of grinding corn for the surrounding country,
And in particular for a great college
That people call the Solar Hall at Cambridge,
Whose wheat and malt were always ground by him.
It happened that its manciple suddenly
Fell sick; most people thought that he would die.
At this the miller soon began to steal
A hundredfold more of their corn and meal;
He'd only filched politely, earlier;
But now he was a barefaced plunderer.

And so the Warden makes a great to-do,
For which the miller doesn't give a straw,
Loudly defies and swears it is not so.
Now at the college of which I've been speaking
Were two young hard-up students, headstrong chaps,
And game for anything. And just for kicks
They plagued the Warden for short leave, until
They'd leave to see their corn ground at the mill.
And each of them was game to stake his neck
The miller couldn't pinch a half a peck
Of corn off them, whether by force or cheating;
And in the end the Warden gave permission.
One of them was called John; Alan the other;
Both born in the same town, a place called Strother.

John and Alan eventually manage to cheat the Miller, and in the meantime seduce his wife and daughter. The Reeve in his tale has not only 'quitted' the Miller but quitted the reputation of Oxford against its rival.

Soon after the Peasants' Revolt began in June 1381, it spread from Essex over the Thames to the Kent estuary towns on the route of the pilgrims from Southwark to Canterbury. At Erith, the site of one of the royal palaces, the leader of the revolt was a soldier, Abel Ker, who had fought for several years in France. At Rochester, as at Fobbing in Essex, a baker was the spokesman of hostility to the poll tax; he managed to win control of the four-storey castle. Kent also produced the two rebel leaders, Jack Straw and Wat Tyler, whose names have lived on in the history lessons and folklore. Both men were linked to the salacious legend that royal officials rudely examined adolescent girls to see if they were liable for the poll tax.

The story was first told by Henry Knighton, a monkish chronicler with the mind of a modern tabloid journalist. He relates how one of the tax commissioners came to a certain village and called together all the men and women: 'Then, horrible to relate, he shamelessly lifted the girls to see which of them had enjoyed intercourse with men.' This tale was seized upon by later historians who understood that the test was not of the girl's virginity but whether she yet had sufficient pubic hair to be classified as nubile. In *The Life of Jack Straw*, published in 1594, when the Peasants' Revolt had come to be seen as an anti-papist demonstration, the hero is heard telling the tax collector: 'My daughter's not fourteen years old, therefore she goes clear.' Collector: 'And because thou sayest so, I should believe thee?' Jack Straw: 'Choose whether thou wilt or not. Thou gettest no more of me.' Jack Straw then kills the collector.

In a seventeenth-century booklet *The Just Reward of Rebels*, a similar story is told of Wat Tyler and his fourteen-year-old daughter Alice. In this version the tax collector takes the girl in his arms 'and most uncivilly and dishonestly took up her clothes and bared her before her mother, saying he would see whether she had any *pubes* upon her or no, and in many places the like barbaric demeanour had been used; at which her mother, hearing her daughter screech out and seeing how in vain she struggled against him, being therefore grievously offended, she cried out also and leaving the house ran into the street among her neighbours, clamouring that there was one within who would ravish her daughter.' According to *The Just Reward of Rebels*, Wat Tyler returned at this point and struck the taxman 'such a blow on the pate that he broke his skull and the brains flew about the room'.

Whether or not their daughters had been insulted, both Straw and Tyler joined in a protest march on Canterbury, where the rebels were led by John Ball. Like Wrawe in Suffolk, Ball was a disgruntled priest who had twice been imprisoned by Simon Sudbury, the Archbishop of Canterbury. He is also credited with the most famous slogan of the Peasants' Revolt, the rhyming question: 'When Adam delved and Eve span/ Who was then the gentleman?'

For these two reasons, Ball became a hero first to the Protestants, who saw the Peasants' Revolt as an anti-papal demonstration, and then to the left who saw it as England's moment of revolutionary glory. The nineteenth-century socialist and pre-Raphaelite painter William Morris wrote *A Dream of John Ball* in which he imagines him as a tall, big-boned man with a ring of dark hair surrounding his priest's tonsure, a shaven face with bluish chin, a large firm mouth and grey eyes which at times could light up his whole face. Others might imagine Ball with grey straggly hair, aggrieved, shifty eyes and a self-righteous smirk for the television cameras.

Archbishop Sudbury twice jailed Ball and twice released him, for which leniency he paid with his life. After the first occasion, Sudbury complained that Ball 'had slunk back to our diocese like the fox that eludes the hunter and feared not to preach and argue both in churches and churchyards, and also in markets and other profane places, putting about scandals concerning our own person and what is worse concerning the Holy Father himself'.

If Ball sometimes attacked the Pope, he usually took up a tone of generalized moral outrage – as, for instance, in this doggerel quoted in *Chronicon Angliae*:

Now reigneth Pride in price
And Covertise is holden wise
And Lechery withouten shame
And Gluttony withouten blame
Envy reigneth with treason
And Sloth is take in grete season
God give aid for now is
The time. Amen.

Ball frequently preached on the theme that 'things would not go well with England until everything was held in common', as well as asking his listeners: 'Are we not all descended from the same parents, Adam and Eve?' However it seems that John Ball was one of the few socialist voices of that time. John Wyclif and his Lollards attacked the wealth of the Church but not of the Crown or the secular lords.

William Langland's allegorical poem *Piers Plowman* is rightly seen as expressing popular discontent with the vice and luxury of the age, but it does not advocate redistribution of wealth. When Piers Plowman asks Lady Holy Church, '. . . the money in this worlde/ That man so fast holdeth/ Tell me to whom, Madame, the tresor appendeth?', Lady Holy Church replies with the words of Christ about rendering unto Caesar that which is Caesar's, then goes on to explain: 'Rightful reason should rule you alle/ And kind wit be warden your wealth to keep.'

About the middle of June 1381, the rebels in Kent and Essex began to converge on London. Although these ramshackle armies on either side of the estuary seem to have kept in touch, there is no reason to think that they followed the orders of some revolutionary organization or 'Great Society', as it was called by the fearful Londoners. In their progress westward, the rebels frequently broke into big houses to burn the manorial rolls, leases and deeds relating to feudal tenure but seldom destroyed buildings or murdered the occupants. The exceptions were manors belonging to government counsellors such as John of Gaunt, the Duke of Lancaster, or the Treasurer Robert Hales, who were held responsible for the poll tax. In Kent the rebels caught up with the king's mother Princess Joan, who was hurrying back to London from a pilgrimage to Canterbury. Since she was Countess of Kent in her own right and popular enough to be known as 'The Fair Maid of Kent', Joan was treated with deference by the rebels, though her lady attendants had to endure some ribaldry.

By the time the rebels had reached Blackheath, the authorities in London were still undecided on how to deal with the crisis. When the King's Council met at the Tower of London, its most experienced member, John of Gaunt, the Duke of Lancaster, was campaigning in Scotland, and some of the earls present were scarcely older than the boy King Richard. The Treasurer Robert Hales and the Lord Chancellor Archbishop Sudbury were nervous and close to panic – with good reason, for they would soon be murdered.

At a separate meeting in Guildhall, the Lord Mayor of London William Walworth and his aldermen showed more resolution. On 12 June Walworth ordered the closure of London Bridge and the main gates into the city. He also sent delegates to Blackheath to talk to the rebel leaders. In turn, the rebels sent one of their hostages, the constable of Rochester Castle, to pledge their loyalty to the king and request a meeting. On Sunday 13 June, King Richard attended Mass in the chapel of the Tower, then boarded a barge for Greenwich where a crowd of 50,000 rebels (according to the *Anonimalle Chronicle*) were gathered on the south bank of the Thames, facing another 60,000 or so on the Essex side. The barge came to a halt about twenty yards from the river bank, amid a hubbub of noise but with no sign as yet of physical assault. The rebel leaders quickly wrote and sent to the royal barge a list of their demands, including the heads of Robert Hales ('Hobbe the robber'), Archbishop Sudbury and Thomas Bampton, who had provoked the first trouble in Essex. Since these demands were unacceptable, the barge turned back upstream without an arrow fired.

The alderman John Horne, who had been sent to Blackheath to try to persuade the insurgents to return to their homes, had become convinced that their leaders were reasonable men who could be won over by friendliness, or what we might now call a dialogue. He apparently told them that most of the Londoners were sympathetic and would welcome them into the city. Accordingly, on 13 June, Alderman Horne gave orders to let the Kentish men cross London Bridge and the Essex men to enter the city at Aldgate.

Although London bolted its doors and shuttered its windows, the strangers at first behaved politely. The Kent men crossing London Bridge respected the newly erected shrine to Thomas Becket, and at first refrained from attacking the Temple, the seat of Robert Hales and his Knights of St John of Jerusalem. The Londoners were relieved to find that at first the rebels paid for their food, and refrained from annoying the local women. However, during the course of a hot June day, the crowd became thirsty, and drank to revive themselves, upon which they remembered their oath to avenge themselves on the king's uncle, John of Gaunt, the Duke of Lancaster, whose Savoy Palace beside the Thames was the wealthiest private residence in the country. From Smithfield, the City and Fleet Street, a call went up for a march on the Savoy. The mob broke down the gates where the present Savoy Hotel gives on to the Strand, and then in the words of the *Anonimalle Chronicle*:

> They entered into the place and came to the wardrobe. And they took all the torches they could find, and lighted them and burnt all the sheets and coverlets and beds and head-boards of great worth, for their whole value was estimated at 1,000 marks. And they burnt the hall, and the chambers and all the buildings within the gates of the said place or manor . . . they found three barrels of gunpowder, and thought it was gold or silver and cast it into the fire, and the powder exploded, and set the hall in a greater blaze than before, to the great loss and damage of the Duke of Lancaster.

The mob made its way to the cellars and opened the ducal wine. Those who were sober enough then started to pilfer the valuables on their own account, while those who were drunk passed out and were burnt to death in the general conflagration. Wat Tyler did his best to prevent the criminals taking over and had a man executed for stealing a silver goblet.

Having wreaked revenge on John of Gaunt, the mob went east to Clerkenwell, where Robert Hales and the Knights of St John had taken over the priory formerly owned by their rival order, the Templars. Since Hales was sheltering in the Tower of London, the rebels vented their anger on some Flemings, who were dragged from behind the altar and murdered.

This was the start of a massacre of the Dutch or Flemish weavers who had been brought to England by Edward III to build up a national cloth manufacture.

The hard work and enterprise of these immigrants did not endear them to the indigenous people. Like the Jews who had been expelled or hanged by Edward I in the thirteenth century, the Flemish were often engaged in money-lending and other disreputable business. As Ronald Webber explains in *The Peasants' Revolt*, which appeared at the time of the sixth centenary, the Flemish were prominent in the 'Stews' or brothels across the river in Southwark. 'The Stews belonged mainly to [Mayor William] Walworth and were run chiefly by madames brought over from Flanders for this purpose. The brothels had signs painted on the wall facing the river, signs such as a boar, cardinal's hat, bull and swan . . . At the rear of the Stews was the Bear Garden, another source of much disturbance.'

Perhaps because of its brothels with their Flemish madames, Southwark suffered worse than London north of the river from violence and looting. This may have influenced Chaucer's fellow poet and friend John Gower, who lived there during the troubles and now lies buried in Southwark Cathedral, one of the buildings sacked in 1381. He expressed his contempt for the Peasants' Revolt in his poem *Vox Clamantis* by interspersing the Latin verse with the vernacular names of the rebels:

> *Watte vocat, cui Thomme venit neque Symme retardat*
> *Bette que fibbe sumul Hykke venire iubent:*
> *Colle furit quem Geffe iuvat nocumenta parantes*
> *Grigge rapit, dum Dawe strepit, comes est quibus Hobbe.*

On 14 June King Richard left the safety of the Tower to talk with the men from Kent at Mile End. In his absence, the rebels surrounding the Tower were either admitted or forced an entry as Froissart suggests: 'for no sooner had the King come out than Wat Tyler, Jack Straw and John Ball entered the castle by force with some four hundred men and went from room to room until they found the Archbishop Simon of Canterbury.

That wise and worthy man, Chancellor of England, who had just celebrated divine service and said Mass before the King, was seized by these scoundrels and instantly beheaded. So was the Grand Prior of the Hospital of St John [Sir Robert Hales, the Treasurer] and a Franciscan friar who was a physician attached to the Duke of Lancaster, which was the reason why he was killed, to his master's subsequent anger, and a sergeant-at-arms of the King called John Legge. Their four heads were placed on long lances and carried before the crowd through the streets. When they had sported with them long enough, they set them up on London Bridge, as though they had been traitors to the realm.'

This account by Froissart and those of the other chroniclers do not explain how the rebels made their entrance into the Tower of London, the most impregnable fortress in the land. Was there someone in the King's Council, like Alderman Horne in the City of London, who hoped to win over the rebels by a policy of appeasement?

The Peasants' Revolt reached a climax on 15 June, when Richard II once more confronted the rebels, this time at Smithfield where they had made an encampment. Although Froissart's well-known account is, as usual, heavily biased against the insurgents, it conveys the haphazard nature of the events, and the undecided behaviour of the participants. The leaders in 1381 had no more idea of what was happening than those in the British General Strike of 1926, the Paris *événements* of 1968, or the overthrow of Communism in Eastern Europe during the 1980s:

> On the morning of the same day [15 June], all the bad men, led by Wat Tyler, Jack Straw and John Ball, had assembled together and gone to a confabulation at Smithfield where the horse market is held on Fridays. There were over twenty thousand of them . . . Many more were still in the town breakfasting in the taverns and drinking Languedoc wine and Malmsey in the Lombards' houses, free of all charge.*
>
> Anyone able to provide them with food and drink was only too happy to do so. The crowds assembled at Smithfield had with them the royal banners given them on the previous day, and the scoundrels were contemplating running amok through London and looting and plundering. The leaders said: 'We have achieved nothing yet. The rights the

---

* The Lombard merchants, like the Flemings, had been the victims of popular envy and xenophobia. However, Froissart may be suggesting that the Lombards supported the revolutionaries, as Jews were accused of doing in the twentieth century.

King has granted us won't bring us in much. Let's sack this rich and mighty town before the men of Essex, Sussex, Cambridge . . . Lincoln, York and Durham come – for they will all come.'

They were all agreeing to this plan when suddenly the King appeared, accompanied by perhaps sixty horsemen. He had not been thinking about them but had been intending to go on and leave London behind. When he reached the Abbey of St Bartholomew which stands there, he stopped and looked at the great crowd and said that he would not go on without hearing what they wanted. If they were discontented he would placate them.

When Wat Tyler saw this, he said to his men: 'Here's the King. I'm going to talk to him. Don't budge from here unless I give you the signal, but if I make this sign (he showed them one) move forward and kill the lot. Except the King. He's young, we will make him do as we want, we can take him with us anywhere in England and we shall be lords of the realm.'

With that he struck his spurs into a horse he had mounted, left his companions and went straight up to the King, going so near that his horse's tail was brushing the head of the King's horse. The first words he said to the King were: 'Well, King, you see all those men over there?' 'Yes,' said the King. 'Because they are all under my command. They've sworn their sacred oath to do anything I tell them.' 'Good,' said the King. 'I see nothing wrong in that.' 'So,' said Tyler, who only wanted a quarrel, 'do you think, King, that these men here, and as many again in London, all under my command, are going to leave you without getting their letters?' (These were the letters the rebels wanted, freeing them from all feudal ties and obligations.)

'It's all in hand,' said the King. 'They have to be drawn up separately and given out one after another.'

At this point, according to Froissart, Wat Tyler looked across at one of the King's squires who was behind Richard and bore his sword. Tyler had encountered this man before and now picked a quarrel.

'Well,' said Tyler, 'so you are here. Give me your dagger.' 'Never,' said the squire, 'why should I?' The King looked at his servant and said 'Give it him.' Very unwillingly the squire did so. When Tyler had it, he began toying with it and then turned again to the squire and said 'Give me that sword.' 'Never,' said the squire, 'it's the King's sword. It's not for such as you. You're only a boor. If you and I were alone in this place, you would never have asked me that – not for a heap of gold as high as that church of St Paul's over there.' 'By God,' said Tyler, 'I'll have your head if I never touch food again.'

Just then the Lord Mayor of London (Walworth) arrived on horseback with a dozen others, all fully armed beneath their robes, and broke through the crowd. He saw how Tyler was behaving and said to him in the sort of language he understood: 'Fellow, how dare you say such things in the King's presence? You're getting above yourself.' The King lost his temper and said to the Mayor: 'Lay hands on him, Mayor.' Meanwhile Tyler was answering: 'I can say and do what I like. What's it to do with you?' 'So, you stinking boor,' said the Mayor who had once been a King's Advocate, 'you talk like that in the presence of the King, my natural lord? I'll be hanged if you don't pay for it.' With that he drew a great sword he was wearing and struck. He gave Tyler such a blow on his head that he laid him flat under his horse's feet . . . One of the King's squires called Sir John Standish dismounted and thrust his sword into Tyler's belly so that he died.

The abrupt killing of Tyler must have paralysed the crowd, for nobody moved against Walworth, or the king himself. Later historians, like contemporary chroniclers, have praised young Richard for his composure in the face of the rebels at Greenwich, Mile End and Smithfield. Indeed, he behaved more sensibly at the age of fourteen than he did later on in his reign when he had a higher opinion of his own dignity and wisdom.

Richard has been accused of reneging on the concessions he made when the rebels were threatening London. He went to Essex to warn his subjects on 23 June that they should not believe the rumour that he supported the rebellion. When a deputation in Essex demanded ratification of the promises made at Mile End, specifically on the question of the labour laws, he is said to have answered, 'Villeins ye are and villeins ye shall remain.' After another outbreak of violence in Billericay, Richard issued a proclamation from Chelmsford on 2 July that, by the advice of his Council, he was revoking the letters patent of pardon 'lately granted in haste' to the rebels.

In the judicial inquiry which then, as now, followed any public disturbance or catastrophe, the king and his new chief justice made a tour of the recently disaffected areas. In Hertfordshire as in Essex, the severity of the sentences shocked even the monkish chroniclers who were ill-disposed to the rebels, but there was no reign of terror comparable with James II's 'Bloody Assizes' after the Monmouth rebellion of 1685. According to May McKisack in her Oxford *Fourteenth Century*:

> On the whole, the judicial proceedings reflect credit on the government. No mass reprisals were allowed; there were no tortures and very few attempts to convict without trial, and a surprisingly large number of persons whose guilt seems to have been clear were either acquitted or punished with moderation; Jack Straw was executed in London after confessing his guilt, John Wrawe was condemned to death after an elaborate trial in the course of which he tried to turn King's evidence; the Cambridgeshire captains were all hanged; and John Ball was tried and executed at St Albans . . . On 30 August the King ordered that all further arrests and executions should cease, and all cases pending be transferred to the King's bench. The effect of this order was virtually to put an end to the capital sentences; and the parliament which met in the autumn, though it confirmed the King's revocation of his charter of manumission to the rebels, demanded also a general amnesty for all but a few specified offenders.

The causes of the Peasants' Revolt were clear even to contemporaries. The desire to be free of villein status and of the hated labour laws was manifest in the burning of manorial records and in the attacks on judges and lawyers. Sir Richard Waldegrave, the Suffolk Knight who acted as Speaker in the Parliament of 1381, blamed the rising on the extravagance of the court and the royal household, the burden of taxation and the inadequacy of national defence, which especially worried Kent and Essex, the counties most vulnerable to invasion.

Those politicians and priests who favoured conspiracy theories continued to blame the Peasants' Revolt on the Lollards, the friars or the Great Society (*magna societas*) whose cryptic circulars were reproduced by the chroniclers. One chronicler, Walsingham, anticipated the attitude of modern sociologists by blaming the crimes of the Peasants' Revolt on the fault of the nation at large. After singling out the mendicant friars for contributing to the trouble, Walsingham ended with the catchphrase: '*Sed ne videamur livore scripsisse* [But lest it should seem that we have written these things out of spite] *fateamur nos omnes in culpa* [let us admit that we are all guilty]'.

Chaucer's attitude to the Peasants' Revolt – as to Wyclif, the war, the Jews and the women's question – has to be surmised from his writings and from his position in society. As a civil servant, a member of Parliament and justice of the peace for Kent, one of the most affected counties, Chaucer must have deprecated the loss of life and property. Chaucer's long-time friend and patron John of Gaunt, the Duke of Lancaster, had suffered personally from the burning of the Savoy Palace and the murder of his physician in the Tower of London. Even if Chaucer had been a secret democrat and socialist, hundreds of years before such ideas were entertained, he would have been prudent enough to keep his thoughts to himself at a time of insurrection. However, the evidence of the poetry suggests that Chaucer was neither a democrat nor a socialist, except in the utopian world of *The Former Age*, his version of Boethius, which could also be taken as an endorsement of pacifism, naturism and New Age diet.

As I have tried to suggest with reference to the *Clerk's Tale*, in which a ruler is told by his subjects whom and when he should marry, Chaucer had no great respect for the voice of the people and its spokesmen. As we shall see in *Troilus and Criseyde*, Chaucer is contemptuous of the Trojan parliament and even inserts a sly reference to Jack Straw. The Greeks have threatened to call off their truce and what we might call the 'peace process' if Troy does not hand over Criseyde in exchange for a captured warrior, Antenor. Hector, the brother of Troilus, speaks out against this deal, but is shouted down by the 'breme' or angry voice of the demagogues who want peace at any price, like those who tried to appease Jack Straw and Wat Tyler.

> Hector which that wel the Grekes herde
> For Antenor how they wolde have Criseyde
> Gan it withstonde and sobrely answerde
> 'Sires, she is no prisoner' he seyde;
> 'I noot on yow who that this charge layde
> But on my part, ye may eft-sone him telle,
> We usen here no women for to selle.
>
> The noyse of people up-starte then at ones,
> As breme as blaze of straw y-set on fyre
> For infortune it wolde, for the nones
> They sholden her confusion desyre . . .

There is a more specific reference to Jack Straw in that wonderful passage from the *Nun's Priest's Tale* when Chaunticleer has been carried off by the fox and the whole farm sets up a hue and cry:

> The silly widow and her doughtres two
> Herden these hennes cry and maken woe
> And out at dores starte they anon
> And saw the fox towards the grove gon
> And bar upon his bak the cok away;
> They criden 'Out! harrow and wayleway!
> Ha, ha, the fox!' and after him they ran,
> And eek with staves many another man;
> Ran Colle our dog, and Talbot and Garlond,
> And Malkyn with a distaff in her hond;
> Ran cow and calf and eek the veray hogges
> Were sore fered for barking of the dogges
> And shouting of the men and wymmen eke,
> They ronne that they thought their herte breke.
> They yellen as feendes do in helle;
> The duckes criden as men would them kill;
> The gees for fere flowen over the trees;
> Out of the hyves came the swarm of bees;
> So hideous was the noise, a *bencite*!
> Certes Jack Straw and al his compagnie
> Ne made shoutes never half so shrille
> When that they wolden any Flemyng kille,
> As on that day was made upon the fox.

After reading this passage it is possible to imagine that the whole of the *Nun's Priest's Tale* is a political satire, not least because of its likeness to that twentieth-century masterpiece, George Orwell's *Animal Farm*. Indeed, Stephen Coote says in his introduction to the *Nun's Priest's Tale* in the Penguin Critical Studies series: 'While we should always remember that the great chase in the *Nun's Priest's Tale* is above all things comic – in terms of the poem a superb explosion of noise after so much debate – such an activity could not but have its darker, more ambiguous side in the 1390s. These villagers may seem harmless enough, but even as we think of them as actively protecting the widow's property, so we should place this in a wider context of men and women rising up to protect what they now thought of as theirs: the wealth of the country.'

Unlike Mr Jones in the Orwell story, the owner of the farm in the *Nun's Priest's Tale* is not a greedy exploiter but a widow bent with infirmity, and condemned by poverty to a life of thrift and privation:

> A pore widow somewhat stooped in age
> Was whilom dwelling in a narrow cottage
> Bisyde a grove, standing in a dale.
> This widowe, of which I telle you my tale,
> Syn that same day that she was last a wif
> In paciens led a ful symple lyf.
> For litel was her catel and her rent;
> By housbandry of such as God her sent
> She fond herself and eek hir daughtres two.
> Three large sowes had she and no mo,
> Three kyne and eek a sheep that highte Malle.
> Ful sooty was her bower and eek hir halle
> In which she eet ful many a slender bit,
> Of poynaunt sauce hir needed never a whit.
> No deynte morsel passed through her throte
> Her dyet was according to her cote.
> Repletion had never made her sick;
> Ful modest diet was al her physick,
> And exercise, and labour and singyng.
> The qoute stayed her not in her daunsing,
> The apoplexie shooke not hir head;
> No wyne drank she, neither white ne red;
> Hir bord was served most with white and blak
> Milk and brown bread, in which she found no lak,
> Rost bacoun and som tyme an egg or two . . .

We get the impression that Chaucer admired the poor widow as much as he did the poor Parson and his brother the Ploughman, as described in the *General Prologue*:

> A better priest I trow there nowhere none is,
> He wayted after no pompe or reverence

Nor made himself spiced in conscience
But Criste's love and his apostles twelve
He taught, and first he followed it himselve.
With him there was a Ploughman, was his brother,
That had i-lad of dung ful many a fother.
A trewe worker and a good was he
Lyvinge in pees and perfit charitee . . .
He wolde threshe and thereto dyke and delve
For Cristes sake with every poore wight
Withouten hyre if it laye in his might.
His tythes payed he ful faire and wel
Both by his own work and his catel.

Both Chaucer and Orwell took a delight in the life of the farm and the character of its denizens, which gives their stories a realism and humour seldom found in animal fables of ancient or modern literature, but a comparison of the *Nun's Priest's Tale* with *Animal Farm* reveals once again the difference between a religious and a political view of the world. As a man of the fourteenth century, Chaucer regarded life in terms of the Christian faith and specifically of his own and mankind's salvation. As a man of the twentieth century, Orwell regarded life in terms of political ideology, specifically of the struggle between his own democratic socialism and what he discerned as the evils of Communism and fascism.

The *Nun's Priest's Tale* is above all a sermon, the wittiest and the wisest preached on that pilgrimage to Canterbury. After the Prioress's diatribe against the Jews, the Monk's ponderous homily on the vagaries of fortune, and the Pardoner's cheeky attack on his own failing, avarice, the Nun's Priest uses a barnyard fable to launch a wide-ranging commentary on the topics of the day such as medicine, dreams, Predestination and, above all, marriage.

After making fun of Chaunticleer as a pretentious intellectual, the Nun's Priest relates how he falls into the jaws of the fox through pride and lust, for he is led astray by his passion for Pertelote. He condemns Chaunticleer because he copulates 'more for delyt than world to multiply'. Nor does it make things better that Pertelote as his favourite hen is in effect Chaunticleer's wife, for as Chaucer's Parson explains in his sermon on adultery: 'The third species of avouterie is sometimes between a man and his wife.'

Moreover, Chaunticleer's lust for Pertelote is only one expression of his kingly pride and complacency as the cock of the roost:

> And with that word he flew down from the beam
> For it was day, and eek his hennes all,
> And with a chuck he gan them for to calle,
> For he had found a corn lying in the yard.
> Royal he was, he was no more afeard;
> He feathered Pertelote twenty times
> And trod as often, ere that it was prime.
> He looketh as it were a grim lioun;
> And on his toes he roameth up and down
> He deyned not to set his foot to grounde.
> He chuckith when he hath a corn i-founde
> And to him rennen then his wifes alle.

Although Chaunticleer could be seen as one of the leaders of the Peasants' Revolt, or indeed as the king, John of Gaunt or the Archbishop of Canterbury, I think Chaucer intended the tale as a sermon or moral lesson.

Fourteenth-century men like Chaucer lived under the guidance of the Church and could not separate secular from religious affairs. Fourteenth-century politicians were just as greedy as ours for wealth and office, but did not try to disguise that greed with high-sounding principles of political philosophy. From the reign of Edward I, it had become accepted in England that the propertied classes, as represented in Parliament, should raise the money to pay for the government of the kingdom. Parliament slowly acquired the unwritten right to advise the monarch on how the money was spent and whom he should have as his ministers. It was not until the reign of Richard II that Parliament tried to shift the burden of tax from themselves, the propertied class, to the people at large through a poll tax.

After the warning given them by the Peasants' Revolt, the ruling classes in England kept to the unwritten law of 'No taxation without representation'. When in the eighteenth century they disregarded this principle, and tried to make the American settlers pay for the cost of the British army, the subsequent protest led to another revolt and the founding of the United States.

12

Troilus: War and Chivalry

CHAUCER WAS IN HIS fifties when he reached the top of his twin careers as civil servant and poet, and wrote *Troilus and Criseyde* which many consider his masterpiece.*

As early as 1374, Chaucer had been appointed Comptroller of the Customs and Subsidies of Wools, Skins and Tanned Hides, but in spite of the grandiose title he was obliged to keep the accounts in his own hand and do his duties in person, or hire a substitute when he went abroad. Then in 1382 he was promoted to the post of Comptroller of Petty Customs, which gave him a full-time deputy. In 1385 he was appointed a justice of the peace for the county of Kent, and the following year a member of Parliament for the county, presumably in the king's party, although no record exists of his having spoken.

These appointments suggest that Chaucer stayed out of trouble during the Wyclif affair and the Peasants' Revolt. His patron at court, John of Gaunt, had begun an affair with Katherine de Swynford, née de Roet, who happened to be the sister of Chaucer's wife Philippa.

Although there were already hints of trouble between the Duke of Lancaster and his brother the Duke of Gloucester in their rivalry for influence over their nephew King Richard II, Chaucer remained in favour at court throughout the 1380s, if not till the end of his life. He continued to turn out poetry for the amusement of the courtiers, including the *House of Fame*, the *Parliament of Fowls*, the *Romaunt of the Rose* and *Troilus*.

---

* Although for reasons of brevity I shall call the work *Troilus*, it is important to bear in mind that Chaucer's name for Cressida was pronounced Cri-*side*, which is often used as a rhyme. I have mainly used the Nevill Coghill version, which brilliantly renders the flow of Chaucer's narrative without disturbing the sense.

An illustrated frontispiece to a fifteenth-century manuscript shows Chaucer reading *Troilus* to the king and his court from a kind of pulpit or lectern. The poem also contains a compliment to the king's first wife Anne of Bohemia, whom he married in 1381 when they were both fifteen. It comes when Troilus first sees Criseyde in the temple:

Among thise othere folk was Criseyda,
In widowes habite black but natheless
Right as our firste lettre is now an A
In beautee first so stood she matcheless.

Such gallant compliments had been expected from court poets since the days when Eleanor of Aquitaine surrounded herself with troubadours in her exile at Poitiers, and it appears that Anne of Bohemia entered into the spirit of chivalry. At any rate she affected to be annoyed with Chaucer for having shown Criseyde unfaithful in love, and subjected him to the penance of writing the *Legend of Good Women* to make amends to her sex. But although *Troilus* was written to be recited to the king and later became a subject of the queen's light-hearted banter, it is not for those reasons a trivial work, performed under royal command. On the contrary, it is Chaucer's most ambitious poem which for centuries was regarded as his masterpiece, combining the comedy of the *Canterbury Tales* with a theme of 'double sorrow', for which he coined a new word in the English language: 'Go litel book, go litel my tragedye.'

As well as containing some of Chaucer's most beautiful poetry, *Troilus* reveals a narrative skill, a sympathy and feeling for character that have led some critics to call it the first great novel in English. *Troilus* is also the key to an understanding of Chaucer and his age. It is here that we see a distillation of his ideas from a lifetime of reading, from Virgil and Ovid in classical times, from Boethius in the interim age, from the early Christian fathers down to St Bernard, from the twelfth-century troubadours, *Le Roman de la Rose*, and then Dante, Petrarch and Boccaccio, who had the same story in his *Filostrato*.

In *Troilus*, more than in all his other works, not excluding the *Canterbury Tales*, we get an idea of what Chaucer thought about chivalry, love and the seemingly endless war against France. Also, although *Troilus* takes place in the pre-Christian era, it gives a truer idea than any other poem of what Chaucer really believed about religion, life and death. Finally, because of its timeless and universal appeal to human beings, *Troilus* gives us a means of comparing Chaucer with writers and artists of other ages and countries, with Shakespeare's long poems as well as his play *Troilus and Cressida*, with Byron and Pushkin, the novels of Dickens, Jane Austen and Tolstoy, and not least with the makers of the Hollywood film *Casablanca*, which echoes the story of Troilus and Cressida.

Chaucer's poem, like Shakespeare's play, takes place near the end of the siege of Troy, and revolves around the love affair between Troilus, a son of Priam, the King of Troy, and Criseyde, the daughter of Calkas, a seer and politician who has defected to the side of the Greek besiegers. When Criseyde is expelled from Troy to join her father, she abandons Troilus for Diomede, one of the Greek captains.

Chaucer's *Troilus* differs from most later stories of Troy, at any rate in the English language, because it is seen from the Trojan rather than from the Greek perspective, and it mostly takes place inside the besieged city rather than in the encampment of the besiegers. Even in Shakespeare's *Troilus and Cressida*, written two centuries later, a far greater importance is given to Greeks such as Achilles and Ulysses, who were more famous with English audiences. This is largely because the later accounts of the fall of Troy were based on Homer's *Iliad* and *Odyssey*, while Chaucer's version came from the Latin poets, who sympathized with the Trojans as the ancestors of the Romans.

Like Dante before him, Chaucer was ignorant of ancient Greek and does not appear to have read any Homer in translation. He probably shared the received fourteenth-century view that Homer's work was spurious because it showed gods fighting with men, because it was written long after the fall of Troy, and because it was biased against the Trojans. In a passage about historians of Troy in the *House of Fame*, Chaucer remarks:

> Oon seyde Omere made lyes
> Feigning in his poetryes
> And was to Grekes favorable
> Therefore held he it but fable.

Chaucer took his view of the Trojan War from Virgil and Ovid, who propagated the legend that Aeneas and other survivors of the débâcle sailed west to begin a new civilization in Rome, now ruled by their patron the Emperor Augustus who, they claimed, was a descendant of Aeneas. As the Roman empire and later the Christian Church became divided between a Greek and Latin wing, so the western or Roman Catholic part identified with the Trojans. During the Middle Ages the French and the English, as well as the Italians, came to see the Trojans as the ancestors of their nation. The seventh-century Frankish chronicler Fredegarius wrote that a party of Trojans, after the fall of their city, had settled between the Rhine, the Danube and the sea under their ruler, King Francio. The idea that the Trojans were the ancestors of the Franks and the French may explain why the capital of the Tricasses people in the Champagne-Ardennes came to be given its present name Troyes.

In ninth-century England a similar legend began, that Aeneas's great-grandson, Brutus or Brut, had created the British people and founded the city now called London. The story was popularized by the twelfth-century writers Geoffrey of Monmouth and Wace of Jersey. Chaucer's friend John Gower was among those Englishmen who took the Trojan connection seriously and wanted London to be renamed Troynovant.

While Virgil and Ovid gave a poetic account of the fall of Troy, Chaucer looked for historical verification to two very much later Latin authors in prose: Dares Phrygius, who gave the Trojan viewpoint, and Dictys Cretensis, who spoke for the Greeks. In a list of notable figures on the Trojan side, Dares mentions Troilus and 'Briseida', which would eventually transmute into Cressida. His Briseida has several features in common with Chaucer's Criseyde, including *superciliis junctis* (joined eyebrows) and *capillo flavo et molli*, corresponding to 'the mighty tresses of her sunnish hair'.

Dares mentions Diomed among the notable Greeks but does not link him with Troilus and 'Briseida'. Their conjunction in a triangle of love and hatred can first be found in the twelfth-century *Roman de Troie* by Benoit de Sainte Maure, who also invented Cressida's lament at the shame she has brought on herself: 'Henceforth no good will be written of me, nor any good song sung. Evil and senseless was my thought when I betrayed my lover, for he deserved it not at my hands . . .'*

It is worth remembering that Benoit de Sainte Maure was writing

---

* The translations of Benoit and Boccaccio are from R. K. Gordon, *The Story of Troilus*, University of Toronto Press, 1978.

under the patronage of Eleanor of Aquitaine who must have identified with Criseyde, as with Helen, whose abandonment of the Greek Menelaus for Paris, the brother of Troilus, was the cause of the war. Eleanor's divorce from King Louis VII of France to marry King Henry II of England was blamed, even in Chaucer's time, for the war between the two countries.

Dante followed the Latin poets in siding with the Trojans and regarding them as the ancestors of Rome and therefore modern Italy. Dante's guide through Hell, the poet Virgil, ranks with Homer among the chroniclers of the fall of Troy. Dante condemned to his inferno the prophet Calchas, father of Cressida, who had foreseen the defeat of Troy and therefore thought it expedient to desert to the Greeks. Indeed, Dante reserved a circle of Hell for what we would now call futurologists, who were condemned forever to look back over a shoulder, so that when they wept their tears ran down the crack in their buttocks.

Dante also describes an encounter with Diomed, the Greek who seduces Criseyde when she is parted from Troilus. Diomed and his friend Ulysses burn in torment for having invented the stratagem of the Wooden Horse to overthrow Troy from within. Chaucer's Diomede uses the same cunning to take advantage of Criseyde's loneliness in the camp of the Greeks.

As well as taking ideas from Dante, Chaucer translated Petrarch's Sonnet 88 for the 'Song of Troilus' in Book One of his poem: 'If no love is, O God what fele I so.' But if Chaucer borrowed ideas from Dante and Petrarch, he lifted the bulk of *Troilus* from Boccaccio's poem *Il Filostrato* (The man prostrated by love). Boccaccio in turn had taken his story from Virgil, Dictys, Dares, Benoit and an Italian version of these, *Historia Trojana* by Guido della Colonna. As he says at the start of his poem, Boccaccio seized on the story of Cressida because it reminded him of his own fickle mistress, Maria d'Aquino, or Fiametta, 'the little flame' who had just 'departed the delightful city of Naples and gone to Sannio'. Resolved to relieve his suffering in a poem, Boccaccio found 'none more suited to meet my need than that of the valiant young Troilus'. True to his purpose he turns himself and Fiametta into Troilus and Cressida, down to their meeting at a Naples church, now a temple in Troy. Boccaccio improved on Benoit's *Le Roman de Troie* by adding another important character, Pandarus, a cousin and friend of Troilus, who advises him on how to win Cressida's love.

Although *Troilus* is half as long again as *Filostrato*, it stays fairly close to Boccaccio's original and a French translation he used as a help to his Italian. The puzzle remains that neither in *Troilus* nor in the *Knight's Tale*, which is derived from Boccaccio's *Il Teseida*, does Chaucer credit the name of the Italian. He frequently mentions that he is taking his story from some foreign authority, but pretends that this is a Latin writer 'Lollius'. Perhaps Chaucer thought it was grander to quote from the Latin 'Lollius' than from a modern Italian. The plagiarism does not discredit Chaucer. Almost anyone who can read both Italian and English would judge *Troilus* a better poem than *Filostrato*, though the same would probably not be said of the *Knight's Tale* and *Il Teseida*.

Whereas *Filostrato* is a young man's poem, full of conceit and self-dramatization, *Troilus* reflects the wisdom, sadness and experience of Chaucer's middle age.

> Before we part my purpose is to tell
> Of Troilus, son of the King of Troy,
> And how his love-adventure rose and fell
> From grief to joy, and, after, out of joy,
> In double sorrow; help me to employ
> My pen, Tisiphone, and to endite
> These woeful lines, that weep even as I write . . .
>
> And pray for those who now are in the case
> Of Troilus, which you shall later hear,
> That love may bring them to his heaven of grace;
> And also pray for me to God so dear
> That I may show, or at the least come near
> To show the pain of lovers suffering thus,
> In the unhappy tale of Troilus.

Chaucer's expressions of sorrow for his hero and heroine should not be written off as a literary device. The reader quickly senses that Chaucer has come to love these creatures of his imagination, just as Dante loved Paolo and Francesca, Shakespeare loved Romeo and Juliet, and Tolstoy loved Prince Andrei and Natasha. Just like any star-crossed love affair in literature, the opera, the theatre or the cinema, these 'woeful lines' have us reaching for our handkerchiefs.

Even if Chaucer himself called *Troilus* a 'tragedye', for the first time using the word in the English language, it is not a tragedy in Aristotle's sense of inspiring pity and terror, for the second of these emotions is absent. Chaucer himself may have studied a Latin translation of Aristotle, the bedside book of his Clerk of Oxenford, but western Europe was not yet aware of Aeschylus and Sophocles, nor, obviously, of Racine and Shakespeare. It is the essence of tragedy that the heroes and heroines bring down destruction upon themselves through some flaw of character such as Othello's jealousy or Macbeth's ambition, but this does not apply to Troilus and Criseyde who are victims of circumstance or the turn of Fortune's wheel. It is war that has blighted the love of Troilus and Criseyde, as well as giving their story its timeless poignancy.

Although Chaucer begins his poem before the fall of Troy, the story is overshadowed by a sense of impending catastrophe in which Troilus and Criseyde are willy-nilly involved:

> It is well known the Greeks in all their strength
> Of arms, and with a thousand ships, set out
> For Troy, and they besieged it at great length
> – Ten years it was before they turned about –
> With one design (by many means, no doubt)
> To take revenge upon the ravishment
> Of Helen by Paris; that was why they went.

Chaucer then introduces us to Calkas, who was to desert to the Greeks and advise them on how to capture Troy through the stratagem of a wooden horse.

> Now it fell out that living in Troy town
> There was a lord of great authority,
> Calkas by name, a priest of high renown
> And learned in the art of prophecy;
> He, by the answer of his deity,
> Phoebus Apollo, whom they also call
> Apollo Delphicus, knew Troy must fall.
>
> And so when Calkas knew by calculation,
> And by the answer this Apollo made,

The Greeks would mount so great a preparation
That Troy must burn and be in ruin laid,
He sought to flee the city, to evade
The doom he knew she was to undergo,
To be destroyed whether she would or no.

And so this wise, foreknowledgeable man
Took purpose quietly to slip away,
And, to the Greek host, following his plan,
He stole in secret from the town, and they
Received him courteously, with great display
Of reverence; they trusted to the skill
Of his advice to ward off every ill.

When this was known, noise of it far and wide
Spread through the town and it was freely spoken
'Calkas has fled, the traitor, and allied
With those of Greece!' Their vengeance was awoken
Against a faith so treacherously broken.
'He and his family and all he owns
Ought to be burnt,' they shouted, 'skin and bones!'

Before explaining how the defection of Calkas threatened the life of his daughter Criseyde, Chaucer inserts a stanza to remind his readers of what was to be the fate of Troy:

But how this city came to its destruction
Is not my present purpose to relate,
For it would make too long an introduction
So to digress, and you would have to wait;
But, of the Trojan war and Trojan fate,
All those who can may study the vagaries
In Homer and in Dictys and in Dares.

The story of 'how this city came to its destruction' was certainly well known to most of Chaucer's contemporaries, as to most Englishmen down to the twentieth century, but it is always in danger of being forgotten. It was Virgil in the *Aeneid* who immortalized the stratagem of the Wooden Horse. After ten years under siege, the Trojans were so sick of the war that they longed to believe the Greeks were too. The Greek captains Diomed and Ulysses knew how to exploit war weariness. They ordered their army on to the ships and made as if to return to the Aegean, but in fact disembarked at an island near Troy. Before leaving, the Greeks built a huge wooden horse which they said was an offering to the goddess Minerva. The defector Calchas let it be known to his fellow Trojans that if they accepted the Wooden Horse, their city would be protected. A double agent, Sinon, was sent into Troy to spread what we would now call disinformation.

According to Virgil, the Trojans could not agree on whether to trust the Greeks. 'Some gazed at the fatal offering to the virgin goddess Minerva and marvelled at the huge size of the horse. Thymoetes was the first to urge them to drag it inside their walls and set it in their citadel, whether it was treachery that made him speak or whether the fates of Troy were already moving towards that end. But Capys and those of sounder judgement did not trust the offering. They said it was some trick of the Greeks and should be thrown into the sea or set fire to, or that they should bore holes in its hollow belly and probe for hiding places.'

Then Virgil describes how the seer Laocoon 'came running down in a blaze of fury, shouting from a distance as he came: "O you poor fools! Are you out of your minds, you Trojans? Do you seriously believe that your enemies have sailed away? Do you imagine Greeks ever give gifts without some devious purpose? Do not trust the horse, Trojans. I fear the Greeks, especially when they bear gifts.'

These last words of Laocoon, *Timeo Danaos, et dona ferentes*, became one of the most familiar Latin tags in the English language, repeated over the centuries by politicians and newspaper leaderwriters whenever peace was discussed with a foreign enemy.

Laocoon was so enraged with his gullible fellow countrymen that he hurled his spear at the side of the Wooden Horse, alarming the Greeks who lay inside it. However, the Trojans ignored his warning. Then two serpents came writhing out of the sea and seized Laocoon and his two sons, strangling and devouring them. Nor did the Trojans heed the similar warning of the prophetess Cassandra, whose fate it was to be able to see the future but never to be believed. But when the Greeks leapt out of the Wooden Horse and opened the gates of Troy to their army, Cassandra was raped and murdered.

Cassandra's name and Laocoon's warning against the Greeks 'even when bearing gifts' are constant reminders not to indulge in wishful thinking and in particular not to trust those who mean to destroy us.

The story of the Wooden Horse was just as relevant in the fourteenth century when cities frequently came under siege and tried to buy off their enemy. Occasionally the attacker was lenient, but more often the victor behaved as the Greeks did to the Trojans, or as Sir John Hawkwood's White Company did to the burghers of Cesena. The danger of letting an enemy into the city was shown once again in the Peasants' Revolt when the rebels crossed London Bridge and even entered the Tower.

By reminding us from the start of the forthcoming betrayal and fall of Troy, as told in the *Iliad* and the *Aeneid*, Chaucer increases the sense of doom which runs through the poem. Criseyde's misery and shame at the treachery of her father Calkas is made more poignant by our awareness that he is planning the Wooden Horse. Chaucer's emphasis on the youth and courage of Troilus, who rides out daily to battle against the Greeks, only serves to remind us of his eventual pitiful fate as described by Virgil:

Troilus, a mere boy, and no match for Achilles, had lost his armour and was in full flight. His horses had run away with the chariot and he was being dragged along helpless on his back behind it, still holding on to his reins. His neck and hair were trailing along the ground and the end of his spear was scoring the dust behind him.

Some of the other famous Trojans appear in Chaucer's *Troilus*. It is Hector who first takes Criseyde's side against those who want to kill her because of her father's treachery:

This Hector was by nature full of pity
And saw she was in misery and dread
One of the fairest too in all the city
So in his kindness, cheering her, he said
'Your father's treason – put it out of your head!
A curse upon it! You yourself in joy
Shall stay amongst us, while your place is Troy!'

It is Cassandra the prophetess who warns her brother Troilus that, when Criseyde goes to the camp of the Greeks, she will be unfaithful to him with Diomed. Even Helen of Troy and her lover Paris appear at a dinner party given for Troilus and Cressida by Pandarus.

Through Pandarus, the gossip and social fixer, Chaucer conveys how life and love take on a new intensity during a time of danger and siege. This was a phenomenon all too familiar in fourteenth-century Europe and down to the present day. We have heard how the elderly poet Guillaume de Machaut, during the siege of Reims, imagined himself as a warrior on the battlements of Troy, and no doubt Chaucer, in the besieging army, imagined what it was like to be among the Greeks.

The same heightened sensibility must have been present in south-east England in 1940 during the Blitz and fear of invasion, for many survivors now concur with Churchill's boast of the Royal Air Force at the time that this was their 'finest hour'. But the atmosphere of Chaucer's Troy or Reims in 1359 was probably more akin to civil wars between people of similar race and language, to the United States in 1861–5, to Spain, Vietnam and Yugoslavia. When a pair of young lovers from opposite sides were killed in Sarajevo in 1992, the newspapers called them Romeo and Juliet, but they were more like Troilus and Criseyde.

Although *Troilus* is set in the ancient world and still rings true in the twenty-first century, it is also the clearest expression of Chaucer's views on chivalry, the medieval code of conduct in war and love. The concept of chivalry started about the time of Charlemagne, when Christian Europe was facing the first Islamic onslaught. Two of the first heroes of chivalry were the Frankish knights Roland and Oliver, who were killed at the Roncevalles Pass in the Pyrenees through which Chaucer himself had travelled on his mission to Spain. The exploits of Roland and Oliver were a favourite subject of verse and song for the troubadours who flourished in south-west France from the tenth century onwards. Their *gestes* or stories of feats of arms inspired the early crusaders and generations of knights down to the age of Chaucer. But while the early *gestes* were devoted to deeds of combat, the troubadours and poets found that their women listeners demanded a feminine and romantic interest.

In the *General Prologue* of the *Canterbury Tales* Chaucer describes two practitioners of chivalry in the 'verray parfit gentil Knight' and his son the amorous Squire, who steps straight out of the *Romaunt of the Rose*. But it is Troilus who combines the bravery of the old Knight with the youthful exuberance of the Squire to produce Chaucer's model of chivalry. The gusto and apparent admiration with which Chaucer recounts his hero's prowess in battle cast doubt on the theory that Chaucer disapproved of war and chivalry.

When Pandarus undertakes to plead the cause of Troilus with Criseyde, his niece, he emphasizes the young man's valour before turning the conversation around to love:

> So after that with many happy rallies,
> Gay looks and gossip, talk began to range;
> They joked on this and that, and there were sallies
> On many matters, pleasant, deep and strange,
> Such as good friends together will exchange,
> When newly met; and then she asked of Hector,
> Scourge of the Greeks, the town's wall and protector.

> 'He's very well, thank God,' said Pandarus,
> 'Save for a slight arm-wound – not to be reckoned
> As serious; and then there's Troilus,
> His fresh young brother, Hector, indeed, the Second;
> There's one who has followed virtue where she beckoned,
> A man all truth, as noble as his birth,
> Wise, honoured, generous – a man of worth.'

> 'O I'm so glad! And Hector's better since?
> God save them both and keep them from all harms!
> How nice it is, how fitting to a Prince
> To be so valiant in the field of arms!
> And to be so well-natured! That's what charms
> Me most; such goodness and such strength, I mean
> So royally combined are seldom seen.'

Pandarus persists in comparing Troilus with his more famous brother, until at last Criseyde has to concur:

> 'By God,' she said, 'of Hector that is true,
> And it is true of Troilus, I agree:

Everyone talks of what they've seen him do
In arms, day after day – so gallantly!
And then at home he is all courtesy
And gentleness, in fact he wins attention
From everyone whose praise is worth a mention.'

Having won his point, Pandarus goes on to tell of the latest exploits of Troilus:

'You certainly are right in what you say'
Said Pandar, 'anybody's heart would warm
To see him as I saw him yesterday!
Never fled bees in such a mighty swarm
As fled the Greeks; he was in fighting form,
And through the battlefield, in every ear,
There ran no cry but "Troilus is here!"

'Now here, now there, he hunted them and coursed them;
Nothing but Greek blood! There was Troilus
Dealing out doom; he wounded and unhorsed them
And everywhere he went it happened thus;
He was their death, but shield and life to us;
That was a day! Not one dared make a stand
Against him, with his bloody sword in hand.'

After a few more words in praise of Troilus, 'the friendliest fellow, considering his rank, I ever met', Pandarus abruptly leaves, understanding that he has roused Criseyde's curiosity, and it is not till later that he reveals how Troilus, the hero, is dying for love of her since he saw her in the temple. Now Criseyde in turn becomes interested in Troilus but does not return his love till one day she sees him coming back from the battlefield. Here Chaucer suggests that Criseyde may have been one of those women who were excited by bloodshed and battery in the joust, as today they might be in the boxing ring or at the motor races:

This Troilus sat high on his bay steed,
Fully and richly armed, showing his face.
His horse, being wounded, had began to bleed;

He rode him homeward at a gentle pace,
And truly such a sight of knightly grace,
As seen in him, was never seen before,
Even in Mars, who is the god of war.

His helmet, which was hewn in twenty places,
Hung by a tissue down behind his back;
His shield was battered in by swords and maces,
With arrows lodged in it in many a crack
That had pierced horn and rind and sinewy pack;
And still the shout went up 'Here comes our joy,
And, next his brother, holder up of Troy!'

Like every young lover in medieval romance, Troilus suffers the physical torments of love, from sleeplessness to fainting fits and even a trance indistinguishable from death. Only the intervention of Pandarus prevents such histrionics becoming absurd.

Although Criseyde has more to lose if the love affair becomes public knowledge, she is generally more level-headed and cool than Troilus, in part because she trusts his discretion:

She found him so dependable in all,
So secret, so obedient to her will,
That she could truly feel he was a wall
Of steel to her, a shield from every ill;
To trust in his good management and skill
She was no more afraid; he seemed inspired
(No more afraid, I mean, than was required).

Troilus in turn is so jealous of Criseyde's reputation that he will not take up her cause in parliament in case this reveals their association. He continues to worry about her honour even when she has left him for Diomede.

Even Pandarus, whose name has become a synonym for pimp, is eloquent on the need for discretion. 'The first virtue is to keepe tongue,' he says, pointing out that sexual boasters are often liars.

'O tongue, alas, that has so often torn,
And from so many a lady fair of face,

The cruel cry "Alas that I was born!"
And has kept fresh so many a girl's disgrace,
When that is boasted of in any case
Is oftenest a lie, when brought to test;
Braggarts are natural liars at the best.'

In the superb passage where Criseyde debates in her own mind
whether to start an affair with Troilus, she rehearses his noble qualities
and his kindness, his high position at court which ensures her
protection, and not least her need for a man in her life. But above
all she wants to conform to the rules of chivalry that govern a lady in
her position:

'Let us suppose the worst that could befall
People might know he was in love with me,
Would that dishonour me? Why, not at all!
Can I prevent him? Not that I can see.
One hears about such cases constantly;
A man will love a woman without permission
From her; is she the worse for that condition?

'Think, too, that he is able to pick out –
Out of the whole of Troy – the loveliest
To be his love (her honour not in doubt);
For he is out and out the worthiest
Except for Hector, to save his life now lies in me!
But such is love and such my destiny.

During his courtship of Criseyde and later when they are sleeping
together, Troilus never neglects his military duties:

In all the dangers of the town's defences
He was the first to arm him as a knight,
And certainly to trust the evidence
Was the most dreaded soldier in a fight,
Except for Hector; hardiness and might
Came to him out of love – the wish to win
His lady's love had changed him so within.

Even during the pauses in the fighting, Troilus behaves like a fourteenth-century knight:

> In time of truce, out hawking he would ride,
> Or else out hunting – lion, boar, or bear –
> (For lesser beasts than these he left aside);
> And riding back, would often be aware
> That she was standing at her window there,
> Fresh as a falcon coming from her pen,
> And she was ready with a greeting then.

The tragedy that divides Troilus and Criseyde is brought about by a change in the fortunes of war. The Greeks beat the Trojans in a battle and capture their general, Antenor. At the suggestion of Calkas, the Greeks offer to hand back Antenor in return for Criseyde. When the exchange is debated by the Trojan parliament, Hector takes the side of Criseyde. However, the members of parliament insist on exchanging Criseyde for Antenor, who, as Chaucer reminds us, was soon to betray the city to the Greeks.

> 'Hector!' they cried. 'What evil spirits inspire
> You thus to shield this woman, and to lose
> Prince Antenor? That is no way to choose.'

When parliament votes to send Criseyde back to her father, Troilus at first considers leaving Troy and the war to start a new life with the woman he loves. But honour and chivalry soon reassert themselves. Criseyde too is against a plan that would ruin both his and her reputations:

> 'As for the thing you spoke of – thus to go,
> Abandon all your friends and steal away,
> May God forbid you ever should do so
> For any woman! Troy has need today
> Of all her men; and there is this to say;
> If this were known, my life and your good name
> Would lie in balance. Save us, Lord, from shame!
> What do you think people round about
> Would make of it? That's very easily said;

They'd think, and they would swear to it no doubt,
It was not love that drove you, but you fled
Out of voluptuous lust and coward dread.
Then all your honour would be lost, my dear,
That honour which has ever shone so clear.'

Here Criseyde too is obeying the rules of chivalry:

'And think a little of my own good name,
Still in its flower; how I should offend,
What filth it would be spotted with, what shame,
Were we to run away, as you intend
What justice could I ever hope to win?
I should be lost; that would be grief and sin.'

The code of chivalry which governs the rules of war is even more strict when applied to affairs of the heart. So when Criseyde reproaches Troilus for even having considered deserting his post, she is also fearful about her own reputation. Their love affair is conducted throughout by the rules laid down in the *Song of Roland*, the story of Sir Lancelot and the *Roman de la Rose*.

13

Troilus: Chaucer and the Novel

While working within the conventions of poetic chivalry, which still held sway at the court of Richard II, Chaucer allowed his characters to develop as human beings with their distinctive charm and foibles. Chaucer's originality is obvious when we compare the three main characters in his *Troilus* with those in *Filostrato*.

Chaucer's hero, like Boccaccio's Troilo, begins as a vain and callow young man who chases women but laughs at the very idea of falling in love; however, he soon develops into a worshipper who cares about Criseyde more than about himself. He not only becomes a braver warrior but a better person, more at ease with himself and the world at large:

> For he became the friendliest of men,
> The noblest, the most generous and free,
> The sturdiest too, one of the best that then
> In his own times there were, or that could be.
> Dead were his jesting and his cruelty;
> His loftiness, the arrogance that hurt you,
> Yielded their place, exchanging with a virtue.

When Boccaccio's Troilo hears that Criseyde is to be sent away, he shows no concern for her feelings in his nakedly egotistical outburst: 'What shall I do, poor wretch that I am, if I lose Criseida in this way? How much better were death for me, or never to have been born. Alas, what shall I do? Despair is in my heart. Ah death, come to me who crave thee.'

Unlike Troilo, who wallows in adolescent self-pity, Chaucer's Troilus goes to the temple to pray and to meditate on the workings

of Fortune, before he and Criseyde debate their future. In deference to
her feelings, it is decided that Criseyde shall join her father but come
back to Troilus within ten days. On the morning of the tenth day, by
which Criseyde has promised to return, we the readers know that she
has betrayed him, but Troilus is waiting eagerly at the gate of Troy.
His slow realization of her betrayal turns Troilus into a tragic figure
and makes this a painful passage to read.

> Then Troilus said to Pandar with a frown,
> 'For all I know, it will be noon for sure
> Before Criseyde will come into the town;
> She has enough to do and to endure
> To win her father over, nothing truer,
> For the old man will force her to have dinner
> Before she goes – God torture the old sinner!'

Morning becomes afternoon and Troilus convinces himself that
Criseyde must have been forced to stay with Calkas very late. He
goes to make sure that the porters keep the gates open:

> Day dwindled fast, night fell and the moon hove
> Into the sky. Still there was no Criseyde . . .

Troilus now persuades himself that she was planning to ride back
secretly under cover of darkness.

> 'We've nothing else to do, and anyhow –
> Look there she is, I see her! Yes, it's she!
> O Pandarus will you believe me now?
> Heave up your eyes, look there, man! Can't you see?'
> Pandar replied: 'It's not like that to me.
> All wrong again. You gave me such a start;
> The thing I see there is a travelling cart.'

The days go by but still Troilus cannot bring himself to lose faith in
Criseyde:

> The third, the fourth, the fifth, the sixth ensued
> After those ten long days of which I told;

His heart between the fears and hope renewed
Half trusted to her promises of old;
But when at last he saw they would not hold
And there was nothing left for him to try,
He knew he must prepare himself to die.

Cassandra warns Troilus that Criseyde has deserted him for Diomede, which Criseyde confirms in what we would now call a 'Dear John' letter. Only then does Troilus prepare himself for death in battle. In the course of the poem, Troilus has changed from a randy and empty-headed young knight into a poet and philosopher who despises 'vanitee' and finally soars to the eighth sphere of Paradise among the 'virtuous pagans'.

It was Chaucer's treatment of Pandarus which showed the great advance he had made on Boccaccio's *Filostrato*, and helped to establish *Troilus* as his masterpiece. Many eminent critics still regard Pandarus as one of the first great comic characters in a tradition embracing Falstaff, Polonius, Pickwick and Micawber.*

While this garrulous old busybody quickly endears himself to the readers, we tend not to notice that his talk is seldom as funny as that of the Wife of Bath, the Nun's Priest or even the Eagle in the *House of Fame*. Pandarus is a master of small talk and comic banter but he remains one of those people of whom it is said that you have to hear them to realize how funny they are. We fail to see why his jokes have such an effect on Criseyde:

At that she laughed and said 'Let's go to dinner'
He fell to jesting at himself and passed
To other matters: 'Niece, I'm getting thinner;
It's love and every other day I fast
I suffer so.' All his best jokes at last
Came tumbling out until his chaffing
Made her afraid that she would die of laughing.

When he is chattering to Troilus, Pandarus sometimes refers to his love for 'a certain lady', and even claims to suffer the torments of

---

* See, for example, G. T. Shepherd's essay in *Chaucer and Chaucerians*, edited by D. W. Brewer, 1966.

passion. In the same way, Criseyde sometimes teases her uncle about his real or imagined mistresses. We are left uncertain as to whether Pandarus actually has a woman friend or whether, like many an ageing bachelor, he wants to assert an interest in the opposite sex.

Thanks to Shakespeare's play as well as Chaucer's *Troilus*, the very word 'pander' has come to mean a go-between, a pimp or even a voyeur. This last interpretation surfaced again in a recent television drama, *An Evil Streak* by Andrea Newman, in which Alex, a middle-aged academic, introduces his niece to a handsome 'resting' actor, David, whom he employs as a cleaner. When Alex hears from David that 'the fish is hooked, it was like seducing a child', he sets up a two-way mirror to observe the result of his match-making. As James Walton observed in a review of *An Evil Streak* in the *Daily Telegraph*: 'If this plot sounds familiar, that's because it's based on Chaucer's *Troilus and Criseyde*, which Alex, the academic who apparently has to do very little work to support his comfortable life-style, has been translating for years. Yet if I remember my university reading right, the chief characteristic of Chaucer's second most famous work was ambiguity and subtlety. Neither is in any evidence at all in Newman's version.'

It is true that Chaucer's Pandarus arranges the time and place for Troilus and Criseyde to consummate their love, and even brings them together in the bedchamber, as was customary on a bridal night in the Middle Ages, but nowhere is it suggested that he gets any sexual excitement from his offices as a go-between. He is fond of Troilus his friend, as of Criseyde his niece, and he relishes their happiness when he brings them together, just as he grieves over Criseyde's unfaithfulness.

Nor is there any suggestion in Chaucer's poem that Pandarus is an ageing misogynist who wants to prove the fickleness of women, like Don Alfonso in Mozart's opera *Così fan tutte*. There are hints of such a message in Boccaccio's *Filostrato* but he puts them into the mouth of his hero Troilo, who voices his own resentment against his mistress Fiametta. But Pandarus, like his creator Chaucer, clearly loves Criseyde and forgives her all her sins. Indeed, Criseyde is one of the most convincing and memorable heroines in all English literature.

Chaucer's Criseyde bears only a superficial resemblance to Boccaccio's Criseida, who was modelled on his unfaithful Fiametta, and has more than her share of vanity and lasciviousness. When Boccaccio's heroine ponders whether to start an affair with Troilo, she does so matter-of-factly, paying no heed to sentiment or morality: 'I am

young, beautiful, charming and gay, a widow, rich, noble and beloved, without children and with a carefree life. Why should I not give
myself to love? . . . Each day my youth slips from me; must I lose it so
miserably? I know no lady in this land without a lover and most, as I
know and see, are in love, and am I to lose my youth for nothing?'

Like Boccaccio's heroine, Chaucer's Criseyde knows she is beautiful
and does not want to live as a nun, but she understands that love will
constrain her selfish pleasure:

> The fear was this: 'Alas since I am free
> Am I to love and put myself in danger?
> Am I to lose my darling liberty?
> Am I not mad to trust it to a stranger?
> For look at others and their dog-in-manger
> Loves, and their anxious joys, constraints and fears!
> She who loves more has little cause for tears.'

Criseyde understands from the start that an affair with Troilus will
bring her responsibility and sorrow as well as sensual gratification:

> 'For love is still the stormiest way of life,
> In its own kind, that ever was begun;
> There's always some mistrust, some silly strife
> In love, some cloud that covers up the sun;
> We wretched women! What is to be done
> In all our grief? We sit and weep and think;
> Our grief is this, that it's our grief we drink.'

Chaucer's Criseyde is a vulnerable and uncertain woman, torn by
conflicting loyalties to her country, her father Calkas, her uncle
Pandarus and then to her lover Troilus. Yet she remains outgoing
and friendly, modest but cheerful and even funny, always able to hold
her own in banter with Pandarus. But Chaucer makes clear she is not a
tomboy, or one of the lads:

> Now she was not among the least in stature
> But all her limbs so answerable were
> To womanhood, there never was a creature
> Less mannish in appearance standing there.

And when she moved, she did so with an air
Of ease and purity, so one could guess
Honour and rank in her, and nobleness.

That description of Criseyde as she appeared to Troilus at the temple should also be read in Chaucer's original:

She nas not with the leste of hir stature
But alle her limes so well answeringe
Werren to womanhode, that creature
Was never lasse mannish in seminge.
And eek the pure wyse of here meninge
Shewede wel, that men might in her gesse
Honour, estat and womanly noblesse.

By the third of the five books that make up the poem, Criseyde is in love with Troilus, and ready to go to bed with him. This consummation and climax of the affair, before the last two books of separation and tragedy, are told with a subtlety, humour and tenderness that are almost unmatched in romantic literature, as well as with many stanzas of enchanting poetry. It is all the more moving, and even erotic, because there is no explicit description of the sexual act or any appeal to the reader's prurience.

Here in book three we see the merits of Chaucer over Boccaccio in their interpretations of Cressida. Although Chaucer's Criseyde has made up her mind to surrender herself to Troilus, the time and place of the rendezvous are left to the wiles of Pandarus, with a little help from the weather. (It is typical of Chaucer that his Mediterranean lovers are stranded together because of an English-style wet weekend.)

In Boccaccio's *Filostrato* it is Criseida who plans and directs the encounter, without the avuncular blessing of a Pandarus. She and Troilo embrace, undress and throw themselves on the bed without physical or verbal foreplay. In Chaucer's version, the preliminaries are conducted in many stanzas of lyrical wooing by Troilus and gradual surrender by Criseyde. When at last she has accepted his embraces, she admits that she had intended to do so all along.

And then this Troilus began to strain
Her in his arms and whispered, 'Sweetest, say,

Are you not caught? We are alone, we twain,
Now yield yourself, there is no other way.'
And soon she answered him, as there she lay,
'Had I not yielded long ago, my dear,
My sweetest heart, I should not now be here.'

At this point, Chaucer explains the virtue of what we would call
'deferred gratification':

And now the sweetness seemed to be more sweet
Because they had endured the bitter thorn;
For out of woe and into bliss they fleet,
Such as they had not known since they were born.
And better so than both to be forlorn!
For love of God, let women all take heed
And do as did Criseyde, if there be need.

The next three stanzas, descriptive of sexual bliss, seem all the more
wonderful if we pause to compare them with similar efforts in
modern novels like D. H. Lawrence's *Lady Chatterley's Lover* or
in the still more ludicrous naked scenes in the cinema and on
television:

Criseyde, unloosed from care or thought of flight,
Having so great a cause to trust in him,
Made much of him with welcoming delight,
And as the honeysuckle twists her slim
And scented tendrils over bole and limb
Of a tall tree, so, free of all alarms,
They wound and bound each other in their arms.

And as a nightingale that is abashed
And holds her peace, having begun to sing,
Because she may have heard the hedges crashed
By cattle, or the shout of shepherding,
Then, reassured, will let her music ring,
Just so Criseyde, now that her fears were still,
Opened her heart to him and showed her will . . .

Her delicate arms, her back so straight and soft,
Her slender flanks, flesh-soft and smooth and white,
He then began to stroke, and blessed as oft
Her snowy throat, her breasts so round and slight,
And in this heaven taking his delight,
A thousand, thousand times he kissed her too,
For rapture scarcely knowing what to do.

After making love in a sleeping-bag in *For Whom the Bell Tolls*, Ernest Hemingway's hero asks his girlfriend, 'Did the earth move for you?', which has long since entered the repertoire of cartoonists and stand-up comedians. Chaucer's Troilus in a similar situation, when most men suffer from *post coitum triste*, offers a hymn of thanks to Venus, beginning 'O love, O Charity . . .' To this Criseyde replies with a hymn of love for Troilus, beginning:

'Indeed' said she, 'dear heart of my desire,
Ground of my joy, my garner and my store,
I thank you for it with a trust entire
As it is thankful; let us say no more,
It is enough; for all was said before.
And, in a word that asks for no release
Welcome, my lover, my sufficing peace.'

Criseyde's happiness comes to a sudden end when the Trojan parliament votes to exchange her for Antenor. Quite apart from her grief at separation from Troilus, she knows she is still in political danger both from the Trojans, because of her father's betrayal, and from the Greeks, who might look on her as a Trojan spy. To add to her misery as she prepares to leave, she is tormented by well-meaning women friends who have no idea what she really feels:

And every fool of those who sat about her
Supposed that she was weeping for the pain
Of having to depart and do without her
And never be amused by her again.
Her older friends were ready to explain,
Seeing her weep, that it was human nature
And they wept too for the unhappy creature.

And so these women busily consoled her
For things of which she had not even thought . . .

Criseyde is guided to the Greek encampment by Diomed, the man who will become her lover. Even in this first encounter, he urges Criseyde:

To drop her Trojan friendship in exchange
For one of Greece, people you never knew
But God forbid there should not be a few
Among the Greek hosts that you will find
As true as any Trojan and as kind.

Although Chaucer's Criseyde (unlike Shakespeare's Cressida) did not intend to collaborate with the Greeks, she soon loses hope of keeping her promise to return to Troy within ten days. For one thing she knows her father will not allow it – 'I cannot find a way to wheedle him' – and she lacks the physical courage to make her way through the Greek lines:

And if I were to put myself in danger
Stealing away by night, might I not fall
Into some sentry's hand, and as a stranger
Be taken for a spy? But worst of all
Some ruffian Greek, fresh from a drunken brawl,
Might come on me and, true as is my heart,
I should be lost, dear Heaven, take my heart.

Near the end of the poem Chaucer gives us a second portrait of Criseyde, including the information that she had joined-up eyebrows and golden or 'sunnish' hair; then he gives a summary of her virtues and weaknesses:

She was discreet and simple and demure
And the most kindly natural there could be;
And she was pleasant spoken to be sure,
Stately and generous and joyous; she
Had a free nature, having a quality
Of pity; but she had a sliding heart.

It is this 'slydinge of corage', to use Chaucer's original words, that drives Criseyde into the arms of Diomed. He plays on her fear, like a German in conquered Europe in 1940, advising a woman to take the side of the victors:

'Troy is in jeopardy, and Troy will bow
There is no remedy to save it now.
Among the Greeks, believe me, you will find
A love more perfect, ere the fall of night,
Than any Trojan love, and one more kind.'

Soon Criseyde is presenting Diomede with a brooch that was given her by Troilus. Although she knows she is doing wrong, she tries to console herself with the thought:

'Since there is nothing better I can say
And grieving comes too late, what shall I do?
To Diomede at least, I will be true.'

But she is not true even to Diomede, assuring him she never before loved any man except her 'wedded lord'. Criseyde's famous lament for her reputation is roughly taken from Benoit de St Maure.

Allas of me, un-to the worldes ende
Shal neither been y-written nor y-songe
No good word, for thise bokes wol me shende
O rolled shal I been on many a tonge!
Through-out the world my belle shal be ronge
And wommen most wol hate me of alle.
Allas that swich a cas me sholde falle.

Although Criseyde's name has indeed been vilified by generations of poets, including Shakespeare, many readers fall in love with her early on in the poem, and forgive her everything.

Chaucer critics too have made elaborate excuses for Criseyde's 'slydinge of corage'. For example, Professor Howard Schless (in an essay 'Chaucer's Use of Italian' in *Chaucer, Writers and their Background*) thinks that Criseyde has failed to keep up with Troilus in his philosophical development. He recalls Chaucer's maxim that 'women are wise in the short avysement' – that is, in short-term thinking. 'But the long avysement belongs to Troilus, to that universal view that is dragging him ever forward and indeed up to the beatitude of the eighth sphere. Nor is this contrast of distance an unusual one, literature is replete with works that show the truism that in the end women fall in love with the man and then with love, while men are in love with love and then with the woman.' Professor Schless argues that Chaucer 'universalized the differences . . . to the point where we are forced to admit the ultimate presence of a cosmic irony'.

A homelier explanation is given by Grace Hadow (*Chaucer and His Times*) whose sympathy disproves Criseyde's fear that 'women most will hate me':

> Cressida is incapable of being swept away by a great passion. She has a cat-like softness and daintiness and charm, a cat's readiness to attach herself to the person she is with at the moment, and a cat's adaptability to circumstances. She is genuinely distressed at being parted from Troilus, she cries till her eyes have double rings around them, and even Pandarus is moved at the sight, but she is incapable of exposing herself to any danger or inconvenience for her lover's sake . . . The whole character is drawn with extraordinary delicacy and insight and with a tenderness which marks Chaucer's large-hearted tolerance.

Observant readers are sure to remark that characters in *Troilus* sometimes appeal to God, the Lord or Heaven rather than to one of the pagan deities. Indeed, when Troilus himself first comes under the spell of Criseyde, he sarcastically likens the strict code of courtly love to the rules of poverty, chastity and obedience to which the monastic orders were bound by oath:

> 'Lord what a happy life!' he said, 'how blest
> A lover leads! The cleverest of you, now
> Who serve love most effectively and best
> Comes to more harm than honour, you'll allow
> Your service is requited, god knows how,
> Not love for love, but scorn for service true
> That's a fine rule to bind an Order to!'

Although Troilus meets Criseyde at the temple of Palladion, and Pandarus can invoke Minerva, Jupiter and 'blissful Venus' all in the same stanza, Chaucer does not suggest that his characters pay more than lip service to pagan religion. Even the beautiful hymn 'O love, O Charity', in which Troilus gives thanks to Venus and Cupid after making love to Criseyde, is actually taken from Dante's hymn to the Blessed Virgin Mary in *Paradiso* XXXIII, lines 14–18, which in turn is taken from a devotional work by the twelfth-century mystic St Bernard of Clairvaux. Chaucer uses the subsequent lines of Dante in his *Second Nun's Tale*.

The confusion of the Christian with the pagan and of the erotic with the divine is still more strange in the scene where Troilus and Criseyde are talking together in bed after making love:

> Lord, how he gazed at her, how blissfully.
> His hungry eyes never left her face
> And still he said, 'Dear heart, O can it be
> That you are truly in this blissful place?'
> 'Yes, yes I am, by heaven's grace.'
> Criseyde gave answer with so soft a kiss
> His spirit knew not where it was for bliss.

If the happiness of the lovers is blessed by the Christian God, their separation and tragedy are blamed on Fortune's wheel and the avenging furies. Soon Troilus is cursing the pagan gods from Jove to Venus and looking for comfort to the idea of Predestination:

> 'And certainly I know it well' he said
> 'That in His foresight Providence Divine
> Forever has seen my losing my Criseyde
> (Since God sees everything and things combine
> As He disposes them in His design
> According to their merits and their station
> As it shall be by predestination).

Although most of this passage is taken from Chaucer's prose translation of Boethius, he brings in the latest debate from Oxford and even adapts a well-known saying of Wyclif: *Omnia quae eveniunt de necessitate eveniunt* – All things that happen of necessity happen.

However, the stanza suggests that Troilus, unlike Boethius, found little consolation in philosophy:

> And to speak briefly, it would be no lie
> To say he was so overcome by care
> That day, all argument had led him there
> Telling him he was lost, and to despair;
> 'Since all that comes, comes by necessity
> Thus to be lost is but my destiny.'

In this way, Wyclif's theology adds to our sense of foreboding about the doom awaiting Troilus. However, the poem's apparent conflict between the pagan gods and the Christian Church is resolved in the last twelve stanzas, sometimes known as a Palinode – 'an ode or song in which the author retracts something said in a former poem'.

In this wonderful Palinode, Chaucer tries to reconcile the classical with the Christian view of life by raising the soul of Troilus into the eighth sphere of heaven, among the 'virtuous pagans' who have rejected earthly desires for divine love. From his voyage in the skies, Troilus even takes notice of us who live in 'this litel spot of earth that with the sea embraced is' – perhaps the inspiration for Shakespeare's 'sceptred isle . . . this precious stone set in a silver sea'. Whether Chaucer subscribed to the theory of London as Trojanovant, he begins his Palinode by excusing the infant state of the English language, compared with Greek and Latin.

> Go little book, go little tragedy,
> Where God may send thy maker, ere he die,
> The power to make a work of comedy;
> But, little book, it's not for thee to vie
> With others, but be subject, as am I,
> To poesy itself, and kiss the gracious
> Footsteps of Homer, Virgil, Ovid, Statius.

> And since there is such great diversity
> In English, and our writing is so young,
> I pray to God that none may mangle thee,
> Or wrench thy metre by default of tongue;
> And wheresoever thou be read, or sung,

I beg of God that thou be understood!
And now to close my story as I should.

The wrath of Troilus, I began to say,
Was cruel, and the Grecians bought it dear,
For there were thousands that he made away,
Who, in his time, had never any peer
Except his brother Hector, so I hear,
But O alas, except that God so willed
He met with fierce Achilles and was killed.

And, having fallen to Achilles' spear,
His light soul rose and rapturously went
Towards the concavity of the eighth sphere,
Leaving conversely every element,
And, as he passed, he saw with wonderment
The wandering stars and heard their harmony,
Whose sound is full of heavenly melody.

As he looked down, there came before his eyes
This little spot of earth, that with the sea
Lies all embraced, and found he could despise
This wretched world, and hold it vanity,
Measured against the full felicity
That is in Heaven above; and at the last,
To where he had been slain his look he cast.

And laughed within him at the woe of those
Who wept his death so busily and fast,
Condemning everything we do that flows
From blind desire, which can never last,
When all our thought on Heaven should be cast;
And forth he went, not to be long in telling,
Where Mercury appointed him his dwelling.

Lo, such an end had Troilus for love!
Lo, such an end his valour, his prowess!
Lo, such an end his royal state above,
Such end his lust, such end his nobleness!

And such an end this false world's brittleness!
And thus began his loving of Criseyde
As I have told it you, and thus he died.

After bringing the story of Troilus and Criseyde to its emotional close, Chaucer abruptly turns from the human tragedy, from carnal love, from Troy and the ancient world, to preach a Christian sermon to the 'yonge, fresshe folk' among his readers. This conclusion to Troilus is all the more surprising when we find that Boccaccio in his *Filostrato* also addresses 'youths in whom amorous desire springs up as your age increases', but sends them a quite different message. While Chaucer advises them to turn to religion, Boccaccio merely warns against putting their trust in a woman 'who is inconstant and eager for many lovers'. Indeed, Chaucer is addressing not just men but 'he or she' among the 'yonge fresshe' folk, here in the original:

O yonge fresshe folkes, he or she,
In which that love up groweth with your age,
Repeyreth hoom from worldly vanitee,
And of your herte up-casteth the visage
To thilke God that after his image
You made, and thinketh al nis but a fayre,
This world that passes sone as floures fayre.

And loveth him, the which that right for love
Upon a cross, our soules for to beye
First starf [died] and roos and sit in hevene above;
For he nil falsen no wight, dare I seye,
That wol his herte al hoolly on him leye.
And syn he best to love is, and most meke,
What nedeth feyned loves for to seke?

Chaucer then dismisses the pagan rites of Jove, Apollo and their rascally kind, before dedicating the book to his fellow poet Gower and to the Wyclifite theologian, Ralph Strode of Oxford. This was as near as Chaucer ever came to making a declaration of where he stood on a controversial issue. In the final stanza, Chaucer once more turns to Dante (*Paradiso* XIV, lines 28–30) for his imagery of the infinite and eternal Trinity:

Lo here, of payens cursed olde rites!
Lo here, what all hire goddes may availle!
Lo here, these wretched worldes appetites!
Lo here the fyn [end] and guerdon for travaille
Of Jove, Appollo, of Mars, of swich rascaille!
Lo here, the forme of olde clerkis speche
In poetrie, if ye hire bokes seche.
O moral Gower, this book I directe
To thee, and to thee, philosophical Strode
To vouchen sauf, ther nede is, to correcte
Of your benignities and zeles goode,
And to that sothfast Crist that starf on rode [died on cross],
With all myn herte of mercy evere I preye
And to the Lord right thus I speke and seye.

Thow oon, and two, and thre, eterne on lyve,
That regnest ay in three, and two, and oon,
Uncircumscript and al maist circumscrive,
Us from visible and invisible foon
Defende, and to thy mercy, everichon,
So make us, Jesus, for thi mercy digne,
For love of mayde and other thyn benigne.

Amen.

The translator Nevill Coghill has called the Palinode 'among the nearest approaches to sublimity in the secular language of our literature' and *Troilus and Criseyde* itself 'the most beautiful long poem in English'. While I would not want to enter it in a competition for the 'top ten' poems of any category, *Troilus* until recent times was considered Chaucer's masterpiece. It also allows us to see him not just as a pioneer but as part of the mainstream of European literature. For one thing, *Troilus* is more than usually steeped in the works of Chaucer's precursors, from Virgil and Ovid to Boethius and *Le Roman de la Rose*, as well as the three Italians, Dante, Petrarch and Boccaccio. For another thing, Chaucer's story of Troilus and Criseyde became a model or inspiration to subsequent poets, not least Shakespeare. Finally *Troilus*, even more than the *Canterbury Tales*, allows us to think of Chaucer as a pioneer of the novel.

As Chaucer's Criseyde had prophesied, most of the subsequent chroniclers of the story turned her into a villainess. The fifteenth-century Scottish poet Robert Henryson, one of Chaucer's many disciples north of the border, condemned her in his *Testament of Cresseid* to condign punishment by leprosy, to the grief of her father Calchas.

> He luikit on her ugly lipper face
> The quhilk before was quhyte as lily-flour;
> Wringing his hand, oftymes he said 'Allas!'
> That he had levit to see that wofull hour!
> For he knew well that their was no succour
> To hir seiknes; and that doublit his pane
> Thus was their care enough betwix them twane.

There were several versions of Chaucer's poem published in England during the seventeenth century, including one translated into Latin and another into 'modern English', for the benefit of those 'who cannot or will not take ye paines to understand the excellent author's Farr more exquisite and Significant Expressions though now grown obsolete and out of use'. Unfortunately the author of this anonymous seventeenth-century version (apparently a translator named Jonathan Sidnam*) became so enraged by the behaviour of Cressida that he broke off his work at the end of Book III with a stanza of his own composition:

> But yet let him that list go on to tell
> The wanton slips of this deceitful dame,
> And what misfortunes afterwards befell
> Poor Troilus, who underwent the shame
> Of her misdeeds, though he deserved no blame;
> For I am loath to do true love that wrong
> To make her fall the subject of my song.

By the time Sidnam's truncated version appeared in the 1630s, Shakespeare's *Troilus and Cressida* had already been staged, though it did not enter the repertory until the twentieth century, when it was

---

* For an account of Sidnam's work and an example of two stanzas of his translation, see the appendix in Coghill's Penguin *Troilus and Criseyde*.

sometimes interpreted as a pacifist or left-wing statement. Shakespeare's play has also been understood as an attack on socialism and even on democracy. Chaucer's anger against the Trojan parliament for its treatment of Criseyde was transmuted by Shakespeare into a speech by Ulysses in favour of class distinction:

> Take but degree away, untune that string
> And hark, what discord follows.

Most of the action in Shakespeare's play occurs among the Greeks, who are shown as scheming like Ulysses or depraved like Achilles. Chaucer's three main characters of Troilus, Cressida and Pandarus are reduced by Shakespeare to empty caricatures. Indeed, if the poets were to be judged by the way they handled the subject of Troilus and Cressida, one would have to say that Shakespeare had mangled and vulgarized the work of his predecessor two centuries earlier.

Whereas Chaucer's *Troilus* was his masterpiece, Shakespeare's play is a hybrid work which teeters uncertainly between tragedy and comedy. It is when we compare Chaucer's *Troilus* with, for instance, *Julius Caesar* or even *Romeo and Juliet* that we remember Shakespeare's genius as a tragedian and poet.

Nevill Coghill's claim for *Troilus* as the most beautiful long poem in the language stands up against Shakespeare's *Rape of Lucrece* and Spenser's *Faerie Queen*, though not perhaps against Milton's *Paradise Lost*. Because of its conversational, humorous style, *Troilus* has more in common with Byron's *Don Juan*, or Pushkin's *Eugene Onegin*, which also ends in tragedy and is also compared to a novel. *Troilus* resembles *War and Peace* in the way it conjures the atmosphere of society under military threat, as in the character of its fickle heroine. Yet, on reading Chaucer's *Troilus* I am more often reminded of Jane Austen's novels, also describing society under threat of foreign invasion. The banter of Criseyde and Pandarus could easily be transposed to a drawing room in *Emma* or *Pride and Prejudice*.

However, the nearest modern parallel with Chaucer's *Troilus* is neither a poem nor a novel but the Hollywood melodrama *Casablanca*, with Humphrey Bogart and Ingrid Bergman as star-crossed lovers. It is once again a story of love in a time of war and political upheaval, during and after the fall of France in 1940. Since *Casablanca* was made as a propaganda film in 1942, it plays down the division among the French, which was as bitter as among the ancient Trojans. Just as many Trojans welcomed the Wooden Horse, so many Frenchmen preferred defeat to four more years of war like 1914–18.

There were French politicians like the Trojan prophet Calkas, who feared all along that the enemy were invincible, and wanted to be on the winning side. There were many Germans like Diomede the Greek, who promised that the winning side would be kind and useful lovers; and many French women, like Criseyde, who slept with the Occupation.

The story of *Casablanca* begins in Paris in 1940, when the anti-fascist American Rick (Humphrey Bogart) meets Ilsa, a refugee from a Nazi-occupied country. Their springtime romance, to the sound of champagne corks and the music of 'As Time Goes By', is brought to an end by the German tanks. Ilsa promises to escape with Rick on the last train leaving for the south of France, but she fails to turn up at the station, just as Criseyde does not go back to Troy.

Some two years later Rick is running a bar in Casablanca, where the French colonial authorities are collaborating with the German occupation. A now embittered Rick refuses to help the anti-fascist refugees in Morocco who hope to reach Portugal and the United States. Then Ilsa arrives with her anti-fascist husband, who had rejoined her as Paris was falling. Both Rick and Ilsa are torn between the demands of love and duty, he to his anti-fascist beliefs and she to her husband. The sense of impending tragedy is relieved by a Pandarus figure, the Casablanca police chief, and other comic patrons of Rick's bar. At last Ilsa escapes with her husband to Lisbon, and Rick flies off to join the Free French.

Like Chaucer's *Troilus*, *Casablanca* is all the more satisfying because it does not have a conventional happy ending, because it puts duty before physical pleasure. However, we have the compensation of knowing that Rick and Ilsa, like Troilus and Cressida, have had their moments of sexual bliss. As Rick says to Ilsa: 'We'll always have Paris.'

14

The Knight's Tale

AT ABOUT THE TIME that Chaucer was writing *Troilus and Criseyde*, he began work on another very long poem adapted from Boccaccio and also dealing with chivalry in love and war, which eventually appeared as the *Knight's Tale* at the start of the pilgrimage to Canterbury. The Host, Harry Baily, who respected persons of quality as much as he looked down on scholars such as the Clerk of Oxenford or Chaucer himself, somehow arranged that the Knight had the honour of speaking first:

> Were it by aventure or other case
> The sooth is that the cut fell to the Knight,
> Of which full glad and blyth was every wight

The *Knight's Tale* is a much abridged adaptation of Boccaccio's *Il Teseida delle nozza d'Emilia* (The Story of Theseus about the Nuptials of Emily) although here, as in *Troilus*, Chaucer omits to credit Boccaccio by name. It begins as Theseus, Duke of Athens, is returning home from a victory over the Amazons with his new Amazon duchess and her beautiful sister Emily. On the way he meets a group of women in black from Thebes who are mourning their menfolk killed or wounded by a tyrant. From among the wounded, Theseus rescues two young cousins Palamon and Arcite, whom he shuts up in a castle, under their word of honour not to escape. From their prison window the two young men see and fall in love with Emily, the sister-in-law of their captor.

For a time the two young men stay friends in spite of their rivalry in love and the frustration of captivity, which Chaucer was familiar with from his time as a hostage in France. But when Arcite escapes and declares his love to Emily, Palamon denounces him to the duke for breaking his parole. The duke commands them both to settle their difference by taking part in a joust, or tournament, to the death at the head of a party of knights, like the 'Combat of the Thirty' which had taken place in Brittany. Before this bloody climax, Palamon, Arcite and Emily go to pray at the temples of Venus, Mars and Diana respectively. Palamon kills Arcite, whose body is then burnt on a funeral pyre, so huge that the nymphs, birds and beasts of the forest 'fledden for feere when the woode was falle'.

When I first read Chaucer as a schoolboy, I found the *Knight's Tale* heavy going, and slogged through it only because the *Miller's* and *Reeve's Tales* were to follow. It was like having to eat up the boiled potatoes and cabbage before going on to the chicken or meat. Reading Chaucer again as an adult, I once more found the *Knight's Tale* dull compared with those of the other pilgrims. Apart from a beautiful passage about the Temple of Mars, much of the poetry is laboured, as though Chaucer was driving himself to the work of translation. Palamon and Arcite are as indistinguishable and brattish as Tweedledum and Tweedledee; the duke is a boor and bully, while Emily is as vapid as a fashion model.

It was therefore with great delight that I started *Chaucer's Knight*, by Terry Jones, the actor and writer of the *Monty Python* television show, which opens with the admission: 'When I first read Chaucer at school . . . I liked the witty and compassionate man behind the portraits of the Prioress, the Monk and the Friar, but I could not understand why such a man could have written such apparently dull and interminable poems as the *Knight's Tale*, the *Monk's Tale* and the *Tale of Melibeus*.'

Pursuing his study of Chaucer and medieval history, Jones came to see the Knight as a soldier of fortune from one of the 'Companies' which then were afflicting Europe, and the *Knight's Tale* as a 'sparkling and witty parody rather than as the philosophical but wooden romance it is usually regarded to be'. Jones's research led him to challenge the idea of Chaucer as a 'cool, courtly writer detached from the turbulent politics of his own day, but to see him as a writer more consistent, concise, humorous and politically aware than he is normally given credit for being'.

Terry Jones begins his book by analysing Chaucer's description of the 'verray parfit gentil knight' in the *General Prologue*, which includes a catalogue of his many campaigns 'as well in Cristendom as in hethenesse'. Jones argues that the Knight 'with his stained tunic and meagre retinue' (consisting of his son the Squire, a yeoman 'and servants no more') would have been instantly recognizable to contemporaries as 'that familiar character, the poor knight'. He might be a small landowner ruined by having to meet his military obligations, or a young man hoping to make his fortune, 'but by far the commonest kind of poor knight were the footloose mercenaries of the Free Companies, thrown up by the incessant wars with France, with no other way of making a living (or no other intention) but to rob and plunder'.

Jones makes much of the fact that Chaucer had been on a mission to meet Sir John Hawkwood in Lombardy. He even suggests that the branded 'M' on the rump of the Knight's horse in the Ellesmere illustration of the *Canterbury Tales* may have stood for 'Milan' where Hawkwood served Bernabo Visconti (although this could also refer to Dante's enigmatic references to the letter 'M', perhaps for monarchy).

The most original passage in Jones's book is his analysis of the foreign campaigns where the Knight is said to have fought, suggesting that they were not in defence of Christianity but on mercenary expeditions for pay and plunder, not least the first of them: 'At Alisaundre was he when it was won.' According to Jones, the attack on Alexandria led by King Peter of Cyprus 'was more like the recent massacre at My Lai [in Vietnam] than some glorious exploit of chivalry'. He supports this with the evidence of contemporaries such as the French poet Guillaume de Machaut and modern historians such as Sir Steven Runciman.

Jones has no trouble in stripping the glamour from the exploits of the knights 'in Pruce . . . in Lettow and in Ruce' where Knights of the Teutonic Order were waging a war of extermination against the pagan Slavs and Baltic peoples. The savagery of the Teutonic Order in guarding the Hanseatic towns may have delighted German nationalists from Henry the Fowler to Adolf Hitler, but disgusted some Englishmen from the thirteenth century onwards. Roger Bacon pointed out that the heathens of Poland and Lithuania were not resisting the arguments of a superior religion but fighting against oppression.

Jones then examines the Knight's adventures in southern Spain: 'In Gernade at the siege ek had he been/ of Agezir.' He argues that the

Castilian campaign against the Moors in Granada was not a holy war 'but simply a political war on behalf of the ruling classes in Spain'. He points out that in North Africa and Asia Minor, where the Knight had also fought, the Christians would often ally themselves with Muslims. He contends that when the knights were not after plunder, they went to these distant places to impress their sweethearts. He reminds us that Chaucer in the *Book of the Duchess* praises Blanche because 'She did not send men to Wallachia/ To Prussia and into Tartary/ To Alexandria, not into Turkey.'

Even if Chaucer's Knight was really a crusader, Jones argues, we should not assume 'that all Chaucer's contemporaries shared the unbounded enthusiasm of modern commentators for knights who went off to kill Arabs, Turks and Lithuanians in the name of Christ'. He quotes many opponents of crusading 'whose golden age had by now lost its lustre'.

Terry Jones thinks that the other pilgrims would have found it ironic that the Knight had fought so often abroad but not in France or in England itself, which was then under threat of a French invasion. He produces a chart to prove that some of the knights with whom Chaucer's Knight has been compared (notably three of the Scropes and Sir William Chandos) 'only went off crusading during lulls in the Hundred Years War, and all of them at some time served in France or defending their country'. He believes that the listeners to the *General Prologue* and to the *Knight's Tale* would have perceived Chaucer's ironic intention.

Jones also suggests that during the *Monk's Tale*, which chronicles the downfall of several employers of mercenaries including King Peter of Cyprus, Pedro the Cruel of Spain, and Bernabo Visconti of Milan, the other pilgrims would have understood this as a satire on the Knight and 'must have been holding their sides with suppressed glee'. He reminds us that the Knight interrupts the Monk. 'Hoo!' quod the Knight. 'Good sire, namore of this!' The Host supports the interruption.

> 'Sire monk, no more of this, so God ye blesse;
> Your tale annoyeth all this company;
> Such talking is not worth a butterfly . . .
> I pray you heartily, tell us something else
> For, but for all the jingling of the bells

> That on your bridle hang on either side,
> By heaven's king that for us alle died
> I should ere this have fallen down for sleep,
> Although the slough had never been so deep.'

Most readers have been grateful to the Knight for interrupting the tedious Monk, especially as it brings on the *Nun's Priest's Tale*, but Jones insists that the Knight was really trying to stop the aspersion on the employers of mercenaries.

At about this point, I realized that Terry Jones was using Chaucer to make a political statement. My suspicions had been aroused at the very start of the book when he quotes from earlier praise of Chaucer's Knight, and voices his own amazement that 'Chaucer the humanist should choose a man who has dedicated his life to war and bloodshed as a pattern of perfection against which all the other pilgrims should be measured'. Whether Chaucer was a humanist in the modern sense of humane, enlightened and often irreligious, or even in the medieval sense of a classical scholar, there is no reason to think that he disapproved of war or soldiering, as Terry Jones apparently does. It seemed to me that Jones was trying to turn Chaucer into a pacifist, just as others have tried to turn him into a friend of the Jews, in spite of the evidence of the *Prioress's Tale*.

There are other passages in Jones's book where it seems to me that he is looking at Chaucer's Knight through the eyes of the modern liberal left. For example, he compares the medieval mercenaries with our modern multinational companies: 'In the same way that the Ford motor company can now dictate terms to the British government, and ITT to the Chileans, so the Free Companies of the fourteenth century were able to dictate terms to popes and emperors.' He compares Chaucer's Knight who has fought in other countries' wars but not in his own to 'a twentieth-century American hero who has fought in Spain, in China, in Biafra, the Congo, Angola and Chile without any mention of the Second World War, Korea or Vietnam'.

Leaving aside for a moment the catalogue of the Knight's battles, there is little in the *General Prologue* that is derogatory of the Knight. Terry Jones does his best to show that Chaucer intended satire in the opening lines:

A Knight ther was, and that a worthy man,
That fro the tyme that he first bigan
To riden out, he loved chivalrie,
Trouthe and honour, fredom and curtesie.
Ful worthy was he in his Lordes warre . . .

Perhaps these words could be construed as having another meaning, but it is just as likely that Chaucer meant us to think of them as virtues. Chaucer used the *General Prologue* to heap scorn and ridicule on the Friar, the Summoner, the Pardoner, the Physician, the Merchant and the Prioress. Had he wanted to show the Knight as a bloodthirsty soldier of fortune, he would have done so without the ambiguity that Terry Jones professes to find. Since most readers have never detected irony or *double entendre* in the praise for the Knight's noble qualities, this suggests either that Chaucer did not intend it or he was failing as a satirist.

Even the details of the account in the *General Prologue* are open to a benign as well as a malicious interpretation. The Knight's shabby appearance could mean that he was one of the poor mercenary class, but it could also be appropriate to a pilgrim riding to Canterbury. His meagre retinue did him credit. His son, the Squire, is shown as a paragon of filial and chivalrous virtue: 'Courteous he was, lowly and servisable/ And carved before his father at the table.' If Chaucer thought the Knight was shirking his patriotic duty in France, he would not have mentioned that the Squire, his son, had been some time in chivalry 'In Flanders, in Artois and Picardy'.

The Knight and the Squire are accompanied by a Yeoman, who sounds like a model English archer of the Hundred Years' War:

And he was clad in coat and hood of green,
A sheaf of peacock arrows bright and keen
Under his belt he bare full thriftily.
Well could he dress his tackle yeomanly;
His arrows drooped nought with feathers low,
And in his hand he bare a mighty bow.
A round-head had he with a brown visage
Of wode-craft well knew he all the usage.
Upon his arm he bore a gay bracer
And by his side a sword and buckeler,

And on that other side a gay dagger . . .
A horn he bare, the girdle was of green;
A forester was he soothly, as I gesse . . .

From Chaucer's evidence at the Scrope coat-of-arms case, we get the impression that he was proud of his army service in France, his knowledge of coats of arms and his friendship with military men. His previous poem, *Troilus*, displays an admiration for chivalry and courage. Nor did he ever express the contempt for crusaders that Terry Jones feels.

Chaucer's friends among the Lollard Knights were as much involved in crusading as was the Knight of the *General Prologue*. Although their mentor John Wyclif denounced war between Christians, he maintained that 'wars waged for God's justice, or for the honour of Christ are right and no other'.*

In accordance with Wyclif's teaching, Sir Lewis Clifford, Sir John Clanvowe, Sir John Montague and Sir John Neville had joined a crusade in Tunis in 1390, while Montague in the following year had joined the Teutonic Knights in 'Lettow and Pruce'. In 1394 or 1395, Chaucer's particular friend Sir Lewis Clifford joined the Order of the Passion for the recovery of the Holy Places, a new organization similar to the Templars and Hospitallers of St Bernard's time.

Terry Jones's contempt for crusading was not apparently shared by Chaucer, though no doubt Chaucer and other elderly gentlemen often deplored the decline of chivalry and the upstarts like Hawkwood who claimed the honour of knighthood. In the centuries that followed, these were favourite objects of satire, as we see from Don Quixote, Sir John Falstaff and Sir Toby Belch.

Jones is well versed in the arguments of Thomas Aquinas, Roger Bacon and other thirteenth-century writers against the attempt to spread the faith by making war on heathens. Although crusading may have begun defensively to recover Jerusalem and other holy places lost to Islam, it had turned into aggression against non-Christians. Jones argues persuasively that some of the Muslim states in the fourteenth century enjoyed a higher level of civilization than Christian Europe, particularly in the sciences of medicine and astronomy on which Chaucer wrote with authority.

---

* *John Wyclif* by H. B. Workman, Oxford, 1926.

Jones points out that, during the fourteenth century, crusading was often directed not against pagans but fellow Christians, especially after the schism within the papacy. John Wyclif was one of the first to denounce Sir John Hawkwood's massacre of the people of Cesena on behalf of the Avignon papacy.

But Jones goes too far in saying that by the time of the *General Prologue* 'the golden age of crusading had long since lost its lustre, and more and more men were questioning whether killing the infidel was the best way of converting him to the religion of love and peace'. In fact, by the time Chaucer was writing about his Knight, crusading was very much back in fashion – not to gain converts but to protect Christian Europe from the advance of the Ottoman Turks and their fanatically Muslim army, the most dangerous threat since the Saracens were defeated at Tours in the eighth century.

When the Ottoman Turks, named after their chieftain Osman, overthrew their Seljuk masters in 1300, they soon proved to be the most resolute and disciplined of the eastern hordes threatening Europe during the Middle Ages. Their crossing of the Hellespont in 1345 was seen by Gibbon as the last and fatal stroke in the death knell of the Roman empire. They captured Gallipoli in 1353; a century later they took Constantinople itself. Meanwhile they established control over the shores and islands of most of the eastern Mediterranean. King Peter of Cyprus appealed to the princes of Europe for help before hiring mercenaries for his disastrous expeditions to Alexandria and Asia Minor.

In the 1360s, St Catherine of Siena led demands for the papacy to call a crusade against the Ottoman advance – a call she also saw as a means of stopping the war between France and England, perhaps of getting rid of the mercenaries who infested Italy. She even appealed to Sir John Hawkwood in a letter: 'Messer Giovanni Condottiere: Since you delight so much in making war and fighting, make no war upon Christians because it offends God. Rather go to fight the Turks, so that from being a soldier and servant of the Devil, you might be a manly and true knight.'

The popes and princes of western Europe ignored Catherine's appeal, and the Turks continued their march through the Balkans. It was left to the Orthodox Christian Greeks, Bulgars and Serbs to confront the Turks at the Battle of Kosovo (Field of Blackbirds) on 28 June 1389. The Ottoman sultan Bajazet celebrated his victory by having his brother strangled and then, in the words of Gibbon, 'turned his arms against the Kingdom of Hungary . . . He boasted that he would lay siege to Budapest, then conquer Germany and finally feed his horse with a bushel of oats on the altar of St Peter at Rome.'

Four years after the Battle of Kosovo, Bajazet's army captured the Bulgar fortress of Nicopolis on the lower Danube, commanding the route up river to Belgrade, Budapest and Vienna. Frantic emissaries from Hungary and Constantinople arrived at the court of Charles VI of France with stories of how the Turks were raping Christian maidens and forcing the boys to convert to Islam and serve as janissaries of the sultan. King Charles was still embroiled in war with England, and in schemes with the Avignon popes to conquer Italy. However, in both France and England there were voices urging an end to the war between them and for a crusade in the Balkans. The University of Paris was following Wyclif at Oxford in calling for an end to the schism within the Church. The dons were supported by eminent scholars like Robert the Hermit, and Philippe de Mesière, a poet and former royal tutor who had long been urging a crusade.

Richard II of England was in favour. He admired France and was sick of the war he had inherited from his grandfather Edward III and his bellicose father, the Black Prince. He was lonely after the death of his first wife Anne of Bohemia, and wanted to marry Princess Isabella of France. But his hopes for peace with France were opposed by a 'war' party led by his uncle, the Duke of Gloucester. Terry Jones compares the two factions with the 'hawks' and the 'doves' in America during the Vietnam War.

Jones seems not to appreciate that the doves in France and in England were as eager for the crusade, which began in 1395. The flower of French chivalry, including Enguerrand de Coucy, another of Froissart's patrons and hero of Barbara Tuchman's *A Distant Mirror*, took the Cross and joined in an expedition which ended in another defeat at Nicopolis. Coucy ended his life in a Turkish prison near the ruins of Troy, that holy place of medieval myth and chivalry. Chaucer's patron John of Gaunt, the Duke of Lancaster, and Gaunt's son, the future Henry IV, were meant to have joined the crusade but called off at the last moment, ostensibly to attend the king's wedding but more probably to be in London in case of a *coup d'état* by the Duke of Gloucester.

Terry Jones assumes that Chaucer favoured a truce with France, as he seems to do in the prose *Tale of Melibeus*, about the peace-keeping efforts of Prudence, a medieval Mo Mowlam or Madeleine Albright. But if Chaucer was really a dove, why would he ridicule the Knight for fighting in distant battles rather than for his country in France? By the time of the *General Prologue* it was the hawks who wanted to fight the French rather than joining them against the Turks.

Jones examines the various critical theories of how the *Knight's Tale* might have a meaning or message imperceptible to the general reader. He compares it with Boccaccio's *Teseida*, showing how Chaucer has changed it, generally for the worse. In particular he explains that the cousins Palamon and Arcite, who in *Teseida* are loyal and friendly to one another, are transformed by the Knight into jealous and spiteful brats. Jones concludes that Chaucer, by telling the story through the persona of the Knight, a greedy and coarse-grained soldier of fortune, wants to convey the decline of chivalry in love and war. One might object that since Boccaccio's work was still unknown in England, the listeners to the *Knight's Tale* had no standards of comparison, as they would with *Le Roman de la Rose* or Dante's *Inferno*, both of which were familiar.

Moreover, if Chaucer wrote the *Knight's Tale* to send up the character of the teller, why did he not do it more amusingly, as in the *Pardoner's* or the *Wife of Bath's Tale*? One can agree with Terry Jones that the description of the jousts and battle in the *Knight's Tale* gives an absurd and repulsive impression of medieval chivalry. Yet paradoxically the *Knight's Tale* also contains some of the most powerful anti-war poetry in the English language, describing the interior of the Temple of Mars (here in the Everyman version by Arthur Burrell). Neither Brueghel nor Goya has given a more frightening picture of the effects of war on the countryside than Chaucer has done in these verses, perhaps from memories of his time as a soldier in France. Yet he puts them into the mouth of a man whose profession was war and bloodshed:

> Ther saw I first the dark imagining
> Of felony, and all the compassing;
> The cruel wrath as any furnace red;
> The pickepurs and eke the pale Dread;
> The smyler with the knife under his cloke;
> The stables burning with the blake smok;
> The treason of the murthering in the bed;

The open warres with woundes al y-bled;
Conflict with bloody knyf and sharp menace.
Al ful of shrieking was that sorry place.
The slayer of himself yet saw I ther,
His herte-blood hath bathed al his hair;
The nayl y-dryven in the skull at night;
The colde death with mouth gaping upright.
In midst of al the temple sat mischaunce,
With sorry comfort and evil countenaunce.
Ther I saw madness laughing in his rage;
Armed complaint, alarm and fierce outrage.
The body in the bushe with throte y-bled:
A thousand slayne and none of sickness dead;
The tiraunt with the prey bi force y-refte;
The towne distroyed, ther was no thing lefte.
Ther burnt the shippes daunsing up and down;
Ther died the hunter by wilde lion:
The sowe eating the child right in the cradel;
The cook y-skalded for all his longe ladel.
Nor was forgot the ill-fortune of Mart;
The carter over-ridden by his cart,
Under the wheel ful lowe he lay adown.

The description of the Temple of Mars is one of the passages in the *Knight's Tale* in which Chaucer has amplified Boccaccio's *Teseida*, adding his own unforgettable imagery such as 'the smyler with the knife under his cloke'. Too often, though, he dully translates Boccaccio – for instance, giving a catalogue of the trees cut down for Arcite's funeral. Sometimes, when he appears to get bored, Chaucer abridges the text, using a literary device known as *occupatio* – mentioning something only to say that he is not going to describe it any further. This occurs at the beginning of the tale, when the Knight compresses more than a whole book of *Teseida* into a few lines simply by mentioning its main events and regretting that he has not the time to say more about them:

And certes if it were not too long to hear
I would have told you fully the manere
How wonnen was the regne of Femenye.

But the central weakness of the *Knight's Tale*, which makes it so inferior to most of Chaucer's work, is not in the poetry but in the portrayal of the three main characters: Palamon, Arcite and Emily.

Although Chaucer may have been proud of the *Knight's Tale*, he must have realized that it would bore some of the pilgrims, not to mention readers in the third millennium. Rather than making the tale more amusing by turning it into a joke against the Knight himself (as Terry Jones has suggested), Chaucer allows the Miller to send it up with a coarse and outrageous parody. As soon as the *Knight's Tale* is finished, the Host calls on the Monk to 'quit' or 'match' it with a tale of his own; but the boorish Miller interrupts to demand the next go, although he is so drunk he can scarcely remain on his horse.

> But in Pilate's voice he gan to cry,
> And swore by armes and by blood and bones,
> 'I can a noble tale for the nonce
> With which I will now quyte the knightes tale'.

Although, oddly enough, Terry Jones does not mention this, the *Miller's Tale* was seen as a parody of the *Knight's Tale*, even in the Victorian times when the *Miller's Tale* was considered too obscene for delicate or female readers. Now, on reading the two tales again, I can understand why Chaucer arranged them to run in sequence. Reading the *Miller's* after the *Knight's Tale* is like watching a *Carry On* film or *Monty Python* instalment after a more pretentious item on television. The Miller begins by admitting that he is drunk, and asks his hearers to blame any mistakes in his speech on the ale of Southwark. He then announces that he is going to tell a tale about a carpenter, for his enemy, the Reeve, follows that trade.

As the two men start to quarrel, Chaucer interrupts the poem to warn his readers that the *Miller's* and *Reeve's Tales* may be told in a coarse and vulgar style – rather as television announcers warn of strong language and scenes of explicit sex. Again like those television companies which tell us that we can always switch to one of the channels on current affairs or religion, Chaucer advises:

> And therefore whoso listeth not to hear,
> Turn over the leaf and choose another tale;
> For he shall find enough both great and small

Of storied thing that toucheth gentilesse,
And eek morality and holinesse.
Blameth not me if that ye choose amiss.
The Miller is a churl, ye know well this;
So was the Reeve and other many mo
And harlotry they tolden bothe two.

The action of the *Miller's Tale* takes place not in Athens but in Oxford, at the house of a carpenter who may correspond to Theseus the Duke. The young-men equivalents of Palamon and Arcite are the undergraduate Nicholas and Absolon, the clergyman. Both love or lust after Alison, the carpenter's wife, the equivalent of Emily in the *Knight's Tale*.

The Knight describes Emily in the stale clichés of a popular song of the day, calling her fairer to be seen 'Than is the lilie on her stalke green/ And fresher than the may with flowers new/ For with the rose colour strove her hue/ I know not which was fairer of the two.' The Miller tells of Alison in homely down-to-earth terms as a woman worthy 'For any lord have lying in his bed/ Or yet for any good yeoman to wed.'

It needs David Wright's translation to do justice to the Miller's description of Alison:

Young, comely was this wife; a lovely girl;
Her body slim and supple as a weasel.
She wore a cross-striped sash, all made of silk;
An apron also, white as morning milk,
She wore about her loins, gored to flare.
White was her smock; its collar, front and back,
Embroidered with black silk inside and out.
The ribbons of the white cap that she wore
Were also coal-black silk, to match the collar.
She'd a broad silken headband set back high
And certainly she'd a come-hither eye.
Plucked to a slender line were her eyebrows
And they were arched, and black as any sloes.
Sweeter was she by far to look upon
Than is a pear-tree in its early bloom;
And softer than the wool upon a wether . . .

Brighter the brilliance of her colouring
Than a new-minted Tower sovereign.
But when she sang, it was as brisk and clear
As any swallow perching on a barn.
And she would skip and frolic, and make play
Like any kid or calf behind its dam.
Her mouth was sweet as mead, or ale and honey,
Or store of apples laid in heather or hay.

Chaucer has introduced to the pilgrims a woman far more real and desirable than the vapid Emily. He has also incidentally shown that the drunken brute of a Miller, with his head that can batter a door down, is capable of producing poetry as beautiful as the Knight's description of the Temple of Mars.

Any man who has heard the Miller's description of Alison will know why Nicholas and Absolon lusted for her. Their rivalry is expressed not in malicious plotting and mortal combat, as with Palamon and Arcite, but in a series of coarse practical jokes. First Nicholas gets Alison into bed with him by convincing her that this is the place to escape an imminent flood and the end of the world. When Absolon arrives at the house imploring Alison for some promise of love, she shows him her naked arse to kiss.

Determined to revenge himself for the insult, Absolon comes back to the house with a coulter, or farming iron, red-hot from the black-smith's furnace. This time it is Nicholas who tries to repeat the jest by baring his backside and farting in Absolon's face.

But Absolon, half-blinded by the blast,
Had got his iron ready, smoking hot;
Smack in the middle of the arse he smote
Nicholas . . .

With this same blow, the Miller has 'quitted' the boring pomposity of the *Knight's Tale*.

15

The Wife of Bath on Women and Marriage

As I HAVE TRIED to suggest throughout this book, our attitude to Chaucer and his age is coloured by the experience and the ideas of the twentieth century, especially with regard to the Black Death, war, class, race, religion and social justice. The revolution in attitudes during the twentieth century is nowhere more evident than in the way we regard Chaucer's treatment of marriage and the relationship between the sexes. Perhaps this is best explained by quoting the thoughts on women of two representative Chaucer critics, one from the start of the twentieth century and one from the end. Their ideas also reveal the changing nature and style of literary criticism. The first is from Arthur Burrell's Introduction to his Everyman edition of the *Canterbury Tales*, first published in 1908:

> For this is Chaucer's secret: he loves; and it is this that makes him so lovable a poet. No student of the *Canterbury Tales* can escape from this reflection. He loves good women; he loves the Virgin Mary and he loves Jesus Christ. Respect, admiration, even worship we find in many writers: in Chaucer they are all there but above all *Amor vincit omnia*.
>
> Mention has been made of Chaucer's good-humoured laughter at the Wife of Bath: but if one trait stands out above all others in his work, it is the worship of good women. No one can read the *Canterbury Tales* without being struck by the idealism which has created Griselda, Constance, Emelye. We may find rarely in Homer, Virgil, Dante, Shakespeare, pictures which crowd to the memory when Chaucer is describing the ladies of his dreams. All of them pale, of course, before Griselda.
>
> The reason, I think, can easily be found. All good women are to

Chaucer reflections of the Virgin Mary, who is 'the lady bright', 'the haven of refuge', the 'bright star of day', 'the glory of motherhood'. She is eternal womanhood in heaven . . . Not even in Shakespeare do we find such an abandonment of worship as we do here. Women have not yet learnt to study the women of Chaucer, their own poet, their defender, their glory. If apology be needed for the poet's coarseness, let the white figures of Constance, Emelye and Griselda atone . . .

By way of comparison, here are two passages from the beginning of *Chaucer's Approach to Gender in the Canterbury Tales* by Anne Laskaya, published in 1995:

Academic discussions of gender issues within Chaucer's texts have tended to align themselves with the postmodern distrust of the sign, for if we ground an inquiry on more or less stable categories of gender, the 'masculinist' and misogynist aspects of Chaucer's writings are undeniable. Finding these elements of the text disconcerting or distasteful after having spent years of one's life preparing to 'profess' literature, many of us take comfort in the reading strategies of postmodernism or gender studies. When we do discuss gender or deconstruct the categories male/female . . . as a feminist I find it noteworthy that we are often trying our best to slide past gender differences . . .

So while deconstruction can indeed add much to our understanding of gender, the deconstructive move can also be a way to ignore gender's power as an on-going discourse and institution, one which persists in categorising human beings as 'men' or as 'women', as 'boys' or as 'girls' . . .

As teachers, we are, I hope, aware of the pain, anger, frustration and disgust our students (particularly our female or gay students) experience when they read the *Reeve's Tale,* the *Clerk's Tale*, the *Wife of Bath's Tale*, the *Pardoner's Tale* and the *Second Nun's Tale* . . .

In the course of the twentieth century, Chaucer has somehow been changed from Arthur Burrell's 'defender and glory' of women into Anne Laskaya's 'masculinist' who enrages and disgusts her female students.

It is not just some of the tales which have upset feminist readers but the prevailing mockery of the *General Prologue* and some of the badinage on the road to Canterbury.

We get the impression that the pretentious, simpering Prioress is also a hard-headed career woman who bullies her underlings such as the Second Nun and the Nun's Priest. Whether or not Chaucer really believed the anti-Semitic slanders which he puts in the *Prioress's Tale*, he goes out of his way to make her ludicrous by showing that her table manners are those of La Vieille, the ageing prostitute in *Le Roman de la Rose*.

Although Prudence, the heroine of the *Tale of Melibeus*, supposedly told by Chaucer himself, is a high-minded diplomat who seems to call for an end to the war with France, the tale is made the excuse for another misogynistic outburst from Harry Baily, the Host, who cannot believe that a woman could be so patient and serene:

When ended was my tale of Melibee,
And of Prudence and hir benignitee,
Oure Host sayde, 'As I am faithful man
. . . I had rather than a barrel ale
That good woman, my wife, had herd this tale.
For she is no thing of such patience
As was this Melibeus wife Prudence.
By Goddes boones! When I bete my knaves,
She bringeth me forth the grete clubbed staves,
And crieth "Slay the dogges everyone!
And break of them the back and eek the bone!"
And if that any neighbour of mine
Will nought unto my wife in chirch inclyne,
Or be so hardy to her to trespace,
When she comth home she rampeth in my face,
And crieth, "False coward, avenge thy wife!
By corpus bones! I wil have thy knife,
And thou shalt have my distaff and go spynne".'

As Chaucer says in the *General Prologue*, the Wife of Bath was also keen to head the queue for Holy Communion:

In all the parish, wife was there none
That to the altar before her shulde goon,
And if there did, certeyn so wroth was she,
That she was thenne out of all charitee.

Although Alison is jealous of her position before the altar, she does not demand to be like those modern-day women who serve or 'preside' (as they call it) at Holy Communion. In this sense she is feminine but she is not a feminist. Chaucer is too often accused by modern critics of being 'anti-feminist' when he is merely making fun of the other sex. But the Wife of Bath, in the prologue which precedes her tale, reveals herself as a feminist as well as a feminine archetype. She is involved in the '*querrelle des femmes*' which had begun in the tenth century and reached a climax during Chaucer's lifetime with the debate over *Le Roman de la Rose*.

The French court poet Christine de Pisan, who dared to complain of the rude language and called the *Roman* 'a handbook for lechers, a cunning trap to ensnare a foolish demoiselle', was in turn compared to the Greek prostitute who had criticized Theophrastus. Six centuries later, Christine's fame was revived by academic feminists who hoped to find a kindred spirit among the patriarchs of the Middle Ages. Some, however, objected to Christine's taking a salary from the King of France. Indeed, Sheila Delany called her the 'Rosemary Woods of her age', a reference to the secretary of President Richard M. Nixon. More charitably, Anne Laskaya suggested: 'Christine was so overwhelmed by anti-feminism that she decided the male attitude must be right, and that women are abominations of nature.'

Christine de Pisan was so much admired in England that in 1400, the year Chaucer died, the new King Henry IV invited her over to London as a poetess in his court. Perhaps because of the war between the two countries, Christine did not accept the invitation and give the English a chance to join in the '*querrelle des femmes*' but by this time Chaucer had written his own immortal portrait of a feminist, in the Wife of Bath.

From her first appearance in the *General Prologue*, we know that she will dominate the pilgrimage to Canterbury. With her enormous head-scarves and scarlet stockings, she cuts an imposing figure, even before we are told that

> Bold was hir face, and fair, and red of hewe.
> She was a worthy womman al her lyfe,
> Husbands at cherche dore hadde she fyfe.

So pleased was Chaucer with his creation that the Wife of Bath is one of the two pilgrims to have an individual prologue to her tale, in which she introduces herself and her private life.

It is here that the Wife of Bath reveals her mature, if not always sober, opinion of men and marriage, giving a blow-by-blow account of her five husbands so far. She begins abruptly as though she had just been shaken out of a sleep, and during the course of her monologue she often seems to be talking to herself, for she is deaf in one ear from a punch by her latest husband. However, her rambling and often outrageous stream of consciousness delights the pilgrims, who frequently interrupt and later make it the subject of a debate on marriage. Six centuries later the Wife of Bath's prologue remains a *tour de force*, unrivalled as the self-portrait of a middle-aged woman. Not even Dickens's Mrs Gamp or Joyce's Molly Bloom can equal the Wife of Bath's prologue for hilarity and pathos.

It begins like a sermon on marriage, which helps to explain why it so enrages professional preachers such as the Friar, the Pardoner and the Clerk of Oxenford.

> 'Experience, though no auctoritee
> Were in this world, were right enough for me
> To speke of woe that is in mariage,
> For, lordynges, since I twelf year was of age,
> Y-thanked be God that is eterne alive
> Housbondes at chirche dore I have had five;
> For I so ofte have y-wedded be;
> And alle were worthi men in there degree.'

Having claimed in advance to speak from knowledge gained in the marriage bed, a knowledge denied to celibate priests and nuns, she goes on to challenge them on their own field of biblical knowledge. She begins with the 'sharp words' spoken by Christ to the woman Samaritan:

> 'Thou has y-had fyve housbondes,' quoth he,
> 'And that same man the which that now hath thee
> Is not thy housbonde;' thus sayde he certeyne.
> What that he ment thereby I cannot sayn;
> But that I axe why the fifte man
> Was noon housbond to the Samaritan
> How many might she have in mariage? . . .
> But wel I wot, withouten any lie,
> God bade us for to wax and multiply.'

Here she cites Solomon and the other Old Testament patriarchs:

'I wot wel Abram was a holy man,
And Jacob eek, as ferforth as I can,
And each of them had wyves mo than two . . .'

It is true, she admits, that St Paul counselled women to keep their virginity, 'but counselling nys no commandement'. Virginity is a state of perfection:

'But Christ, that of perfection is the well,
Bade not every wight should go and sell
All that he had, and give it to the poor . . .
He spake to them that would live perfectly,
But, lordyngs, by your leave, that am not I;
I will bestow the flower of my age
In the actes and in the fruytes of mariage.'

She then challenges the priests to explain why the sexual organs are there if not for procreation. It is ridiculous to pretend

'That they were made for purgacioun
Of uryn, and our bothe thinges smale
Were eek to know a female from a male;
And for no other cause:- say ye no?'

Although she appears to have borne no children, the Wife insists on using her body as God intended:

'In such estate as God hath called us
I wol persevere, I am not precious;
In wifehood I will use my instrument
Als freely as my maker hath me it sent.
If I be dangerous, God give me sorrow,
Myn housbond shal han it at eve and at morrow.'

Here she gives a novel interpretation of St Paul's First Epistle to the Corinthians 7:3–4: 'Let the husband render unto the wife due benevolence: and likewise also the wife unto the husband. The wife hath

not power of her own body, but the husband; and likewise also the
husband hath not power of his own body, but the wife.'

> 'I have the power during all my lif
> Upon his propre body, and not he;
> Right thus the apostle told it unto me.
> And bade our housbondes for to love us well;
> Al this sentence me liketh every del.'

After citing biblical texts for her sermon on marriage, Alison turns to
the lesson she learnt from her own experience, swearing to tell the
whole truth, or never touch liquor again:

> Now, sires, now wol I telle forth my tale,
> As ever more I drinke wyn or ale,
> I shal say sooth of housbondes that I hadde,
> As three of them were goode, and two were badde.
> Two of them were goode, rich and olde;
> Unnethes might they the statute holde,
> In which that they were bounden unto me;
> Ye wot well what I mene of this parde!'

For anyone who has not got the joke, the Wife of Bath means that two
of these rich husbands were so old that they could scarcely fulfil the
marital duty or statute, as prescribed by St Paul. Just to make her
meaning clear, she goes on to explain how she made these old men
give her a present every time they enjoyed her favours, and then made
them toil at the work, no doubt at the risk of a heart attack:

> 'As help me God, I laugh when that I thinke
> How piteously at night I made them swinke,
> But by my faith! I told of it no store;
> They hadde me give their land and their tresor,
> Me needeth not no longer doon diligence
> To win their love or doon them reverence.'

This part of the prologue closely follows La Vieille in *Le Roman de la
Rose* when she advises a younger prostitute how to part a man from
his money. It may also be based on Ovid's Dipsas, for Alison's

monologue grows increasingly drunken. One of the grudges she bears against her fourth husband, the 'reveller', apart from keeping a concubine, was the way he stopped her enjoying a song and dance:

> 'And I was yong and full of ragerie [wantonness],
> Stubborn and strong and jolly as a magpie!
> Lord! how could I dance to a harpe small,
> And singe, y-wis, as any nightingale,
> When I had drunk a draft of sweete wine . . .
> And after wine on Venus most I think,
> For all so certain as cold engendereth hail,
> A liquorous mouth must have a lecherous tail.
> In women, vinolent is no defence,
> This knowen lechours by experience.'

The Wife of Bath's prologue develops a feminist slant when she turns to her fifth husband Jankin, the Oxford theology student whom she met at her fourth husband's funeral, and whom she took 'for love and no richesse'. However 'this jolly clerk' Jankin soon displayed a vicious streak, inflamed by his reading of misogynist authors like St Jerome, Boccaccio and Jean de Meun. It was because she ripped out a page from one of these books that Jankin gave her the punch on the ear which left her 'somdel deef, alas'.

The thought of Jankin, who is seemingly still alive (although some scholars suggest that Alison has murdered him), provokes a diatribe against the priestly enemies of her sex, whose celibate status makes them unfit to comment:

> 'For trusteth well, it is impossible
> That any clerk shall speke good of wyves
> But if it be of holy seintes lyves,
> Ne of noon other wyfes never the mo . . .
> By God, if women hadde written stories,
> As clerks have written their oratories,
> They would have write of men more wickedness
> Than all the mark of Adam can redress . . .
> The clerk when he is old, and may not do
> Of Venus workes, is not worth a shoe;
> Then sit he down and write in his dotage,
> That women cannot keep their mariage.'

The Wife of Bath asks her listeners not to take offence at her uninhibited thoughts on marriage, for her intention is 'nought but to amuse'. However, her thesis, and the examples she uses to back it up, are clearly meant as a challenge to the clerics in the company, and she succeeds in riling them. First the Pardoner and then the Friar interrupt to challenge her errors of theology, while the Clerk of Oxenford, who must have been hurt by some of the rude remarks about Jankin, is biding his time before he replies in his tale about Griselda.

The Wife of Bath's prologue, even more than her subsequent tale with its call for women's 'mastery', proves so controversial that it serves as a theme for the next narrators (apart from the Friar and the Summoner, who have their own private dispute to settle). Indeed, many Chaucer critics follow the eminent G. L. Kittredge* in seeing the Wife of Bath's prologue as the opening of a symposium on marriage, or a marriage group comprising also the *Clerk's*, *Merchant's* and *Franklin's Tale*, as well as some further remarks by pilgrims about their own marital lives.

While I agree that this part of the *Canterbury Tales* should be read and understood as a whole, I think we should not take too literally the idea of the pilgrims exchanging views on the road to Canterbury. Anybody who has ridden among a group on horseback will know that conversation is just as hard as it would be between cars on the motorway today. Although Chaucer remarks early on that the Miller has drunk so much ale at Southwark that he can barely sit on his horse, and, again, that the *Monk's Tale* would have sent his hearers to sleep except for the bells on his horse's bridle, most of us probably think of the pilgrims telling their tales at an inn or 'ale-stake' on the way, or even sitting beside the road. The obvious modern equivalent are the coaches in which the faithful travel to Lourdes or Garabandel, or tour through the Holy Land. On the only occasion I joined a pilgrimage, to visit the Marian apparitions at Medjugorje in Herce-govina, the jolly Irish Catholics in our minibus kept me and themselves amused throughout the trip with their anecedotes, jokes, songs and recitings of the Rosary.

---

* George Lynam Kittredge has summed up his argument in an essay 'Chaucer's Discussion of Marriage', in *Chaucer Criticism: An Anthology*, edited by Richard J. Schoeck and Jerome Taylor, University of Notre Dame Press, 1960.

That is rather how I imagine that marriage debate on the road to Canterbury, with the Host directing affairs through a public address system next to the driver, the Wife of Bath taunting the priests across the centre aisle, while the Miller and the Summoner are happy with their six-packs at the rear of the coach.

The Wife of Bath has opened the marriage debate with a thinly disguised attack on the whole institution. While she does not go as far as La Vieille in *Le Roman de la Rose* in proclaiming *Tous pour toutes, toutes pour tous* (All men for all women, all women for all men), she anticipates modern theories of sexual liberation. In so far as she values the institution of marriage, she sees it as a licence to exploit and dominate men.

After the Wife of Bath's very long prologue and tale, the Friar pays her a grudging compliment as one preacher to another, while also in effect telling her not to bother her pretty head with matters she does not understand:

> 'Dame,' quoth he, 'God give you al good lyf!
> Ye have here touchid, so God prosper me,
> Upon a matter of great difficulte.
> Ye have said moche things right well, I say;
> But, dame, right as we ryden by the way,
> We neede nought but to speke of game
> And leave auctorites, in Goddes name,
> To preaching and to scoles of clergie.'

However, instead of giving his own opinion of matrimony (which would have been informed since we know from the *General Prologue* that 'He had i-made many a mariage/Of yonge wymmen, at his owne cost'), the Friar launches into a scurrilous tale about a Summoner, for which he is amply repaid in kind.

The debate on marriage is not resumed till the Host, Harry Baily, calls on the shy Oxford scholar and priest:

> 'Tel us some mery tale, by your fay;
> For if a man is entred unto play,
> He needes must unto that play assent.
> But preche not as freres do in Lent,
> To make us for our olde synnes wepe,

> Nor let thy tale make us for to slepe
> Tel us some merry thing of aventures.'

The Clerk ignores the demand to tell a funny story, so reminiscent of children's parties and television chat shows, giving instead the sombre tale of Griselda's marriage to Walter. As I explained in the chapter on Chaucer's visits to Italy, I find the *Clerk's Tale* chiefly interesting on the still topical question of royal marriage. However, it must also be seen as the Clerk's reply to the Wife of Bath's prologue.

This becomes obvious early on in the *Clerk's Tale*, when Walter's subjects are pressing him to get married:

> 'Bow then your neck under that blissful yoke
> Of sovereignte, nought of servise,
> Which that men clepen spousail or wedlock . . .'

'Sovereignty' is the very word which the Wife has used in describing her victory over her fifth husband Jankin, another clerk of Oxenford:

> 'He gave me al the bridle in my hand
> To have the governance of house and land,
> And of his tongue and of his hand also
> And make him burn his book anon right tho.
> And when I hadde gotten unto me
> By maistrie, all the sovereignty
> And that he seyde "Myn owne trewe wyf,
> Do as thee lust the term of all thy lyf".'

The suffering of Griselda at the hands of Walter can therefore be seen as the Clerk's revenge for Jankin's defeat at the hands of the Wife of Bath. This is apparent, too, in the 'envoy' to the *Clerk's Tale*, which is sometimes seen as Chaucer's apology for Walter's behaviour. However, the second stanza is addressed to the Wife of Bath and her kind, sarcastically warning them not to be swallowed up by Chichevache the legendary cow, who feeds only on patient wives and therefore is always thin from hunger:

> 'O noble wyves, full of high prudence
> Let no humility your tongues veil;

Nor let no clerk have cause or diligence
To write of you a story of such marvail
As of Griselda's, pacient and kind,
Lest Chichevache you swalwe in her entrail.'

The *Clerk's Tale* greatly impresses two of the men engaged in the marriage debate. The Host Harry Baily says he would give a barrel of beer for his wife to have heard the lesson of Griselda's patience and humility. The newly-wed Merchant grimly remarks on the difference 'Twixt Griselda's grete pacience/And of my wife the passing cruelty'.

The Merchant declines an invitation to talk about his own marital troubles in the confessional style of the Wife of Bath, so instead tells of the marriage of May and January, a girl and a greedy old man, which I mentioned as an example of what Chaucer thought of the merchant class. The *Merchant's Tale* is remarkable for the grimly amusing account of the wedding night of May and January, here in the David Wright translation:

Everyone went away and left the room;
And January clasped into his arms
His paradise, his mate, his lovely May,
Petting and soothing her with many a kiss,
Rubbing the bristles of his gritty beard
(Which was like sharkskin, and as sharp as briars;
After his fashion he was freshly shaved)
Against her tender delicate soft face:
'Now I must take some liberties,' he says
'With you, my wife – and upset you perhaps,
Before the time comes when I shall descend.
None the less, consider this,' says he
'There is no workman of whatever kind
Can do a job both well and in a hurry.
We'll take our time and do it properly . . .'
He laboured on till day began to break,
And then he took a sop of bread in wine,
Then sat up straight in bed; and then he sang
Both loud and clear; began to play the goat,
Kissing his wife, as randy as a colt,
As full of chatter as a magpie is.

> The slack skin round his neck, O how it shakes
> As January sings – or rather, croaks!

The *Merchant's Tale* conveys the pain and sorrow of a loveless marriage. In the *Franklin's Tale*, Chaucer sets out to show how marriage can be redeemed by *gentillesse*. The Franklin himself belongs to the new monied class and rues the fact that his own son does not behave like the Squire, who is a proper gentleman.

The *Franklin's Tale* is set in ancient Britain and follows the ethos of Arthurian chivalry. The hero is obedient to the heroine during his courtship, for this is one of the rules of love. At last she agrees 'To take him for her husband and her lord/ Of swich lordship as men have over their wives'. However, the husband has promised not to assert his authority, and she in turn promises to be obedient in return for his *gentillesse* in renouncing sovereignty.

The Merchant in his tale expresses disgust for marriage in a sarcastic encomium:

> 'A wyf! a seinte Marie! Benedicite!
> How mighte a man han any adversitee
> That hath a wyf? Certes I can not say
> The blisse that is betwixe them tweye
> Ther may no tonge tell or herte thinke.'

The Franklin echoes the same judgement but in all seriousness:

> 'Who coulde telle but he wedde be
> The joy, the ease and the prosperitie
> That is betwixe a housband and his wyf?'

A Scottish admirer, Gavin Douglas, wrote of Chaucer: 'For he was evir (God wait) all women's friend!' The South African poet David Wright, who has written the best modern translation of the *Canterbury Tales*, was nearer the mark when he said in his Introduction that 'Chaucer is the only English writer to treat marriage (as distinct from love) seriously and at length in poetry.' David Wright himself wrote a beautiful elegy for his first wife and went on to make a happy second marriage before he died.

Although the Wife of Bath's prologue is full of satire and jokes

THE WIFE OF BATH ON WOMEN AND MARRIAGE

against women, it is her subsequent tale that most angers feminists, for it deals with the very modern subject of rape. And Chaucer himself had been accused of this crime. 'Perhaps the one biographical fact everyone remembers about Chaucer, if one fact is going to be remembered, is that in 1380 Cecilia Champaign apparently threatened to accuse him of raping her,' wrote Caroline Dinshaw in *Chaucer's Sexual Poetics*, published in 1989. The hyperbole of this judgement (for few people have heard of the accusation) is partly explained by the fact that when Ms Dinshaw was writing, the topic of rape was uppermost in the preoccupations of the feminist movement.

The boxer Mike Tyson and one of the younger Kennedy men were among the famous Americans charged with what has come to be known as 'date rape'. In England a law student was sent to jail for raping a woman friend who got into bed with him naked after a party. Even in France, where the feminist movement was weaker than in Britain or the United States, a man was imprisoned for raping his own wife.

The case of Champaign v. Chaucer was therefore more topical in the late twentieth century than it had been when it first came to light in 1873. On 1 May 1380 there was enrolled in the court of Chancery a formal document in which Cecilia Champaign (or Cecily Champain – both names are variously spelt) agreed unconditionally to release Geoffrey Chaucer from all actions concerning her rape or anything else (*omnimodas acciones tam de raptu meo tam de aliqua alia re vel causa*). Cecilia herself came to court on 4 May to acknowledge the document, which was witnessed by some of Chaucer's most influential friends, including Sir William Beauchamp, the chamberlain of the king's household, Sir John Clanvowe and Sir William Nevill, both Knights of the king's chamber, and John Philpot, collector of customs during Chaucer's controllership. Their presence is an indication of how seriously Chaucer took the action.

Admirers of Chaucer such as G. K. Chesterton have tried to suggest that the *raptus* in the accusation was not really rape but some form of abduction in the course of a civil action; or that Chaucer himself was not the principal in the case, or was the victim of blackmailers. However, the best legal opinions seem to concur that the term *raptus* during the fourteenth century could only have signified violent and completed sexual intercourse. Moreover, it seems from Chaucer's accounts that around this time he sold his house and cashed in some

annuities, suggesting that he needed money to settle affairs with
Cecilia. And he obviously wanted to keep the action as secret as
possible. Those feminists who believe that all men are rapists are
probably right in thinking that this was the nature of Cecilia's
accusation. Still, we have no idea of whether or not she was telling
the truth, or whether, perhaps, she was 'vinolent' at the time. The most
plausible explanation I have read was advanced by Chaucer's recent
biographer Derek Pearsall:

> The strongest likelihood, in my opinion, is that Cecily threatened to bring
> a charge of rape in order to force Chaucer into some compensatory
> settlement, and that she then co-operated in the legal release. The actual
> offence for which she sought compensation is not necessarily the offence
> named in the charge that she used for leverage and did not press: there are
> many things that it might more probably have been than physical rape,
> including neglect and the betrayal of promise by the man, or some
> unilateral decision on his part to terminate an affair that he regarded
> as over but which the woman in retrospect regarded as a physical
> violation. It has often been conjectured that there may be a child hidden
> away too and that 'little Lewis', the ten-year-old son to whom Chaucer
> dedicated the *Treatise on the Astrolabe* in 1391, was the product of the
> union with Cecily, but the evidence is mainly coincidental.

Whatever the truth of Cecilia's accusation, it must have affected the
story about a rape which appears as the tale of the Wife of Bath, after
her very long prologue about her husbands. Most scholars believe that
Chaucer had planned to assign to the Wife of Bath what now appears
as the *Shipman's Tale*, and begins as though it was told by a woman.
However, the present tale of the Wife of Bath is just as appropriate to
her favourite theme of how to acquire and dominate young husbands.
It is only when the Pardoner, the Summoner and the Friar have
interrupted her prologue, then started to quarrel among themselves,
that the Host calls on Dame Alison for a story instead of her rambling
autobiography:

> Our Hoste cride 'Pees and that anoon'
> And sayde 'Let the woman telle hir tale.
> Ye fare as folkes that dronken ben of ale.
> Do, dame, tel forth your tale, and that is best . . .'

The Wife of Bath sets her tale in the distant past:

> In the olde dayes of King Arthour
> Of which that Britouns speken gret honour,
> This lond was al fulfilled of faerie;
> The elf-queen with hir joly companye,
> Dauncede ful oft in many a grene mede . . .

. . . Though now, Dame Alison tartly goes on to say, it is friars and preachers rather than elves who infest the countryside, ready to jump on unsuspecting women and make them pregnant. She is getting her own back on the Friar and the Pardoner for interrupting her prologue.

However, the rapist in the *Wife of Bath's Tale* is one of King Arthur's knights and the kind of 'lusty bachelor' that she herself fancied.

> . . . That on a day came ridyng fro river
> And happed, al alone as she was born,
> He saw a mayde walking him byforn,
> Of which mayden anon, with foule dede,
> By verray force bireft her maydenhed.

The crime causes such fury that the knight is pursued to King Arthur's court and condemned after a trial to execution, for 'such was the statute then'. (By Chaucer's time, rape was more often punished by a fine, although the fifteenth-century poet Sir Thomas Malory spent much of his life in prison for this crime.)

King Arthur's queen and her lady attendants plead for the right to decide the young man's fate and give him a year and a day to save his neck by finding the answer to their question: 'What thing is it that women most desiren?' After almost a year of hearing worthless suggestions, the knight meets an old witch who says she will tell him the answer if he promises to obey her command once he has got his freedom. He returns to face a tribunal of the queen and her ladies:

> With manly voice that all the court it herde,
> 'My liege lady, generally,' quoth he
> 'Women desiren to have sovereigntee
> As well over their housbond as over their love,

And for to be in maistry him above.
This is the most desir, though you me kille;
Do as you list, I am heer at your wille.'
In all the court there was not wyf, or mayde
Or widow, that contraried what he sayde;
But sayden, he was worthy have his lif.

At this point the old crone jumps up to demand that the knight now keep his promise to carry out her wish, which of course is marriage. The comedy of the ensuing scene is all the richer because we know from the Wife of Bath's prologue that she too has a fondness for young men, or what we would now call 'toy boys', just as Chaucer had a fondness for much younger women. Since the old witch does not become a beautiful girl until after the bridal night, the Wife of Bath has time to deliver herself of a lecture on the arrogance of believing that 'olde richesse' can make 'gentil men'.

And with that word upstart that olde wif,
Which that the knight saw sitting on the grene.
'Mercy,' quoth she, 'my soveraign lady queene,
Ere that your court departe, do me right.
I taught this same answer to the knight;
For which he plighte me his trothe there,
The first thing that I wold him requere
He wold it do, if it lay in his might.
Before this court then pray I thee, sir knight,'
Quoth she, 'that thou me take unto thy wif,
For wel thou knowest that I have kept thy lif;
If I say fals, say nay, upon thy fey.'
This knight answered, 'Allas and weylawey!
I wot right wel that such was my behest;
For Goddes love, choose then a new request;
Tak all my good, and let my body go.'
'Nay,' quoth she then, 'beshrew us bothe two.
For though that I be olde, foule and poure,
I would not for the metal or the ore
That under erthe is grave, or lieth above,
But I thy wife were and eek thy love.'
'My love?' quoth he, 'nay, my damnacioun.

Allas! that any of my nacioun
Should ever foully disparagid be!'
But al for nought; the end is this, that he
Constreined was, he needs must hir wedde
And take his wife, and go with her to bedde . . .
For privily he weddyd her on the morrow,
And alday hidde himself as doth an owl,
So woe was him, his wife looked so foul.
Great was the woe the knight had in his thought
When he was with his wife on bedde brought
He walloweth and he turneth to and fro.

The old woman revels in the knight's embarrassment and continues to
chide him for arrogance in demanding a wife of his own age and social
class:

His olde wife lay smiling ever mo
And sayd, 'Deere housbond, *benedicite*,
Fareth every knighte with his wyf as ye!
Is this the lawe of King Arthure's house?
Is every knight of his thus dangerous?
I am your owne love and eek your wife
And I am she that savyd hath your life,
And certes, never did I you unright.
Why fare ye thus with me the firste night?
Ye fare like a man that had lost his wit.
What is my guilt? For Godes love, tel me it,
And it shal be amended, if that I may.'
'Amendid!' quoth this knight, 'Allas! Nay, nay,
It wol nought be amended, never mo;
Thou art so lothly and so old also,
And thereto comen of so low a kynde
That litil wonder is I wallow and wynde;
So wolde God, myn herte wolde brest!' . . .
'Now sir,' quoth she, 'I could amende al this,
If that me list, ere it were dayes three
So that you wolde bear you wel to me.
But for you speken of such gentilesse
As is descended out of old richesse,

> Therefore should ye be holden gentil men
> Such arrogaunce it is not worth an hen.'

Here Chaucer was one of the first to use the word 'gentleman' in the sense it acquired during the nineteenth century.

After teasing the knight and lecturing him on his social arrogance, the crone at last changes into a young and beautiful woman. The Wife of Bath ends her tale with a glorious statement of women's triumphalism:

> And when the knight saw verrayly al this,
> That she so fair was, and so yong thereto,
> For joye he caught hir in his armes two;
> His herte bathid in a bath of blisse,
> A thousand tyme on rowe he gan hir kisse.
> And she obeyed him in everything
> That mighte do him pleisauns or likying.
> And thus they lyve unto their lyves end
> In parfait joye; and Jhesu Crist us sende
> Housbondes meke, yonge, and fresshe on bedde,
> And grace to overcome them that we wedde.
> And eek I pray to Jhesus shorten their lyves
> That wil nought be governed by their wyves.
> And old and angry nygardes of despence,
> God send them some verray pestilence!

In the *Wife of Bath's Tale*, Chaucer has subtly turned a feminist sermon on rape into a light-hearted satire on feminist views about marriage.

The questions asked by the *Wife of Bath's Tale* were once more matters of controversy in England and the United States in AD 2000, the sixth centenary of the death of Chaucer. Two scientists of the Darwinian school published a theory that rape is not an expression of sexual lust so much as the evolutionary need to spread the male genes. An American Jungian psychoanalyst cited the *Wife of Bath's Tale* in trying to answer the very question asked by the queen and her ladies: 'What is it that women most desiren?'

The Darwinist view was advanced in *A Natural History of Rape: Biological Bases of Sexual Coercion* by Craig Palmer, an evolutionary anthropologist at the University of Colorado, and Randy Thornhill, an evolutionary biologist at the University of New Mexico. Their theory, based on a study of scorpion flies, contends that rape is a natural and biological product of man's evolutionary need to reproduce and is therefore 'as much a part of life as thunderstorms and epidemics'. Human males will rape, the authors say, whenever their capacity to reproduce is threatened. Thus every man is a potential rapist and, given the right conditions, may become one.

Even before the book was published its thesis came under attack from feminists in the United States. For example, Susan Brownmiller, whose 1975 treatise *Against Our Will: Men, Women and Rape* was rated by the New York Public Library as one of the hundred most influential books of the twentieth century, called the Palmer/Thornhill argument 'wrong-headed and dangerous' (*Guardian*, 25 January 2000). Susan Brownmiller went on to say that the impulse of men to spread their genes could not explain homosexual assaults in prison or the rape of women past child-bearing age. 'But the most important thing I can say about this book is that I think it will be used as a defence by lawyers in rape cases. These guys will become expert witnesses, for a fee, as part of the defence, and that's dangerous.'

As the debate continued on why men rape, a book was published in Britain which set out to answer the other question posed by the *Wife of Bath's Tale*, and indeed specifically mentions Chaucer's poem. This was *Women and Desire* by Polly Young-Eisendrath, described by her publishers as a 'pyschologist and Jungian pyschoanalyst practising in Burlington, Vermont where she is clinical associate Professor at the University'. Polly Young-Eisendrath begins her book: 'In twenty years of practising psychoanalysis and psychotherapy, I have found that the question "What do you want?" produces bewilderment in most women. We often do not know or we cannot say what we desire.' She had been impressed by the words of the French pyschoanalyst Jacques Lacan that women want to be wanted, not loved, but sees this not as a normal aspect of the female character but as a damaging affliction of female development: 'For in spite of feminism, female power – decisiveness, status, command, influence – cannot be expressed directly at home or in the workplace without arousing suspicion, confusion, fear or dread. Both women and men still tend to experience female power as exotic at best and dangerous and despicable at worst.'

The question of what women really want is often attributed to

Sigmund Freud, according to Polly Young-Eisendrath, but she traces it further back to medieval folktales and literature, specifically to the *Wife of Bath's Tale* and the thirteenth-century *Marriage of Sir Gawain and the Lady Ragnell*, which was probably the source of Chaucer's poem.

16

A Trueborn Englishman

THE LAST FIFTEEN YEARS of Chaucer's life were clouded by the catastrophic career and eventual murder of King Richard II. Although Chaucer must have known Richard well, and was painted reading aloud to him from *Troilus*, his only overt commentary on that woeful reign is the ballade *Lak of Stedfastnesse*. Yet the tragic life of Richard, which passed without comment by Geoffrey Chaucer, his own court poet, inspired one of the most beautiful plays by Shakespeare, writing two centuries later. Furthermore, Shakespeare assigned a leading role and the most famous speech to Chaucer's protector and life-long friend 'Old John of Gaunt, time-honoured Lancaster'. Since Shakespeare had obviously steeped himself in Froissart's *Chronicles* as well as in Chaucer's poetry, it is possible to suggest that he too recognized the fourteenth century as England's national coming of age and Chaucer himself as the first great Englishman.

Richard's father, the grim Black Prince, had tried to force the boy into the kind of military life for which he was not suited in body or mind. As so often happens, Richard developed instead a sensitive and artistic nature. He hired the leading contemporary architect Henry Yevele to build the magnificent hammerbeam roof on the Great Hall in Westminster. He was the first Plantagenet who spoke English equally as well as French, and the first to enjoy having his portrait painted.

Resentment against his father may have augmented the wilful side of Richard's character, which expressed itself in extravagance, temper tantrums and gross indulgence of favourites. As early as 1381, when he was barely fifteen, Richard was seizing the property of his subjects for his private use. He sacked a Chancellor who tried to curb his expenditure, and drew his sword on the Archbishop of Canterbury. As usual he wanted money to bestow on his favourites such as Robert de

Vere. The chronicler Walsingham complained that these frivolous companions taught Richard effeminate habits and discouraged him from such manly pastimes as hunting and hawking. However, even his angriest enemies never seriously claimed that Richard was homosexual.

Nor did these favourites seek power as they did money and titles. The effective running of England was left to the king's uncles, John of Gaunt, the Duke of Lancaster, and Thomas of Woodstock, Duke of Gloucester. Gaunt was too preoccupied with his claim to the throne of Spain to want to replace Richard in England; indeed, he seems to have acted throughout the reign with the selfless patriotism shown to us in Shakespeare's play. Gaunt's younger brother, the Duke of Gloucester, was a belligerent Francophobe who feared, correctly, that Richard wanted to end the war.

Discontent came to a head in 1386 when Richard made his friend de Vere the Duke of Ireland, when dukedoms were still reserved for men of royal blood. To make matters worse, England was then under threat of a French invasion by warships gathered at Sluys, the port of Bruges. This was also the time when Chaucer's imaginary pilgrims were on their way to Canterbury and listening to the *Knight's Tale* of chivalry and war. It was in 1386 that Gaunt left for Spain to pursue his private ambition, while Richard tried to raise money for the defence of the realm. Understandably, Parliament told him that they would not vote more revenue unless he dismissed some of his unpopular ministers. Richard replied that he would not listen to Parliament's advice on sacking a scullion from his kitchens.

During this first confrontation, the Duke of Gloucester warned the king to remember the fate of his great-grandfather Edward II, who also was ruined by favourites. Far from taking this sombre advice, Richard cocked a snook at Gloucester and other critics by trying to have Edward II canonized as a martyr, and even seeking proof of the miracles he performed.

Richard's enemies won control of the Parliament in which Geoffrey Chaucer sat as a knight. The country was now splitting up into two armed camps. Then in 1388 a group of the king's opponents, calling themselves the Appellants, established a kind of tribunal against the royal favourites. Among those who lost their heads in this summary justice was Sir Nicholas Brembre, a former Lord Mayor of London. Among the crimes with which he was charged was wanting to change the name of the city to Troynovant. The Duke of Gloucester and his associates had struck at Richard's friends through their control of what came to be nicknamed the 'Merciless Parliament'. Living and writing as he did in such dangerous and suspicious times, it is hardly surprising that Chaucer concealed his views on politics and religion. Even to call London 'Troynovant' was now a capital offence.

When the threat of a French invasion had subsided, Richard felt strong enough to visit his realm of Ireland where, Froissart tells us, he entertained the kings of Ulster, Leinster, Munster and Connaught, attempted to teach them table manners and to make them abandon the kilt. Shakespeare has put in the mouth of Richard II a traditionally sour English comment on that island's famous absence of poisonous snakes:

> So much for that. Now for our Irish wars:
> We must supplant those rough, rug-headed kerns,
> Which live like venom where no venom else
> But only they have privilege to live.

After his first venture in Ireland, Richard returned to try to exact his revenge on his English opponents. In the course of a decade from 1388, Richard kidnapped and then had murdered his principal enemy Gloucester, but merely banished Henry Bolingbroke, who later came back to England to supplant him.

Shakespeare begins his play with the confrontation between Henry Bolingbroke, son of 'Old John of Gaunt', and Thomas Mowbray, the Duke of Norfolk who helped to kidnap and, perhaps, to murder the Duke of Gloucester. Richard orders them to fight a joust to the death, like Palamon and Arcite in the *Knight's Tale*, then cancels it at the last moment – perhaps because of his own sense of inadequacy as a warrior. He then banishes both these potential enemies. The dying John of Gaunt laments the exile of his son and then like 'a prophet new-inspired' gives us a vision of

> This royal throne of Kings, this sceptred isle
> This earth of majesty, this seat of Mars
> This other Eden, demi-paradise.

Even patriots have found this speech a rather guilty pleasure, like standing up for the national anthem or singing 'Rule Britannia'.

However, it suited the taste of Elizabethan audiences, shortly after the Spanish armada episode of 1588.

After John of Gaunt's death, Richard seizes his property and forbids his son Henry to return for the funeral. At about this point in Shakespeare's play, as in the history of the fourteenth century, we start to lose patience with Richard and welcome Henry's invasion and *coup d'état*.

Shakespeare himself was in two minds, perhaps because he knew that his monarch Elizabeth I identified with Richard II. He gives to the doomed king some beautiful, if self-pitying, speeches ('For God's sake let us sit upon the ground/And tell sad stories of the death of kings'), and changes his child-bride Isabella into a grown-up loving wife. At the same time he shows the usurper Bolingbroke as torn by remorse for having Richard murdered at Pontefract by men who took him too literally, like the knights who killed Becket. Sir Piers of Exton says:

> Didst thou not mark the King, what words he spake,
> 'Have I no friend will rid me of this living fear?'
> Was it not so? . . .
> 'Have I no friend?' quoth he: he spake it twice . . .

Here Shakespeare echoes the words attributed to Henry II. He also shows Bolingbroke as generous to his enemies and a true Plantagenet in the crusading tradition. As soon as Henry IV is crowned, he wants to make up with his former opponent Mowbray, the Duke of Norfolk, only to hear he has died in exile abroad:

> Many a time hath banished Norfolk fought
> For Jesu Christ in glorious Christian field,
> Streaming the ensign of the Christian cross
> Against black pagans, Turks and Saracens,
> And, toiled with works of war, retired himself
> To Italy, and there at Venice gave
> His body to that pleasant country's earth,
> And his pure soul unto his captain, Christ,
> Under whose colours he had fought so long.

This eulogy comes shortly after John of Gaunt's reference to the royal kings:

Renowned for their deeds as far from home
For Christian service and true chivalry
As is the sepulchre in stubborn Jewry . . .

The theme appears again in *Henry IV Part One*, when the king sees a crusade as a way of uniting the divided English:

The edge of war, like an ill-sheathed knife,
No more shall cut his master . . . therefore, friends,
As far as to the sepulchre of Christ,
Whose soldier now under whose blessed cross
We are impressed and engaged to fight,
Forthwith a power of English shall we levy,
Whose arms were moulded in their mothers' womb
To chase these pagans in their holy field
Over whose acres walked those blessed feet
Which fourteen hundred years ago were nailed
For our advantage on the bitter cross . . .

Whatever we think today of medieval crusaders and in particular of Chaucer's Knight, it appears from this that Shakespeare considered them admirable, and even glamorous.

We cannot know the political manoeuvres and compromises that Chaucer had to make to survive the last few dangerous years of his life when Richard, the king he had served for twenty years, was overthrown by Henry, the son of his patron John of Gaunt, the Duke of Lancaster. Chaucer's friend and fellow poet, John Gower of Southwark, whom Chaucer addressed as 'moral Gower', has given an indication of how he trimmed his sails to the change of political wind. Early in Richard's reign, Gower addressed to him a pompous and patronizing lecture on his responsibilities, urging him to be worthy of his father, and reminding him that the God-given beauty of his person should be matched by the virtue of his soul. It speaks well for Richard that, when he encountered Gower on the river, he invited him on to the royal barge and advised him in turn to write more readably and in English rather than French or Latin. Gower must have been flattered by this attention, for he himself has reported the king's admonition:

He hath this charge upon me laid
And bid me do my besynesse
That to his hihe worthinesse
Som newe thing I shoulde boke.

It was probably at the instigation of Richard's supporter Sir Nicholas Brembre that Gower took up the cause of renaming London 'Troynovant', though this did not cost him his head, unlike Brembre. But Gower seems to have understood that Richard's cause was doomed, for as early as 1383 he was dedicating his poetry to Henry Bolingbroke, the future Henry IV.

Chaucer's involvement in politics, as in religious debates, was cautious and non-committal. It took the form of a ballade *Lak of Stedfastnesse*, of which the final stanza is called 'Lenvoy to King Richard':

O prince, desyre to be honourable,
Cherish thy folk and hate extorcioun!
Suffre no thyng that may be reprevable
To thyn estat don in thy regioun.
Shew forth thy swerd of castigacioun,
Dred God, do law, love trouthe and worthynesse
And wed thy folk ageyn to stedfastnesse.

The ballade expresses some uncontroversial sentiments from *The Consolation of Philosophy*, but then Chaucer knew that Boethius was jailed and eventually tortured to death for giving offence to the Emperor Theodoric. When dealing with sovereigns, platitude is safer than frank advice. Neither Richard nor his opponents could have taken offence at *Lak of Stedfastnesse*.

When Bolingbroke seized power and mounted the throne as Henry IV at the end of 1399, Chaucer prudently did not greet him with a pledge of support but with a plea for a renewal of his patronage in the form of a comic address to his empty purse. It appears that 'The Complaint of Chaucer' was written at some point between 30 September 1399, when Henry became the accepted king, and 13 October, the date on the document confirming his pension. But as so often happens to writers anxious for payment, there was a long delay in obtaining cash, so that Chaucer's last five pounds from the king arrived only in June 1400, four months before his death.

In spite of the slowness with which it was answered, 'The Complaint of Chaucer to his Purse' is a most delightful invoice:

> To yow, my purse, and to noon other wight
> Complayne I, for ye be my lady dere.
> I am so sorry now that ye been light;
> For certes but if ye make me hevy chere,
> Me were as leef be layd upon my bier;
> For which unto your mercy thus I crye,
> Be hevy ageyn, or elles must I die.

Since he addresses his purse as his lady love, the word 'hevy' here can also mean pregnant. He goes on to say that his purse is also his 'stere' or rudder.

> Now voucheth safe this day or hyt be nyght
> That I of yow the blissful sound may hear
> Or see your colour lyke the sonne bright
> That of yellowness had never peer.
> Ye be my lyf, ye bee myn hertes stere.
> Quene of comfort and of good companye,
> Beth heavy ageyn, or elles must I die.

After a third stanza likening his shortage of cash to a friar's want of hair on his tonsure ('I am as shave as nye as any frere') Chaucer ends with an Envoy to Henry IV, addressing him as the conqueror and legitimate king of Brutus's Albion:

> O Conqueror of Brutes Albyon,
> Which that by line and free eleccion
> Been verray Kyng, this song to you I sende,
> And ye that mowen [may] alle oute harmes amende,
> Have mynde upon my supplicacion!

Since Shakespeare wrote plays about all the Plantagenet kings from Edward III* to Richard III, as well as about Henry VIII, we have to ask

---

* This little-known play is now generally agreed by scholars to be the work of Shakespeare. It is published as an appendix in John Julius Norwich's *Shakespeare's Kings*, Viking, 1999.

why he chose the reign of Richard II to give his most famous exposition of English nationalism. It is true that the Agincourt speech in *Henry V* is still more stirring of blood and adrenalin, which is why it was so often recited in both world wars, but it does not rival John of Gaunt's for national self-glorification:

> This other Eden, demi-paradise;
> This fortress built by Nature for herself
> Against infection and the hand of war;
> This happy breed of men, this little world,
> This precious stone set in the silver sea,
> Which serves it in the office of a wall,
> Or as a moat defensive to a house,
> Against the envy of less happier lands.

John of Gaunt's speech is so overpowering, as well as shocking to modern received ideas, that we tend not to notice the milder expressions of English national pride which Shakespeare includes in the same Act of *Richard II*. This is especially evident when Richard has sentenced the two quarrelling noblemen, Mowbray and Bolingbroke, to banishment from the kingdom. 'A heavy sentence, my most sovereign liege,' says Mowbray, then goes on to explain:

> The language I have learnt these forty years,
> My native English, now I must forgo:
> And now my tongue's use is to me no more
> Than an unstringed viol or a harp;
> Or like a cunning instrument cased up,
> Or, being open, put into his hands
> That knows no touch to tune the harmony:
> Within my mouth you have engaoled my tongue
> Doubly portcullis'd with my teeth and lips;
> And dull unfeeling barren ignorance
> Is made my gaoler to attend on me . . .
> What is thy sentence then but speechless death,
> Which robs my tongue from breathing native breath?

Bolingbroke sees no remedy for the pain of living abroad except for his national pride:

Then, England's ground, farewell; sweet soil, adieu;
My mother, and my nurse, that bears me yet!
Where'er I wander, boast of this I can:
Though banish'd, yet a trueborn Englishman.

Shakespeare suggests that, even during the reign of Richard II, the enmity between Norman and Anglo-Saxon was giving way to a common sense of nationhood. King Richard observes with dismay that his rival Bolingbroke is popular and at ease with the crowds when he travels through the country:

Off goes his bonnet to an oyster-wench,
A brace of draymen bid God speed him well
And had the tribute of his supple knee
With 'Thanks my countrymen, my loving friends,'
As were our England in reversion his,
And he our subjects' next degree in hope.

The custom of royal pretenders courting the public, which flourished during Shakespeare's lifetime, was carried on by the Duke of Monmouth during the reign of Charles II and by Stuart pretenders in Scotland.

Shakespeare obviously saw the fourteenth century as the age when the English first took pride in their language, their separate nationhood and their common purpose. This pride is also manifest in the poetry of Chaucer, though without Shakespeare's naked chauvinism. The decline of French and the rise of the English language began with the loss of Normandy to the French in 1204. From then on the Norman rulers of England increasingly intermarried with Anglo-Saxons, as did the Chaucers, or Chauciers, of London with the Dynyngtons of Suffolk. The children of such unions probably learnt French from their father, but picked up English from their mother, nurse and servants. When Edward III went to war in the 1330s, he issued an edict to parents to teach their sons French to be able to use it in service on the Continent, and by the end of the century Oxford was taking measures to stop French falling into disuse.

Although legal documents were generally written in French, philologists claim to discern from the syntax that judgements were first thought out in English and then translated. According to Bill Bryson in his delightful *Mother Tongue*, rich parents during the fourteenth century would send their children to Paris to learn the more fashionable central French dialect, which had by this time become almost a separate language. This is why Chaucer's Prioress spoke only the French of Stratford-atte-Bow. Bryson continues:

> The harsh, clacking, guttural Anglo-French had become a source of amusement to the people of Paris, and this provided perhaps the ultimate and certainly the most ironic blow to the language in England. Norman aristocrats, rather than be mocked for persevering with an inferior dialect that many of them spoke badly anyway, began to take an increasing pride in English. So total was this reversal of attitude that when Henry V was looking for troops to fight with him at Agincourt in 1415 he used the French threat to the English language as a rallying cry.

Thus modern philology confirms what Shakespeare's genius had perceived in *Richard II*, that the English language and consciousness came into being during the age of Chaucer.

Chaucer was well aware of his part in creating the language of which he became the first great poet. At the end of *Troilus* he mentions the 'great diversity in English and our tongue', adding a prayer that the scribes will not 'myswrite' or 'mysmetre' him in transcription. Unhappily, most of these scribes altered his English to suit their own fancy or regional custom. Chaucer himself wrote in the London dialect which came to prevail as standard English, but he enjoyed making play with the great diversity of the language, trying his hand at the doggerel 'Rum, ram, ruf' which the Parson dislikes, and the North Country accents of the students in the *Reeve's Tale*.

Although Scotland remained a separate country, its poets during the cultural renaissance of the fifteenth century regarded Chaucer as their model and master, the man who had regularized and purified the language. 'O reverend Chaucer, rose of rhetoris,' wrote Gavin Douglas, the Bishop of Dunkeld, while William Dunbar hailed him as: 'Milky fontane, clear strand and roys royal/ Of fresh endyte, through Albion island braid . . .'. The Scots, Welsh and Irish during the Middle Ages had not come to regard the English language as a threat to their culture and independence, and of English hostility to the Celtic nations we find scarcely a hint in Chaucer's poetry.

The reference to the Irish as 'rough rug-headed kerns' in Shake-

speare's *Richard II* is probably based on Elizabethan experience of the
country or perhaps on Froissart's account of the country in the
fourteenth century. Froissart is also a principal source for the anti-
French feeling which mounted in England during Chaucer's lifetime,
for there is no suggestion of it in Chaucer's poetry. Anti-French feeling
was strongest among the military, who had profited from the looting
of towns like Caen and Calais at the beginning of the war, and from
the ransom of prisoners after the Battle of Poitiers.

Anti-French feeling at the end of the century was personified in the
Duke of Gloucester. Froissart tells us that the duke had 'a constant and
heartfelt dislike of the French', even rejoicing in their defeat by the
Turks at Nicopolis in 1396: 'These frivolous French got themselves
thoroughly smashed up in Hungary and Turkey . . . They are so
overbrimming with conceit that they never bring any of their enter-
prises to a successful conclusion . . . I don't know why we have this
truce with them, for if we started the war again – and we have a
perfectly good reason for doing so – we should make hay of them. By
God, if I live a couple of years longer in good health, the war will be
renewed. I won't be bound by treaties and pacts and promises – the
French never kept any of theirs in the past.'

The Duke of Gloucester's francophobia was more representative
of English feeling than was King Richard's admiration. 'It is absurd,'
wrote Knighton, the chronicler, 'that a King of England should do
homage to the King of France for Aquitaine, since the King of France
may thereby put all Englishmen under his feet.' Even William Langland, whose *Piers Plowman* probably spoke for the common people,
wrote that the devil himself was a proud 'Pryker' or Knight for
France.

In recording sentiments like these, Professor May McKisack sadly
remarks that the victories and still more the reverses of war 'bred a
francophobia which died hard in England'. But if the fourteenth-
century English were often at war with France, they had no quarrel
with 'Europe' in the sense that the word is used about the Common
Market, or the Treaty of Rome or the European Community. Englishmen like Chaucer were conscious of being the inheritors of Greek and
Latin civilization, and of having been part of the Roman empire. They
had never taken so seriously the Holy Roman Empire founded by
Charlemagne, and certainly not its attempts to regain political power.

Since the arrival of St Augustine, the English Church had usually been obedient to the popes at Rome and had remained so when a rival papacy was established at Avignon. Although Chaucer accepted some of Wyclif's ideas, he regarded himself as a Catholic, and England as part of Christendom. Chaucer lived at the very end of the era when western Europe, roughly the EC countries, was still united by a common religious faith.

For Englishmen in Chaucer's age it was much more easy to trace descent from a Norman, Viking, Saxon or Celtic ancestor, and no doubt there were many who bragged of their true-born ancestry and complained of more recent immigrants. As we know from the *Prioress's Tale*, there was hostility to the Jews, while the experience of the Peasants' Revolt showed that the Dutch, or Flemings, were just as unpopular then as they were in William III's time.

However, Richard II's England was not the democratic society Shakespeare describes, in which Norman aristocrats like Bolingbroke went 'wooing poor craftsmen with the craft of smiles' or doffing their bonnet to oyster-wenches. We should not trust those William Morris socialists and Roman Catholic apologists who hankered after a 'Merrie England' before the advent of the Reformation and the rise of capitalism. Even G. G. Coulson, whose *Chaucer and His Age* helped to interpret the Middle Ages for the twentieth-century mind, was not immune to this kind of literary nostalgia. In his introduction, written before the First World War, Coulson compared the pleasure of reading Chaucer to that of foreign travel: 'It is just because we should never dream of choosing France or Germany for our home that we love them so much for our holidays; it is because we are so deeply rooted in our own age that we find so much pleasure and profit in our past.' Yet with all these reservations, I feel that Shakespeare was right to perceive in the reign of Richard II the first flowering of our language, national pride and sense of identity. And Chaucer, our first great poet, can also be seen as the first great Englishman.

Chaucer, as I imagine him from his life and works, has some of the characteristics that we the English find endearing about ourselves, but foreigners find annoying. These could be categorized as tolerance (or complacency), self-deprecation (or arrogance) and diffidence (or standoffishness).

The indifference of the English to the excitements of the Continent was seen with exasperation by George Orwell, on his return from fighting in the Spanish Civil War. He describes at the end of his *Homage to Catalonia* taking the boat train to London from Dover or Folkestone (incidentally the route in reverse of the Canterbury Pilgrims):

And then England – southern England, probably the sleekest landscape in the world. It is difficult when you pass that way, with the plush cushions of a boat-train under your bum, to believe that anything is really happening elsewhere. Earthquakes in Japan, famines in China, revolutions in Mexico? Don't worry, the milk will be on the doorstep tomorrow morning, the *New Statesman* will come out on Friday . . . It was still the England I had known in my childhood: the men in bowler hats, the pigeons in Trafalgar Square, the red buses, the blue policemen – all sleeping the deep, deep sleep of England, from which I sometimes fear that we shall never wake till we are jerked out of it by the roar of bombs.

Like the English in the 1930s who would not get interested in Spain or central Europe, Chaucer appears to have stayed serene throughout the calamitous fourteenth century. As a soldier and diplomat he witnessed the horrors of war in France and met such monsters as the Visconti brothers and their henchman Sir John Hawkwood. Back in England he observed the Wyclif furore, the Peasants' Revolt and the overthrow of Richard II, but did not become involved. Because he did not take one side or the other on any issue, Chaucer has since been claimed both by the Catholics and Protestants, by Parliamentarians and Cavaliers, by jingoist patriots and by pacifists such as Terry Jones. The Marxists, feminists and post-modernists have tried to bring Chaucer into their arguments, and when he was found not to fit, omitted him altogether.

Some Chaucer critics have labelled him a Laodicean – meaning luke-warm or half-hearted – especially about religion. Others have applied to him John Keats's phrase 'negative capability', meaning a general sympathy even with conflicting attitudes and emotions. It might be truer to say that Chaucer did not take anything seriously. Many Englishmen pride themselves on seeing the funny side of everything and everybody. The great comic novelist P. G. Wodehouse, when he was captured and interned by the Germans in 1940, could not resist joking about the Germans during his broadcasts from occupied Europe. He made fun of the Germans, just as before the war he made fun of the British fascist leader Sir Oswald Mosley.

As Wodehouse made fun of the fascists through Sir Roderick Spode and his 'Black Short' movement, so Chaucer caricatured the evils of his age through the Pardoner, the Prioress and the Friar. Moreover, like Wodehouse and generations of English comics, Chaucer was eager to laugh at himself. He joked about his weight when the eagle in the *House of Fame* complains how hard he is to carry. Through the Sergeant at Law he makes fun of his own plagiarizing from Ovid. The only two *Canterbury Tales* which Chaucer attributes to himself are the doggerel *Tale of Sir Thopas* and the prose *Tale of Melibeus*, a boring treatise on diplomacy.

Chaucer's fondness for self-deprecation brings us to what was his own very English failing of shyness, reserve or what foreigners often call aloofness. The description of him by Deschamps as '*brief en parler*' echoes the phrase Chaucer uses in the *General Prologue* about his alter ego, the Clerk of Oxenford: 'Of studie took he most care and most heede/ Not one word spak he more than was need.'

But it is Geoffrey Chaucer himself who is most sharply reprimanded by the Host for his diffidence and for keeping his eyes on the ground in front of him as though he was hoping to catch a hare:

> Til that our host to jape soon bigan
> And that at erst he looked upon me
> And sayde thus: 'What man art thou?' quoth he
> 'Thou lookest as thou woldest find a hare
> For ever upon the ground I see thee stare.'

The Host then holds him up to the ridicule of the company by pointing out the shape of his waist and calling him a 'popet' or toy boy for any woman to embrace.

We all can recognize in Harry Baily the eternal dreaded figure of the party host who insists that you 'talk to some of these fascinating people', the bore in the train who remarks that 'reading is an unsociable habit', or worst of all the compere of a television chatshow who humiliates his guests to increase his ratings. We can recognize in Chaucer the kind of Englishman who still does not 'parade his emotions'.

Chaucer anticipated the sentimentality that took over the English character in the nineteenth century. He gushed over small furry animals and 'briddes', and long before the Victorian Christmas, was singing the pleasures of the 'colde froste seison of Decembre':

> Janus sit by the fyr with double beard
> And drinketh from the bugle horn the wyn,
> Bifore him is the brawn of tusked swyn
> And 'Nowell' crieth every lusty man.

The sentimentality went with his English sense of humour.

Notes on Further Reading:
Background to Chaucer's Age

To UNDERSTAND THE EVENTS of Chaucer's lifetime, the two classic works are Lord Macaulay's *History of England* and Jules Michelet's *Le Moyen Age*, both written during the mid-nineteenth century. These two rival expositions of the English and French national myths were written by brilliant men who saw in history a means of expressing their romantic patriotism. The early chapters of Macaulay's history are a prelude to his account of the 'Glorious Revolution' of 1688 under Macaulay's hero William of Orange, later William III of England, the foundation of the nineteenth-century constitutional monarchy and British imperial power. According to this Whig interpretation of history, the early Middle Ages witnessed a compromise between the Norman invaders and the defeated Anglo-Saxons, the curbing of royal power by the Magna Carta and the development of Parliamentary government.

Macaulay saw the key events as the quarrel of Henry II and Becket, King John's loss of Normandy and the gradual emergence of an English language and culture.

Jules Michelet was a child of the French Revolution of 1789 and remained an opponent both of monarchy and Bonapartism. He was, at the same time, an intense French patriot, deeply suspicious of England and 'Anglo-Saxon' values. He began his immense history of France with this critical work on the Middle Ages, which praises the spirituality of the Christian kings, especially St Louis, and reaches a climax with the career of Michelet's heroine, Joan of Arc, who was burnt to death by the English. The villains of Michelet's *Le Moyen Age* are the Normans, who broke away to conquer England in 1066, and later the first Plantagenet monarch, Henry II, who married the former French Queen Eleanor of Aquitaine and thus acquired her vast inheritance in south-west France.

It was Michelet who created the caricature of the English as coarse eaters of red meat whose success in war depended on commerce rather than courage. Reading Macaulay and Michelet one comes to understand the mutual hostility of the English and French which began in Chaucer's age and still persists into the twenty-first century.

The murder of Becket, which brought Chaucer's pilgrims to Canterbury, was seen both by Macaulay and Michelet as one of the causes of England's eventual separation from France. The most recent book on the subject, Frank Barlow's *Thomas Becket* (Phoenix, 1983), gives a scholarly analysis of the many accounts of the murder by Becket's contemporaries, complementing W. I. Warren's *Henry II*, which gives a sympathetic portrait of the other main protagonist. A Roman Catholic view of Becket is given in the biography by David Knowles and Robert Speaght, the actor who played the role in T. S. Eliot's play *Murder in the Cathedral*.

For those who would like to know more of Henry II's much-maligned wife, there are two excellent recent biographies – Desmond Seward's *Eleanor of Aquitaine, The Mother Queen* (1978) and Alison Weir's *Eleanor of Aquitaine: By the Wrath of God, Queen of England* (1988).

I have relied very heavily on the relevant volumes of the Oxford History of England, especially Mary McKisack's *Fourteenth Century*. For a more European view of the Middle Ages, there is the *Cambridge Medieval History*, Gibbon's *Decline and Fall of the Roman Empire* and Sir Stephen Runciman's books on the crusades and *The Sicilian Vespers*.

A full bibliography to the life and work of Chaucer can be found in the Riverside Chaucer edition (1987) and in Derek Pearsall's excellent *The Life of Geoffrey Chaucer. A Critical Biography* (Blackwell, 1992).

In writing the chapters on the Black Death I have relied on Philip Ziegler's modern classic and on Barbara Tuchman's *A Distant Mirror*, although I cannot accept her underlying thesis.

Since Barbara Tuchman wrote *A Distant Mirror*, the HIV/AIDS epidemic has cast doubt on the capacity of modern science to prevent or even to understand such plagues. The AIDS controversy has inspired a number of books reappraising earlier epidemics such as the Black Death, the plague of 1665 and the Spanish Flu of 1918. Particularly interesting is Alfred W. Crosby's *America's Forgotten Pandemic. The Influenza of 1918*, especially the preface to the new edition of 1989 (CUP).

For further reading on *Le Roman de la Rose* and its influence on Chaucer, there is C. S. Lewis's acclaimed *The Allegory of Love: A Study in Medieval Tradition* (OUP, 1936), Dean Spruill Fansler's *Chaucer and the Roman de la Rose* (Gloucester Press, 1965) and John V. Fleming's witty *The Roman de la Rose. A Study in Allegory and Iconography* (Princeton, 1969). Jill Mann for some valuable insights into the Wife of Bath and other pilgrims in her *Chaucer and Medieval Estates Satire: The Literature of Social Classes and the General Prologue to the Canterbury Tales* (1973). This is altogether one of the sharpest and wittiest studies of Chaucer's social satire.

In comparing Chaucer's *Romaunt of the Rose* with the original, I consulted the three-volume *Roman de la Rose* published by Felix Lecoy (Librairie Honore Champion, Paris, 1976).

In the chapters on Chaucer in Italy, I have tried to convey how the influence of Dante and Boccaccio's tolerant attitude to the Jews was manifest during the Second World War as well as in the novels of Ignazio Silone. The Italian Jew, Primo Levi found comfort from the *Inferno* during his time in Auschwitz, as he recalls in his epic memoir *If This Is a Man*. Dante was also a favourite author to inmates of the Soviet *gulag*, as exemplified by the title of Solzhenitsyn's novel *The First Circle*.

As an antidote to the Whig admirers of Wyclif, it is salutary to read K. B. McFarlane's *John Wycliffe and the Beginnings of English Noncomformity* (published by the English Universities Press, 1952, as part of the Teach Yourself History Library). He says that Trevelyan's stricture on the Lollards for taking the spirit of martyrdom upon them 'comes ill from those who have never been called upon to die for an unpopular opinion'.

The questions posed by Wyclif have not yet been resolved and can best be examined today by listening to the debate within the Church of England.

Index